George Albree

Things of the Kingdom

A Series of Essays

George Albree

Things of the Kingdom
A Series of Essays

ISBN/EAN: 9783337168889

Printed in Europe, USA, Canada, Australia, Japan

Cover: Foto ©ninafisch / pixelio.de

More available books at **www.hansebooks.com**

THINGS OF THE KINGDOM.

A SERIES OF ESSAYS.

BY

GEORGE ALBREE.

A MEMORIAL VOLUME.

PRINTED FOR PRIVATE CIRCULATION.

PHILADELPHIA:
J. B. LIPPINCOTT & CO.
1881.

Copyright, 1880, by JOSEPH ALBREE.

In Memoriam.

GEORGE ALBREE.

Born in Salem, Massachusetts, February 1st, 1803.
Came to Pittsburgh, Pennsylvania, December 25th, 1825.
Married to Martha Curling, March 27th, 1828.
Lost his beloved wife, October 1st, 1867.
Died suddenly in Pittsburgh, February 20th, 1880.

PREFACE.

As this volume is intended for private circulation among our father's personal friends, it seems proper that we, his children, should briefly state the reason for its publication.

During the last fifteen years of our father's life, a gradual but very perceptible change took place in his speculative theological opinions and in his views of religious truth. This divergence from the ordinarily received belief of the Presbyterian Church, in which he had been an elder for forty years, while not affecting his hearty acceptance of the main points of the Calvinistic faith, was nevertheless so positive and distinct in character, that it was not possible for him to manifest the energy, activity, and heartiness which had marked his life in earlier years. He was so conscious of this change in his views, and of the anomalous position in which it placed him towards his Christian brethren, that he was, at times, almost determined to sever his official connection with the visible church organization, and, in the method most in accord with his own theory, devote his energies to the welfare of the criminal classes, with whom he had providentially been placed in contact as one of the directors of the Allegheny County Work-

House, and whose confidence and affection he seemed to gain so easily.

Being firmly convinced by years of careful study of the Bible, and by the results of his own experience, that the views of religious truth he held so tenaciously were clearly taught in Scripture, and that their prevalence among Christians would be followed by the greater triumph of Gospel principles, it was impossible for him to retain them in his own mind as themes of quiet meditation. Finding in them, as he thought, the key that would open many a dark and mysterious problem of human existence, springs of enjoyment in every phase of spiritual experience, and sources of consolation in times of trouble and affliction, he was always ready and anxious to make them known to all, and urge their acceptance by those to whom they might seem scriptural. Being to a certain extent mystical, although eminently practical when applied to every-day life, these views were often misapprehended and their proclaimer regarded as one who, having departed from what were usually accepted as the old and the safe paths, would preach another Gospel. Pained by repeated manifestations of this feeling, and to correct, if possible, the misconception of the truths he loved so dearly, as well as in the hope of leading some of his friends to see the truths of the Gospel of Grace as they appeared to his own mind he concluded to give expression to his views in a volume composed of a series of essays, that he might offer to any who would be sufficiently interested to read it.

In the midst of his work, and before his purpose was completed, he was suddenly called home, leaving these essays in their present shape, some of them only partially finished and awaiting further additions. Two of them—those on "Prayer" and "The Sabbath"—had been published as pamphlets, but are now presented in condensed form.

Knowing well how thoroughly our father enjoyed the preparation of this volume, and the pleasure with which he anticipated its publication, his children determined, after his death, to carry out his purpose, as far as it was in their power, by placing his manuscript in the form of a memorial volume for distribution among his friends.

CONTENTS.

	PAGE
GOD'S MANIFESTATIONS OF HIMSELF	13
THE GOSPEL NOT TO CONVERT THE WORLD	23
CHARACTERISTICS OF THE JEWISH DISPENSATION	47
THE JEWISH NATION AND ITS FUTURE DESTINY	63
THE COMING OF CHRIST	98
PERVERSIONS OF SCRIPTURE	116
ORGANIZATION	133
PARDON OF SIN	153
THE ABIDING COMFORTER	164
PRAYER	174
A DARK PROBLEM	200
APHORISMS AND REFLECTIONS	210
THE SABBATH	225
SUFFERING	250
CRIMINALS AND PRISON REFORM	261

THINGS OF THE KINGDOM.

GOD'S MANIFESTATIONS OF HIMSELF.

"Of Him, and through Him, and to Him are all things: to whom be glory forever."—ROMANS xi. 36.

"All things were made by Him, and without Him was not any thing made that was made. In Him was life, and the life was the light of men."—JOHN i. 3, 4.

"God hath in these last days spoken unto us by His Son, whom He hath appointed heir of all things, by whom also He made the world."—HEB. i. 2.

"And when all things shall be subdued unto Him then shall the Son also Himself be subject unto Him that put all things under Him, that God may be all in all."—1 COR. xv. 28.

THE general facts gathered from these passages are, the statement of creation by Divine power; the object of creation,—God's glory; the agency by which all is accomplished—His Son. God's glory in the creation of the world and the race of men is the theme of revelation. God's purpose in the creation of men, as it has been unfolded in revelation, is a purpose of Love. By the development of this purpose of Love to His creatures, God has connected human life and destiny with His own glory. His love has been so deep and wide that it has made the existence of man an essential part of His glory. That entire union of Himself with the race He had called into conscious life and being,—that transcendent manifestation of love and honor in the assumption of human form,—have inseparably connected the race with its Creator.

The manifestations of this purpose of love, while constant and progressive, have assumed conditions and forms grouping themselves in classes and extending through fixed definite periods of time. They may be designated as periods of *Liberty, Law, Grace,* and *Glory.* Through two the race has passed; in the third, and probably near its close, it is now living; the last is still before it. Through all of these periods two facts have become evident,—the constant, unchanging love of God, the constant and ever-increasing sin of man. The results of liberty—that period when man was left to work out to their proper end all the impulses of his natural heart—were, that "the wickedness of man was great in the earth, and every imagination of the thoughts of his heart only evil continually." In the second period we may discover clearer manifestations of love in the Law of God, which, being a revelation of His own nature and will, is by virtue of its source holy, just, and perfect, given to a chosen people for a special purpose of good to them, and through them to all people. We take the designs of the law to be,—first, a revelation to man of the sin of his heart; and second, a disciplinary process by which men would be prepared for the reception and appreciation of the infinite love of God in His Son. In the third period, called by Paul "the dispensation of the Grace of God," we have a revelation of the kingdom of Heaven as the final result of the great redemptive work of Christ,—the remission of sin by faith in the Son of God,—the gift of the Holy Ghost, with all it implies,—with "life and immortality made manifest by the appearing of our Saviour Jesus

Christ." The fourth and future period, called by Paul "the dispensation of the fulness of times," is an object of lively hope and earnest expectation to all who look for Christ's appearing. It is the dispensation to which all others are preparatory,—the fulfilment of all prophecy. It will be the time of "the restitution of all things, of which God hath spoken by the mouth of all his holy prophets since the world began,"—when the redemptive work of Christ shall have extended so far and wide " that at the name of Jesus every knee should bow in heaven, and in earth and under the earth, and every tongue should confess that Jesus Christ is God, to the *glory* of God the Father." The "dispensations" of the love of God, which we have thus briefly indicated, although intimately connected with each other, and incomplete when separated and viewed alone, are distinct and different in manifestation and circumstances. Having one main purpose, the glory of God, united with the welfare of His creatures, they are various developments of the Divine plan forming one harmonious combination. As liberty was followed by law, and law in turn completed and fulfilled by grace, so will grace be swallowed up by glory. In the first, God selected a man and his family, and in the second a nation, through whom He would bless the race; so in the third has He a chosen company, standing in close and peculiar relations to Himself through Christ the Son, upon whom and through whom He will display the infinite riches of His love, who will be the inheritors of all he hath promised, and who will in a wider and truer sense than Israel under the law " make known to the sons of men His mighty acts, and the glorious majesty of His kingdom."

A retrospect of God's providential dealings with mankind as a race since the creation may make more evident the plan which, to our mind, has been revealed in Scripture for the restoration of His fallen creatures to purity and happiness by the impartation to the human soul of God's own life and holiness. Adam, as he came from the hand of his Creator, was neither a holy nor a sinful man, but was simply an innocent being. Voluntarily transgressing the single restriction laid upon him, he departed from God, thus exchanging for himself and his descendants the original estate of peace and enjoyment for one of pain and misery. The knowledge of sin came by the breach of the one law, and the law worked out its own result,—wrath. Man's deliverance could only be accomplished by the power against which he had rebelled. Scarcely had death—through our mother Eve—entered into the world than the promise of life through her seed was given, and the means of restoration called into operation. Scarcely had man involved himself in trouble ere the anxious cry of a loving parent was heard calling, "Adam, where art thou?" A God of love could not rescue the child that Satan had seduced from loyalty and obedience, for justice demanded satisfaction for the broken law. Thus early in the history of man appeared the apparently irreconcilable conflict between love and justice. But while man was led captive by Satan, a hope of deliverance was imparted by the promise that "the seed of the woman should bruise the serpent's head," a foundation was laid for his faith, an assurance was given that the just would justify the ungodly. The germ of the plan for restoring man to more than pristine glory was already unfolding. The process of redemption leading through liberty, law, and grace to glory was already in course of development. Man, free from the restraint of any law, was at full liberty to choose his own course, could come back to God or depart still farther from Him. Not willingly, it may be, but nevertheless constantly and surely, he was becoming enslaved by Satan and led farther from the Source of life and light, until sin had wellnigh obliterated all traces of his Divine origin, and both body and soul bore the deep brands of his captor. After the catastrophe of the flood, God came nearer to man, in the selection of Abraham as a source of blessing to the race, and, after a trial of his faith, gave the more specific promise that in "his seed should all the nations of the earth be blessed." Moses records God's dealings with His chosen people in Deut. xxxii. 9, 10: "For the Lord's portion is His people: Jacob is the lot of His inheritance. He found him in the desert land and in the waste howling wilderness; He led him about, He instructed him, He kept him as the apple of His eye." From among the idolatrous nations God selected the Hebrews as the channel through which He would manifest Himself to the race, with the design of establishing a kingdom of righteousness on the earth, making that nation the teacher of all nations, placing it as a city on a hill that cannot be hid. He made known His glory and power to them in a peculiar manner, associated His own life with them, gave them a code of laws perfectly adapted to their circumstances,—obedience to which would result in their happiness,—placed them under a course of training and discipline by which they might be fully prepared for the more complete revelation of Himself in the promised Messiah and an active participation in His purpose of love to all the earth. The more God did for them as a nation the more hardened and rebellious were the Jews, until by the mouth of Isaiah He exclaims, "What could have been done more to my vineyard, that I have not done in it? wherefore, when I looked that it should bring forth grapes, brought it forth wild grapes?" Notwithstanding this and other expressions of the apparent failure of the Jews in the fulfilment of their high destiny, the declarations of the Jewish prophets confidently point to a time in the future when their nation will be missionaries to "the isles afar off that have not heard my fame neither have seen my glory, and they shall declare my glory among the Gentiles." (Isa. lxvi. 19.) The "great day of the Lord" will not come until Elijah has prepared the way and the heart of the people. While there is some resemblance between the position offered to the Jews and that of the Church of Christ, there is a marked difference between the boon placed before them and the high glory reserved for the Gospel Grace Church as it is presented in Rev. v. 10 and xxi. 24.

John came in the power and spirit of Elias to prepare the way for the coming of Messiah, but his testimony was rejected, and he was cut off. The Messiah, long promised and hoped for, appeared, was rejected, and crucified by "His brethren according to the flesh." The stream of blessing which would have followed His acceptance by His own nation was diverted from its proper channel and was turned upon the Gentiles; the way was opened for the descent of the Holy Ghost into the hearts of all believers at the Pentecostal season, and by its indwelling in human hearts the Redeemed Church was established on the earth.

As the Gospel of Grace was not manifested until after the death of Christ, His mission on earth was preaching the Gospel of the Kingdom of Heaven, an earthly, sanctified kingdom. After His resurrection the Son of God was never seen by mortal eyes as He had been when He was the Son of man. He spoke only to His own disciples of the Kingdom of God and of the Holy Ghost that was to come upon them. Matthew, a Jew in heart and feelings, presents Christ as the Son of David and the Son of man who would deliver Israel from the Roman bondage and make it the leading nation of the earth. Although a believer in Christ's Divine mission, he evidently looked for its fulfilment in a temporal and carnal sense. Mark, the faithful recorder, presents Christ as the Son of man and the friend of humanity. Luke, the learned Gentile, presents Him as the Son of man and the Son of God. In these three Gospels may be traced the gradual transition from the Jewish to the Gospel Grace system, the latter still retaining many of the legal characteristics of the former, from which it was so soon to be separated. As Christ came to the lost sheep of the house of Israel, He neither preached Himself nor sent His disciples to preach to the Samaritans or Gentiles. When He healed He made no attempt to proselyte, but told the Jew to make an offering according to the law, but the Gentile to "go and sin no more." The barriers had not yet been broken down, the gate had not yet been swung open.

John, who seemed by nature to have had a fuller and more complete apprehension of Christ's mission, presents Him as the Son of God. John was pre-eminently the Christian evangelist. In his Gospel he does not refer to that vision of the latter-day Jewish glory—the Transfiguration—of which he was a witness. In all he wrote, while not forgetting that he was a Jew, and that the promises were the inheritance of his nation, John addresses both saints and sinners, Jews and Gentiles. Passing all boundaries in his Revelation,—the history of time and eternity,—he concentrates the life and essence of the Old and New Testaments, closing with the prayer of the universal Church, "Even so, come, Lord Jesus."

The object of the present essays is to present God as a Being of infinite Justice and Love, whose heart is yearning for the happiness of His creatures, and who would have all men come to the knowledge of the truth as it is in Jesus, but without the least infringement on their moral free-agency; to attempt to make evident that, moral free-agency being a constituent of God's own character, He has granted to men the power and privilege of exercising the same, and given them the liberty of choosing life or death; that salvation is from God, condemnation from ourselves, our good from necessity, our evil from our own voluntary choice; that God's plan began in perfection, and will end in perfection; that God's will will be done in earth as it is in heaven; that the prayer of the Church, as expressed in the ninety-seventh Psalm, will be fulfilled, and it can be said truly, "The Lord reigneth, let the earth rejoice," and the saints can with joy "say among the nations, The Lord reigneth."

While it would seem impossible to have a conception of an all-wise and all-powerful personal Creator and God which does not involve the possession and exercise of predestination and forcordination absolutely free from any influence or restraint beyond God's own choice, consistency with the law of His own Being, and the revelation He has made of His nature and purpose, it is equally important, in our conception, that we should as firmly settle in our minds the truth—as fully declared in Scripture, and just as important in its bearing on human faith and action—that man, by the constitution of his nature, was made, and continues to be, a *moral free-agent*, capable of making in all things an intelligent, voluntary choice, and of experiencing throughout his whole conscious existence the good or evil results consequent upon such choice. Destitute of the divinely-given power, the restoration and salvation of man would reflect no glory on the infinite love of God; without it, the conditions of man's immortality would be only the results of an external constraining influence which he had been powerless to resist.

Our conception of God, of His character, and the whole course of His providential dealings with men, depends in some degree upon the ideas we entertain concerning man as a sinful being. If sin, which has entered into and so fully possessed the race, be only a malady like a bodily disease caused by certain fixed conditions for the resistance and overcoming of which there are lodged within our human nature germs of self-purification and correction, by whose development the cause and its effects may be removed, the process is only a question of time and industry on our part. As in the case of bodily disease strict attention to wise and familiar sanitary laws and avoidance of that which causes or aggravates it will in time sweep the disease from the earth, so may faithful, constant observance of moral law relieve us from the malady of sin. If any such idea holds sway in the mind, there can be seen no absolute necessity of a Plan of Salvation involving a long process of preparation on the Divine part, an incarnation of God, a Divine-human life and death of suffering, a constant, ever-present influence of the Holy Spirit for the restoration of man to purity and holiness. Just in proportion as we have a true idea of the "exceeding sinfulness of sin," of its inborn and all-pervading power and awful results, of the immeasurable distance to which it removes the soul from its Divine source of life and love, so do we have the more exalted views of the infinite love and wisdom of the Father as manifested in His efforts to restore man to purity and happiness by a process attended with the highest glory to Himself and most perfect satisfaction to man,—a plan which, while fully satisfying the attribute of justice, comes into full accord with the deepest wants and feelings of the human soul. A salvation from sin is manifested to man, wherein, by the reception of a Divine principle, he will be guided by truth under all circumstances, and yet be in possession of perfect liberty, in which his power of free choice will not be infringed on or a particle of his individuality be destroyed, while at the same time he will be led in a path that will yield to him the highest and purest satisfaction of which his nature may be capable.

THE GOSPEL NOT TO CONVERT THE WORLD.

The phrase "kingdom of God" occurs in the New Testament seventy times; "kingdom of heaven," twenty times. There are besides about thirty references to either. In many places where the phrase is used by Christ or the Apostles it is in connection with or a synonym of the "Gospel" or "glad tidings." This is specially marked in the passage from Isaiah read by Christ in the synagogue at Nazareth, and made the basis of His declaration, "This day is this scripture fulfilled in your ears." Matthew records the fact that Jesus went about all Galilee "preaching the gospel of the kingdom." Mark, in still clearer terms, writes of Christ " preaching the gospel of the kingdom," quoting his words, "The time is fulfilled and the *kingdom of God* is at hand; repent ye and believe the *gospel.*" The proclamation to be made by the twelve was simply, "The kingdom of heaven is at hand;" the seventy were instructed to say, "The kingdom of God is come nigh unto you." To Nicodemus "the kingdom of God" was presented as a state into which he might enter on certain conditions. It formed the theme of many of the discourses of our Lord, was illustrated by many parables, and was an object of indefinite desire and hope to those whose minds were at all influenced by the Divine teachings. Christ and the disciples after the resurrection talked of "things pertaining to the kingdom of God." That the disciples did not clearly comprehend the nature and object of the "kingdom" is evident from their last recorded question before the Master ascended,

"Wilt Thou at this time restore again the kingdom of Israel?"

In the ordinary Jewish mind the advent of the "kingdom," as spoken of by Christ, called up the long-cherished ideas, gathered from the inspired utterances of the Prophets and the traditions intertwined with the predictions, that Messiah would insure the triumph of Israel over all his enemies, would re-establish the throne of David and make Jerusalem the metropolis of the nations; that the approach of the Messianic period would be marked by some miraculous phenomenon similar to that at Mount Sinai; that peace would reign over all the earth, and the name of Jehovah be universally adored. Whatever may have been the difference of interpretation of the Messianic predictions among the Jews,—whether they were to be fulfilled by *one person* of the House of David, a King, Deliverer, and Prophet, or by the children of Israel as a race,—it was the inwrought and immovable conviction of the national mind that an "everlasting dominion," an "everlasting kingdom," would be "given to the people of the saints of the Most High," an honor and glory of which all of the ancient chosen people would be partakers. It is not strange that these high aspirations should almost exclude an equally important part of the same predictions,—the humiliation and suffering which were to precede the glory and majesty. Cherishing most deeply the temporal and material ideas involving the triumph and exaltation of their nation, prevented by the fatness of heart, blindness of eyes, and deafness of ears, predicted by Isaiah, from any spiritual appreciation of the Divine salvation placed within their reach, the Jews failed to recognize the Founder of the "kingdom" in Him who "had no form nor comeliness," who was "despised and rejected, a man of sorrows and acquainted with grief," "oppressed and afflicted," "taken from prison and judgment, brought as a lamb to the slaughter, cut off out of the land of the living," and having "His grave with the wicked." We may, perhaps, in reading the Messianic prophecies in the light of history, wonder how it was possible that the Jews, with the Books of the Prophets in their hands and read daily in their synagogues, should have failed to see in the words and the life of Christ a literal fulfilment of those predictions on which their hopes were based and which had sustained their faith during long periods of captivity, and yet is it not possible, we might go further and ask, Is it not *probable*, that Christendom of this age entertains ideas of the origin, nature, and object of the "kingdom" as far removed from the reality as those held by the Jews who listened to the gracious words of the Master?

It will scarcely be denied that the general expectation of Christians of the present age is that a wide diffusion of the gospel by the preaching of the word, by the efforts of missionaries, by the distribution of tracts and Bibles, and by the operations of those human agencies of aggression on the domains of Satan which have been multiplied during this century, will insure a visible triumph of pure religion, and that now, without any new or serious pause, truth and piety shall steadily advance, shall conquer larger and still larger portions of the human race, "until all the earth is filled with the knowledge of the Lord." It is fondly believed that all forms of civil and religious despotism, all gigantic political and ecclesiastical corruptions, will surely, though gradually, be disintegrated and swept from the earth by the prevalence and potency of the principles taught by Christ; that righteousness and truth universally prevailing will usher in the long-predicted and hoped-for "kingdom of God;" that the petition, "Thy will be done on earth as it is in heaven," will soon be literally and abundantly fulfilled. While believing firmly that God's purpose of mercy to the race will surely be accomplished, we must say frankly that we do not share in the bright hopes which seem to be cherished by the Church. We cannot accept the prevalent idea, or see that its truth can be sustained either by Scripture or the facts of history.

It is the object of this essay to make evident, 1st, negatively, that the primary design of the "kingdom" or Gospel of Grace, as introduced into the world by the teachings of Christ and his Apostles, *was not the conversion of the world;* that the world from the period immediately succeeding the Ascension of our Lord has not advanced in true knowledge of God, or made substantial increase in spiritual holiness; that there will be no general progress in true holiness during the continuance of the present Grace Dispensation on the earth. 2d, positively, that the Gospel of Grace is a *witness* to be preached in all the world to all people, to call out from the world all those who will believe in the Lord Jesus Christ; that the world, as distinguished from God's people, is constantly developing increasing disloyalty to God, and will continue in the same course until the close of the Grace Dispensation; that at the future period of time when God's purpose of love to His people shall have been completed, the *Church*, composed of all those who by faith have been made one with the Lord Jesus, will be withdrawn from the world and taken to the enjoyment of its Lord in heaven; that God, in the person of Jesus Christ, will then, by power and judgment, not by the Gospel of Grace, begin to subdue the world to Himself, and Christ will receive the fulfilment of the promise of "the heathen for an inheritance and the uttermost parts of the earth for a possession;" and that by the coming of Christ with His saints the Millennium will be ushered in.

I have endeavored to state these propositions so broadly and fully that they may not be misapprehended. While this truth may, as many other deep truths of Revelation, be involved in some obscurity, and some difficulties may seem to cluster about it, yet it may claim acceptance not only because it has a substantial scriptural basis, but for the reason that the experience of the Church and the world for nearly two thousand years gives positive testimony in its favor. Well aware of the fact that it is a doctrine directly opposed to the cherished hopes of the large majority of Christians, and that its prevalence would result in an entire change in the present mode of Christian activity, I would hesitate to advance it were I not so fully convinced in my own mind that it is deeply imbedded in Revelation and is one of the hidden treasures of God's word that will in its proper time shine out clearly.

The general purpose of God in the earthly mission of Christ was the conquering of death, the destruction of the works of the devil, and by one offering to forever perfect them that are sanctified. One special purpose was "to take out from the Gentiles a people for His name" (Acts xv. 14-19), an elect Church, foreordained before the foundation of the world,—a selected people, "called, chosen, and faithful," through and by whom He would manifest His final glory. All who compose this elect Church were "chosen in Him, before the foundation of the world, that they should be holy and without blame before Him in love," "predestinated unto the adoption of children by Jesus Christ to Himself, according to the good pleasure of His will." (Eph. i. 4.) "His workmanship, created in Christ Jesus unto good works" (Eph. ii. 10), "saved and called with a holy calling, not according to works, but according to His purpose and grace given in Christ Jesus, before the world began." (2 Tim. i. 9.)

Christ declares it is the Father's will that " of all which He hath given me, He should lose nothing, but raise it up at the last day" (John vi. 39); and again says positively, " *All* that the Father giveth me, *shall come* to me." These are but a few of the many passages which plainly declare God's purpose to form for Himself a Church,—the " one Body," composed of all who should be " heirs of God, and joint-heirs with Christ," of whom Christ Himself, risen and glorified, would be the Head. To this chosen company God in a measure intrusts His glory. To them in a peculiar manner He reveals His will. To them He grants His Spirit to lead them into all truth. On earth they are to be "a city set upon a hill" that cannot be hid—a " light of the world"—the faithful shining representatives and witnesses, showing forth the praises of their absent Lord, who has gone to prepare a place for them, who will return and take them to Himself. On the earth they are educated and prepared by the Holy Ghost for the high destiny awaiting them when, clothed in glorified spiritual bodies, they shall sit with Christ on the Throne judging the nations of the earth.

The Gospel of Grace is to call out from the world all who will come, all who will accept Christ, and those who by coming and accepting make evident that they are part of that chosen company through whom the Father will manifest His love and mercy, and upon whom He will confer the high glories of His everlasting kingdom. The Dispensation of Grace, perfected in the Eternal Mind before the foundation of the world, but revealed on the earth and made potential for mankind by the Incarnation of the Lord, is an independent system, complete in itself, and while in harmony with, and in one sense developed from, all that had preceded, it has a distinct and definite purpose. Although complete and perfect in itself, the Gospel of Grace must be considered as a parenthesis between the *apparent* failure of the first earthly material dispensation and that "latter-day" judicial dispensation which was the burden of the ancient prophecies, and which will be the consummation of the glory of God on the earth. Rising, it may be, in the material economy, its course is like that of a rapid river, passing through the stagnant waters of a morass without mingling, flowing on through its destined channel. Being a manifestation of a reconciled God to a rebel world, it gives to all, both Jew and Gentile, the invitation to come, —let him that will, come and drink of the waters of life freely; but as only those who realize their need of life will come, it can scarcely be claimed that its purpose is the arbitrary conversion of the world. As the magnet passing over a mingled mass of iron and sand surely attracts to itself all the particles of metal, so the Gospel of Grace passing through the world draws and holds to itself all those who will be sharers with Christ in His final glory.

Its purpose and intent are revealed by Christ and the Apostles, its means are fixed and definite, and, being energized by the power of the Holy Ghost, there is no place for contingencies, nothing can prevent its consummation. The proclamation of reconciliation "that all things are ready," that there is no obstacle in the way of any soul, is to be made to all creatures. If any have no desire to come, or if any by a perverted will transform light into darkness, and choose death rather than life, the responsibility for the result must rest on the creature, not on the Creator. The development and progress of the Grace system are above and beyond any dependence on human wisdom or philosophy, for it is the peculiar province of the Holy Spirit to bring under its power every redeemed soul. Human effort cannot add one to the number, neither can all the powers of hell pluck one from the Shepherd's hand.

The Gospel of Grace is the Life and Righteousness of God manifested or proposed, but not offered (for an offer would involve conditions), through Jesus Christ, to all the fallen children of Adam who realize need of deliverance from spiritual death. It neither implores nor solicits acceptance of the provided Salvation. If a soul chooses to remain in death, the act is one of free choice. The Salvation manifested is worthy of reception, not only from the infinite character of its Author, but from its intrinsic worth and value and its perfect adaptation to the eternal welfare of the soul. By its acceptance only can the soul come into accord with the source of its own true life and become a partaker of the life, love, and holiness of God. Pure acceptance of so rich a blessing can only result from willing choice by the exercise of that free-agency with which the Creator has endowed every reasonable creature. The slightest command or threat, the least constraint of legality, would be a stain on the character of the Giver. The whole spirit of the Gospel of Grace is concentrated in its only solicitation, "Come unto me that ye may have life."

The selection by God of a portion of the human race, and the formation of a Church in the world by the Gospel of Grace, are in harmony with His recorded dealings with the Hebrew nation. When Moses called all Israel together in Horeb and repeated to them the Law, he declared God's choice of them in the clearest and most emphatic manner: "For thou art an holy people unto the Lord thy God;

the Lord thy God hath chosen thee to be a special people unto Himself, above all people that are upon the face of the earth. The Lord did not set His love upon you, nor choose you, because ye were more in number than any people,—for ye were the fewest of people,—but because the Lord loved you, and because He would keep the oath which He had sworn unto your fathers, hath the Lord brought you out with a mighty hand." (Deut. vii. 6–8.) They were to be a "special people" unto the Lord for purposes plainly declared to them by Moses during their journey, and subsequently affirmed by the holy men and prophets of the nation. They were to be teachers of the Divine unity, the declarers of the great truth of Monotheism among idolatrous nations. In the words of Isaiah (xliv. 8), "Ye are even my witnesses." They were to "make known to the sons of men His mighty acts and the glorious majesty of His kingdom" (Ps. cxlv. 10-12); they were to be the channel through which mercy should be conveyed to all nations. (Gen. xxvi. 3, 4; xlix. 10; Isa. xlix. 6.) While many other purposes are revealed, not only by prediction but by the facts of Jewish history, the most remarkable statement concerning the "special people" is connected with their "final restoration." The application is the same regardless of any peculiar interpretation that may be attached to the words. Without throwing any clear light on the future mysterious mission of the Hebrew nation, the prophet Ezekiel in the words, "*Not for your sakes do I this*, saith the Lord God, be it known unto you; be ashamed and confounded for your own ways, O House of Israel" (chap. xxxvi. 32), reveals, yet carefully conceals, the fact that God's dealings with the ancient people had a higher and more glorious purpose than their individual happiness, national glory, or final salvation,—

a purpose of good to them having at the same time an intimate relation to God's glory.

In many points the closest analogy and most perfect correspondence may be traced between the choice of the "special people" of the old dispensation and the Church of the new; while in other points it fails to hold. The choice of either was simply the exercise of Divine Sovereignty; the objects chosen were the subjects of peculiar love and solicitude: all that was essential to the prosecution of the purpose for which they were chosen came to them directly from God, frequently in a manner that might be regarded as supernatural. The high destiny to which both were called was active service for God and the manifestation of His glory and honor. In either the choice is *limited*,—one by birth, the other by sovereign pleasure. In either it is absolute,—in one case as a nation, in the other as the individual. Up to a certain point the Jewish nation, despite its rebellion, folly, and sin, perfectly fulfilled the purpose for which it was chosen. The ancient people were the rulers and teachers of the nations, they were the depository of Divine truth, they were the source from which salvation for the Gentiles came through the Person of Jesus Christ. But still, as a nation, they have thrown away their birthright by refusing to recognize their predicted Messiah; turning away from their traditional idea and hope, they failed to take that high position for which centuries of discipline and training under God's Providence had been designed to prepare them. Their glory has for a time been transferred to others, but the day of ingathering and rejoicing, when the Jews shall be hailed as messengers of light to the nations of the earth, will surely come.

There are now, and have been in the world ever since

the earliest days of the Christian era, two Messianic missions based upon the same revelations of Divine truth, claiming as their own the same prophetic utterances, cherishing hopes of the same ultimate glory. The Supreme law—the strength and hope of the Hebrew nation, the unalterable faith of Israel, the basis of its social and religious existence—is the *absolute unity and invisibility of God*. They have lived for it and by it; for this they have never ceased to struggle and suffer. Accepting with an approving mind and a loving heart the fact that the saving Messiah became a Divine Incarnation, the God who assumed the form and lived the life of men, all Christians believe and assert that the Messianic prophecies were accomplished by the birth, life, death, and resurrection of Jesus Christ. Claiming as their own, in the most definite and exclusive sense, the bulk of the prophecies of the Old Testament,—a heritage the right to which the most rigorous biblical criticism rather confirms than weakens,—the Jews are waiting with imperturbable patience the fulfilment of the Divine promises. They are hoping for the day when the universal proclamation of peace and good-will will re-establish the fraternity of all nations and the reign of God be inaugurated on the earth. Their theory will not admit the "advent of Messiah until universal peace shall be coincident with His era, and until those laws of justice and love shall prevail which are declared to be the providential signs of the Redeemer of mankind." From the more remote period of its historical existence the aspirations of Judaism have not been limited to the development of its internal and individual life. Among the most profound thinkers and writers of the Jews in later centuries, we frequently meet the idea that the whole world is to be their domain and future empire,—not, perhaps, so much under a material but a moral sway. Certain it is that this long and firmly cherished hope has left a deep impress on all the principle and all the events of their history.

Having in another essay enlarged more fully on the great difference in spirit and result between the Legal and Grace Dispensations, we have touched on the two Messianic theories in the hope of bringing out more clearly the facts that in the future development of truth on the earth and the prevalence of the kingdom of Christ the Jews, as the "chosen people," are destined to take an important part, and that the mission they are to perform has been regarded by Christendom too exclusively as the portion of those who are called by the Gospel of Grace. While the Christian Church has properly appropriated to herself all the Messianic prophecies of the Old Testament, she has also strangely and without reason taken possession of truths and declarations to which she has no just claim and which were not intended for her. By a spiritualizing of certain textual expressions, and, indeed, of whole passages, in the books of the Prophets, exclusively addressed to and intended for the Jews, the primary meaning is utterly destroyed and a mode of interpretation introduced which is confusing and misleading to all but those who study the Bible critically. Take as an illustration such phrases as "Israel," "the House of Jacob," "the cities of Judah," "the streets of Jerusalem," very frequently recurring in Isaiah and Jeremiah, and almost without exception bearing a strictly literal meaning. In the ordinary usage among the churches these expressions are symbolically given to the elect Church and the Heavenly Jerusalem. The "Throne of David" is used as synonymous with the "kingdom of Christ." The passage in the first part of the second chapter of Isaiah and the greater part of the thirty-third chapter of Jeremiah,— passages which biblical critics agree have direct and special application to the Restoration of the Jews,—explained in this symbolizing method, are accepted as references to the Christian Church, and believed to be predictions of the triumph of the Gospel of Grace. The fact is, we cannot find in the Prophets any predictions concerning the dispensation under which the Church is now living, this period of delay in the visible exaltation of the Messiah. There is no hint of a, to us, long lapse of time intervening between the humiliation and the exaltation of the "Branch of Righteousness." His appearance is to be immediately followed by "righteousness and judgment in the land." The primitive Christians, finding nothing in the old Scriptures contrary to their hopes, waited with patient eagerness for the reappearing of Him whom they had seen taken up in the clouds. It seems to be a strange perversion of language to apply that which Isaiah expressly says is written "*concerning Judah and Jerusalem*" to the Christian Church of the present parenthetical dispensation. The little practical benefit that may possibly be derived from these erroneous interpretations is gained only at the expense of the definite truth which forms so large a part of the prophecies. Let all the passages of the described import in the prophetic writings be shorn of that mystical, spiritualistic meaning which has been thrust upon them, and it will be found that the prophets give us no substantial basis on which to rest a hope that this world is to be converted to God by the present Gospel of Grace. It will, of course, be understood that I speak only of the statements concerning the Jewish nation, its restoration and future mission. The predictions referring to the person and work of the Messiah, the proclamation of salvation to the Gentiles, are of an altogether different character, and their partial fulfilment serves as a guide to the proper interpretation of those yet unfulfilled. These are so full, so free, and so rich, that the Church of Christ may find entire satisfaction in them without the wrongful appropriation of the large portion of Scripture that is the heritage of the Jew.

I have claimed that the preaching of the Gospel between the time of the Ascension of Christ and His next appearing in the world was not designed to convert the world to righteousness, or to result in that period of comparatively blessed holiness which has been so abundantly predicted and for the advent of which all Christians so ardently hope. Of the ultimate prevalence of righteousness to be enjoyed on the earth under the reign of the Lord Jesus Christ there can be no doubt, unless the Bible be resolved into a collection of myths. But of the means by which this result shall be accomplished or of the time when it shall be fully manifested there have always been widely divergent beliefs taking practical form in correspondingly divergent courses. It is patent that the belief on this vital point—the design of the Gospel of Grace as it is to be gathered from Scripture and as it may appear from a consideration of Divine Providence—is one that will powerfully affect and influence both the interior Christian life and its development in outward activity. Whether our impulses, thoughts, aspirations, and efforts are to flow in harmony with the Divine purpose and thus yield the full measure of satisfaction and success, or whether our whole Christian course shall be one of discord with inexorable law, depends upon the correct apprehension of revealed truth.

On this, as on many other points of Christian doctrine, the negative argument presses with great power. Among the many motives for perseverance in labor and encouragement to steadfastness in duty given to the primitive Christians by the Apostles, we fail to find any assurance that the preaching of the Gospel would convert the world to the service of the Master whom they loved and served. The obstacles they should meet, the persecution they must encounter, the sufferings and martyrdom they should endure, were plainly foretold, but the ultimate success of that Gospel to which their labors and lives were devoted was nowhere assured either by Christ or the Apostles. In the New Testament no promise of success was granted to believers corresponding in any degree with that given by the Lord to the Israelites when leaving Egypt, that they should enter upon and possess a land flowing with milk and honey, the doubting of which caused the death of a generation or the postponement of the fruition of the promise until the sceptics had passed away. We cannot find any such promise of the success of the Gospel in the Old Testament, for that belongs to the Jews. Excepting where its teachings are connected with morality, and by reason of a common origin apply to all mankind, the revealed truths belong in a special manner to the Jews, and are inseparably joined with the ceremonial system of which they formed a part. This system was not universal or general, but national and peculiar. Gentiles as nations had no part in these truths. Individually, any benefit or virtue to be derived from them was preceded by acceptance of rites which marked the believer as a Jew and separated him from his former kindred. But the Gospel of Grace is a new dispensation having a design and purpose altogether different from that of law,—a new revelation of God to mankind, a manifestation of the infinite love of God under dissimilar conditions having reference to the future glory of God, pointing to a culmination above and beyond earth and time, spiritual and eternal in nature, working out a Divine plan of which no intimations had been given in the prophecies of a nation, and following a course indicated by inspiration of the Holy Spirit only when the old Mosaic Law, local, material, and temporal in character, intended for and adapted to one peculiar nation, had been rendered nugatory and vain and its efficacy destroyed by the fulfilment of the purpose for which it had existed. When Christ came—the event to which all the sacrifices, ceremonies, and ritual of the Mosaic economy pointed forward—the virtue of the Law departed, or rather the grace of which it had hitherto been the channel gathered itself in its source and culmination, the man Christ Jesus.

Rejected by the Jews as a nation, refused by those whose whole training would seem to have prepared them for the reception and enjoyment of so great a blessing, Grace, in the person of the Lord Jesus Christ, was manifested to the Gentiles. Then began the Gospel of Grace, that new process of Divine Love of which we find no indications in Jewish prophecy; then appeared the development of the Church of God chosen and perfected before the world began.

Very soon after the Apostles began preaching the "Gospel of the Kingdom," we meet an authoritative statement of its purpose in Acts xv. 14: "Simeon hath declared how God at the first did visit the Gentiles, to take out of them a people for His name," followed by the declaration from the prophet Amos, "*After this* I will return, and will build again the tabernacle of David," etc. Here we have something definite and positive in nature. Moreover, it was given in the first general council of the Christian Church gathered at Jerusalem by James, one in authority, and in itself was made the basis of his decision in the important matter then threatening the peace of the infant Church, and which, decided otherwise, would have laid the heavy yoke of the Jewish law upon all Gentile Christians. To all those who attach more importance to Divine truth because it has been announced and formulated by the highest authorities or office-bearers of the "visible Church," this whole statement of the council at Jerusalem should be of great value. From it we learn that while the blessings of the Gospel Dispensation are *universal* in the sense of manifestation to all men,—Gentiles as well as Jews,—yet the purpose of the Gospel is essentially one of *selection*,—a gathering from the Gentiles "a people for His name." Peter also, on the day of Pentecost, states its universal purpose when he declares, "The promise is unto you, and to your children, and to all that are afar off," but defines its specific purpose of selection in the succeeding words, "As many as the Lord our God shall call." (Acts ii. 39.) The same strongly marked purpose is plainly revealed in Acts xiii. 48. When Paul and Barnabas waxed bold, and preached to the Jews, as the Lord had commanded them, that Christ should "be for salvation unto the ends of the earth," they announced the universal character of the Gospel, but the ulterior purpose is very prominently brought into view by the record of the results following their preaching: "And as many as were ordained to eternal life believed." The same general truth may also be found in Acts ii. 47: "And the Lord added to the Church daily such as should be saved." With these, and many other passages of similar meaning and import scattered through the New Testament, it can scarcely be said that the members of the primitive Church cherished the pleasant delusion, so prevalent in the Church of modern centuries, that their labors and sufferings were to be productive of an era of universal triumph of the faith they professed. Their hopes ran forward to the reappearing of Him whom they had seen ascend into heaven, and their trust was based *on the promise of His coming.*

The same general principle of selection becomes apparent, in a wider sense, after a careful consideration of John's vision of the marriage of the Lamb, in Rev. xix. When the voice of the great multitude is heard announcing in gladness and joy, "The marriage of the Lamb is come, and the wife hath made herself ready," it is evident that many others are present than those who compose the Church, —the Lamb's wife. The angel immediately says, "Write, Blessed are they which are called unto the marriage supper of the Lamb," and enforces attention to the fact by declaring, "These are the true sayings of God." The Church has occupied a peculiar position in the world. It has been formed of those who, by the marvellous and irresistible power of the Holy Ghost, have been united to Christ, who, by virtue of Divine and Sovereign Grace, have been chosen to be the companions of the Son in His heavenly glory, who, having been truly identified with Him, have been His faithful witnesses during His absence from the earth, and have waited patiently, but trustfully, for His glorious appearing. They have been selected to fill the highest place of honor which the infinite love of God could give to any of the human race.

But besides the highly-favored saints, there are many others enjoying so richly the favor of God that they are called "Blessed," and are invited to participate in "the marriage supper of the Lamb." Who they are, and whence they come, are not within the present purpose to inquire. They may be the saints of other dispensations. They certainly will be the recipients of Divine favor, but they are not of the Church,—the Bride. By no process can all of those who sit down to the "marriage supper" be considered as identical with, or a part of, the Bride. The principle of selection seems to make evident that all those who have believed in and accepted Christ, between the time of His ascension to the Father and the time of His reappearance on the earth, will be the Lamb's wife. The fact that these have been selected to high privilege, and called to places of honor and service, does not in any way militate against the truth that God by revelations of himself, and by the operations of His Holy Spirit, has gathered many Saints, to whom will be accorded the privilege of participation in the full manifestation of Divine love to men, and in the completion of His purpose, so far as it is declared in His word.

Of higher authority than any yet quoted are the words of Christ in that wonderful discourse recorded by Matthew (xxiv. 14): "And this Gospel of the Kingdom shall be preached in all the world for a witness, and then shall the end come." Whatever may be the truth contained in these words, whatever may be the interpretation placed upon the word "witness," Christ evidently did not intend to assure His disciples of success—final, universal success—in proclaiming the Gospel. Granting the constant fulfilment of the promise, "Lo, I am with you alway, even to the end of the world," and resting in the assurance that Divine power is always present to energize and make potential the proclamation of the Gospel which Christ commanded, yet, with Christ's own declaration of the *purpose* of that Gospel before us, can we draw from any of His utterances, or from all combined, that which will warrant a *reasonable hope* for the conversion of the world before He comes? Shall we confess that devotion to Christ is not a sufficient motive and impulse to sustain us in Christian life and effort? May we not consistently affirm that, had the ultimate success of the preaching of the Gospel been a purpose in the Divine mind, Christ would not only have declared it, but have presented it as an encouragement to His disciples?

But it is claimed, and indeed asserted, by many as an almost self-evident proposition that the proclamation of the Gospel as commanded by Christ, the bearing witness *to* all nations, will be followed by the conversion *of* all nations. While freely admitting the truth that the faithful performance of duty in proclaiming the Gospel and bearing witness to the Grace of God on the part of those who are called and chosen, with the attendant supernatural power of the Holy Ghost operating on the hearts of men, are the means, and the only revealed means, by which souls may attain a new spiritual life, yet the emphatic and repeated declarations of Scripture do not warrant the cherishing of a hope that the labors of the Church are to be followed by the universal diffusion of the Grace of God.

The consummation of God's eternal purpose relating to time, to be manifested in the coming of Christ, are twofold,—the withdrawal from the world of His own Church, and the conquering of the world by the exercise of power in the person of His Son. In the first aspect the coming of Christ will be the fulfilment of the promise made just before His ascension,—a going away, the preparation of a place, the coming again, and the reception into that place of those who had been called. By this reception into the place provided for His saints, Christ preserves His people from the perilous times which are to come upon the earth. The assurance to them is, "Because thou hast kept the word of my patience, I also will keep thee from the hour of temptation which shall come upon the world, to *try* them that dwell upon the earth." The promise is not that they shall be sustained *in* or carried safely *through* the ordeal, but they shall be kept *from* that trial, the terror and rigor of which we can have but little comprehension. Whatever it may be, believers in Christ may have the assurance that by the coming of the Lord and their presence with Him, they will have no part or share in that which is to be the portion of those upon the earth.

But it must be marked that this Coming of Christ is His coming *for* His people,—the time they long and wait for, when they shall be caught up to meet the Lord in the air; when, in company with the blessed dead who have died in the Lord, they shall enter upon the fruition of hope. The Church, composed of all those, and only those, who moved by the Holy Ghost have exercised faith on the Lord Jesus, as distinguished from those who were saved during the continuance of the former Jewish Dispensation, or who may be saved after the coming of Christ for His people, will then be in reality and in very truth the "Body of Christ" and "the Bride of Christ." Whatever may be their happiness, or whatever may be their blessed employments, we know that they "shall ever be with the Lord." With the taking up of the Church, this present Dispensation of the Grace of God in Jesus Christ ends. Its purpose, the gathering of a people for His name, shall have been consummated.

In the second aspect, as far as the Coming of the Lord for His Church is concerned, its influence on the world will be rather negative than positive. The world may be utterly unconscious of the great phenomenon, and altogether ignorant of the time when it may be taking place. But the negative results of the withdrawal of the Church, and with it the Grace of God as it had been made effectual by the

Holy Ghost, will soon be made apparent in the great "Apostasy," "the falling away," and the appearance of "Antichrist." While the Holy Ghost was present on the earth, working with power in the lives of the Saints, and daily bringing into spiritual life those whom it was calling, the ordinary means of grace, the proclamation of the Gospel, the preaching of the Word, and the power and example of Christians, were all influences which restrained and modified the manifestations of evil. The reflective influences of Gospel truth, while powerless to produce any genuine change of heart or life, were yet effective in restraining the outbreakings of sin. The mind of man cannot conceive the wickedness and sin which will be developed when the depraved human heart is left to follow its own inclinations. Indeed, the light and truth of the Gospel despised and rejected will, like every good thing perverted, be only the means of promoting evil.

There is a period, clearly marked in Scripture, intervening between the time when the Church is taken away and the return of the Lord with His Saints,—that "Coming of Christ" in which the world will be most deeply concerned, for it will be the time of the consummation and fulfilment of all the prophecies of judgment and the exercise of kingly power. How long it may continue has not been revealed. It is not important that we should know, and it might be presumptuous to endeavor to determine, its time or duration. The order of events is clear, but of the time no man knoweth. But this interval, be it long or short, is the time of tribulation, "such as was not since the beginning of the world to this time, no, nor ever shall be," the time when "that wicked shall be revealed," when the nominal Church left on the earth shall become more corrupt than ever,—the time when "the God of

Heaven" begins to "set up a kingdom which shall never be destroyed," and which by its continued progress and power "shall break in pieces and consume all" other kingdoms. The revealed truth that Christ will withdraw His Church from the world at a future time, and the prophecy and statement of the events which will then occur, make it evident that the conversion of the world by the Gospel which Christ preached on the earth was not its design. In addition to the entire absence of any statement upon which a hope could be based, we have the clear prophecy of the existence and intense activity of evil, the development of which will carry the world deeper and deeper into sin and misery.

When this dark and doleful period of the world's history shall have ended, Christ will come to rule as the Son of David, to take possession of the promised inheritance, to rule on earth as he has ruled in Heaven. Then will the promised Millennium begin. Having returned to earth and bound Satan, Christ will take possession of His earthly throne. "All things that offend and them that do iniquity" shall be gathered out. "The righteous shall shine forth as the sun." All those marvellous forces by which evil in man, in the beasts, and in the material universe is subdued will be in full and constant operation, and the final result will be that "the whole earth will be filled with His glory."

A very brief sketch of what I believe to be the revealed purpose of God will close the consideration of this most important question, upon which so much depends,—not a statement of chronology, attempting to fix dates or seasons, but simply the order of times and events as foreshadowed or clearly stated in Scripture and confirmed by history.

First. The period of liberty, extending from the fall of man to God's calling of Abraham.

Second. The period embracing the history of the Jews from the calling of Abraham up to the advent and rejection of Christ, when men were under a process of Law.

Third. The Dispensation of Grace, in which we are now living, the period in which the Holy Ghost is gathering out from the world those who will compose the Church,—the Body and Bride of Christ.

Fourth. That period, be it long or short, intervening between the coming of Christ for His Church and His coming to reign upon the earth,—the time of judgment betwixt the Grace Dispensation and the Millennium.

Fifth. The Millennium, that period of universal peace and happiness which it is ordinarily supposed is to continue for one thousand years on the earth.

Sixth. The little time when Satan shall be loosed for a season.

Seventh. "Then cometh the end, when He shall have delivered up the Kingdom to God, even the Father,"—that Dispensation of Ages of which we have no revelation, that period of which it may be said " *God is all in all.*"

CHARACTERISTICS OF THE JEWISH DISPENSATION.

THE Old Testament is not a sealed book, the importance of which passed away when Christ ascended to heaven. Those Christians are in error who think that the principles which governed the Jewish nation and the remarkable events which crowded its history, can have but little interest or practical benefit for those who are supposed to be in full possession of the promised inheritance. The Church of the present Dispensation accepts the fact that it is in the enjoyment of invaluable blessings because of unbelief on the part of the Jews, but the Church has never fully accepted in its inner consciousness the equally important truths that it is not in the line of direct succession; that it has but slight, if any, portion or lot in the Old Testament prophecies; that the exact and literal fulfilment of all the promises to the Jews is only temporarily suspended; and that the time will come when the Star of Jacob will be in the ascendant and the kingdom be restored to Israel. Vastly important to ourselves and intimately connected with the final destiny of the human race as is the Church of God, its birth, progress, and culmination are not embraced in the general scope of Hebrew prophecy. We deceive ourselves with false hopes if we appropriate to the Church of this Dispensation the promises upon which the ancient Jews based their faith of a future earthly reign of their Messiah. The redemption of the world would have been effected by

Christ at His first coming had He been accepted by His brethren. Their cordial reception of Him and complete recognition of His divine character would have been the prelude to their highest national glory. All that had been promised would have been in immediate process of fulfilment. The conditions would indeed have been altogether different: the race of men would not for eighteen hundred years have borne the awful burden of guilt arising from the crucifixion of its Lord; there would have been the universal and probably sudden manifestation of that "kingdom" which John declared was "at hand." Whatever theories we may entertain on this subject, we may rest assured of the fact that the infinite resources of the Eternal God would then and there have accomplished His designs of love to men had the Jews joyfully accepted instead of bitterly rejecting His Son.

Although the Church of the present was not revealed to the gaze of the prophets, Christ and the Apostles have given us two general truths concerning it. On earth it is to be the faithful witness of its absent Lord. When He comes to take it to Himself, it will be an active participant in His purpose of love and mercy, and a sharer with Him in His glory. Beyond these we have but little of its duties or rewards. We are confident that the grace and love of the Lord are so infinite and His resources so inexhaustible that the blessings granted to the Gentiles will in no way detract from the future glory of the Jews, neither will their possession of the earth and the glorious earthly kingdom of the Jews interfere with or in any way affect the close union between Christ and His chosen Church.

It is impossible to have any correct understanding of the relation in which the Old and New Testaments stand to each other, or to have any true conception of God's great plan of good to the human race, ordered from the beginning of time and extending onward to its close, unless we first gain some distinct idea of His revealed purpose to and with the Jews. The basis upon which rests the whole Jewish economy is found in God's covenant with and promise to Abraham. It was essential to the fulfilment of this promise that God should select from the people of the earth, then sunk in idolatry and sin, a nation that would be a "peculiar people," upon whom He would lavish His favor, and to whom He would make special and definite revelations of Himself and His will.

He would make them not only the prophets of good things for all nations, but also the active participants in accomplishing that which they foretold. That they were called to be the witnesses and teachers of the fundamental truth of Monotheism, is apparent in all the Jewish records. The eternal existence, the Personality, and the Unity of God were indelibly impressed upon their minds and wrought into their hearts. By the revelations God made of Himself to Abraham, Isaac, and Jacob, by the deliverance of their descendants from Egyptian bondage and His guidance of them through the wilderness, by the giving of the Law from Sinai, and the foundation of a new order of religious ceremonials, sacrifices, and worship,—symbolical of still greater blessings in store,—they were taught that all was for their restoration to purity and holiness by the closest possible alliance of humanity with the everlasting God, and that, under certain conditions, Jehovah would establish an assured communion between Himself and the chosen people that would be for their peace and happiness. A loving Father, yearning for His rebellious children, would absorb them into His own life and holiness by placing them under the guidance of His own hand, subjecting them to a Law of absolute purity, with an ultimate design of dwelling within their hearts and establishing a kingdom of Righteousness upon the earth. Leaving out of view, for the time, the symbolism of the ancient worship, we find that these principles give continuity to the whole record of God's dealing with His chosen people and evidence of the wonderful adaptation of the process to accomplish the proposed end. Take, for example, that portion of Jewish history embracing their rebellion and consequent forty years' sojourn in the wilderness. The generation which had been intimately familiar with and constantly tempted by the idolatry of Egypt was cut off and its place supplied by one formed and moulded by God's own hand. Their religious conceptions had been created and fixed, their moral consciousness awakened and deepened, by the authority of the moral law and by the constant influence of the Tabernacle service. The enjoined necessity for and frequent recurrence of the bloody sacrifices assured them of an ever-present sinfulness and corruption, from which forgiveness, at least, might be obtained. Their repeated deliverances from impending dangers by displays of miraculous power had wrought into their souls a feeling of dependence upon that "Jehovah" whose new name had been given to them in their "anguish of spirit" and "deep bondage." They came to the borders of Canaan a strong people, young in years, prepared to take and hold possession of the land promised to their fathers. Their theology was pure, their principles of domestic and social economy were the best in the world, and to-day form the basis of civilized life, and their worship and religious belief had been interwoven into their individual and national life. They were in every way prepared for the work they were to do. The purpose of God in choosing a people, and the successful result of the discipline and training, became evident when they entered into possession of Caanan.

One of the most remarkable characteristics of the Jewish nation, always present with them, and continually finding expression in their prayers, psalms, and prophecies, is their firm belief in a happy state of being on the earth for all its inhabitants, a condition of peace, joy, and prosperity, of which they were to be the channel. As Isaac Taylor says, "It is greatly this steadfast confidence in a bright future for all nations that gives unity and coherence to Hebrew prophecy, and which blends into a mass the various materials of which it consists. It is this hope for the world that has welded into one the succession of the Old Testament writers. The Patriarch of the race received this very promise, that in him should all nations henceforth be made happy." David and the Psalmists take up this same large assurance and say, "All nations whom Thou hast made shall come, and worship before Thee." Isaiah rests often upon this theme, and kindles as he expands it; and one of the last of this company foresees the setting up of a kingdom which should have no end, and which should embrace "all people, nations, and languages." It is true that Palestine was always the Hebrew Prophet's foreground and the Holy City his resting-place; but he looked out beyond these near objects, and with the remoteness of place he connected the remoteness of time, and dwelt, with fervent aspirations, upon the promise of an age when "from the rising of the sun to the going down of the same" the anthems of a universal worship shall ascend from earth to heaven. Singular it is that a people so intensely national and exclusive in thought and feeling, so isolated by the circumstances of their Divine training, should so confidently anticipate and clearly predict a time of peace, justice, and truth for all nations. The dreams and imaginings of the poets of other nations will not compare, for far-reaching extent, with the vision of these ancient seers. Strange as it seems, the Jew, whose high privilege came from birth and blood, who regarded all others with contempt, preached a philanthropy through his prophets that was absolutely unrestricted, embracing an area wide as the world and reaching forward into ages yet to come. The genuine philanthropy of the world bases itself upon and is cherished by the principles of the prophets. In them, rather than in the words of Christ, do we find any warrant for a hope of the ultimate triumph on the earth of justice and benevolence. To them seems to have been revealed with Divine precision what God was to do on the earth with Israel and the nations. In striking contrast with the fulness of their visions is the remarkable silence of the New Testament concerning the destiny of nations, and of the progress and universal diffusion of the Gospel. What we gather from the words of Christ and the Epistles of the Apostles (the Revelation of John only excepted, for that is inextricably combined with the Jewish prophecies) assures us of waning faith, continued and successful aggressions of evil powers, the depredations of "grievous wolves," of "perverse men" drawing disciples after them, and of perilous times for men. Instead of peace, Christ's advent is followed by the sword. The New Testament has no promises of earthly comfort or prosperity as the reward of personal piety. The Christian is to be content with food and shelter, trusting in the continued presence of Christ in the soul, and solacing himself with the thought that "the coming of the Lord draweth nigh" and "hoping unto the end for the grace that is to be brought unto them at the revelation of Jesus Christ."

Aside from the all-pervading influence of inspiration which made these predictions absolute truth, a natural reason for this marked peculiarity may be discerned in the fact that the whole Jewish economy and legal dispensation were *national* in character, *temporal* in duration, and (apart from figurative intent and symbolical design) thoroughly *materialistic* in spirit. They were national by the circumstances of Divine choice,—from the selection of the seed of one man through whom the blessing must flow, a God-given birth which came only by heredity. They are purely national because the burden of the prophecies is the latter-day glory of the Jewish people, when they shall have found and accepted the Messiah, when the Gentile nations have been brought to the knowledge of the truth and the curse removed from the face of the earth.

They were temporal, because they were to have their consummation on the earth, and to fulfil a purpose among the *nations* regarded in the mass. Except, therefore, as an underlying and assumed principle springing from the eternity of God, a future immortality was not an essential part of the Jewish system as such. A promise of individual immortality was very dimly, if at all, revealed, and we search in vain for any definite declaration which can be regarded as confirmatory of the glorious hope. Now, in the authentic announcement of immortality and the incontestable evidence given by Christ, the yearnings and aspirations of the Psalmists and prophets may be regarded as only the gropings and reachings forward of those to whom no clear revelations had been vouchsafed.

In nothing, perhaps, is the difference between the Jewish and Christian systems more clearly marked than in the feelings awakened in pious hearts by the contemplation of the natural death of the body. The Psalmist pleadingly cries out, "What profit is there in my blood when I go down to the pit? shall the dust praise Thee? shall it declare Thy truth?" and again he affirms "that the dead praise not the Lord, neither any that go down in silence." Again he asks the questions, "Wilt Thou show wonders to the dead? shall the dead arise and praise thee? shall Thy loving-kindness be declared in the grave, or Thy faithfulness in destruction? shall Thy wonders be known in the dark and Thy righteousness in the land of forgetfulness?" He clings closely to life because "in death there is no remembrance of Thee. In the grave, who shall give Thee thanks?" When he was afflicted and poured out his complaint before the Lord, he said, "O my God, take me not away in the midst of my days." Solomon gives utterance to the same idea when he declares, "There is no work, nor device, nor knowledge, nor wisdom in the grave whither thou goest."

Hezekiah doubtless expressed the feelings of the pious Jew on his recovery from sickness and deliverance from death: "I said in the cutting off of my days, I shall go to the gates of the grave: I am deprived of the residue of my days. . . . For the grave cannot praise Thee, death cannot celebrate Thee, they that go down into the pit cannot hope for Thy truth. The living, the living, he shall praise Thee as I do this day: the father to the children shall make known Thy truth."

The natural shrinking from death, either as an entrance upon a new condition of being or a ceasing to be, did not arise in the breast of the Jewish saints from any slavish fear of God or from visions of a dread future called up by a guilty conscience. It was because they believed death to be the end of their usefulness. They desired to remain on the earth to serve and honor the Lord, to enjoy the bounties of His hand, to receive, even to a good old age, the blessings which He had joined to the faithful performance of duty. The future being shrouded in darkness, the earth was their portion, and they would gain from it all the satisfaction it could afford.

To Christians all is different. For them death has no terrors, for it has been conquered for them by Christ. Death is only the servant to usher them into the presence of their Lord. The real object of the Christian's hope is not his individual happiness after the life on earth, but the coming of Christ and the resurrection of the saints. To meet death is not the object of a saint: it is merely the entrance upon that eternity of glory which Christ has assured.

"When the Most High divided to the nations their inheritance, when He separated the sons of Adam, He set the bounds of the people according to the number of the children of Israel." The division and separation were not from any inherent goodness in the Hebrews exceeding that of the surrounding idolatrous nations. It was the first step in the process by which God, who is a Spirit, would manifest Himself in a spiritual manner as a reconciled God to every son and daughter of Adam, and raise them from a position of degradation to one of glory and honor far above that forfeited by their progenitor. The Jews were simply the material through which He would reveal Himself and His plan of mercy culminating in the Incarnation of His Son. Descending from the heights of His own glory and meeting the race of men at their lowest point, He would redeem them from sin and lead them by a gradual and long-continued process to the point where He would give them all He had to give,—Himself in the Person of His Divine Son. As the word of the Lord said unto Jeremiah, the whole house of Israel and the whole house of Judah were to be unto the Lord " for a people, and for a name, and for a praise, and for a glory;" they were to form an earthly kingdom of Righteousness, to be a light unto all nations.

The discipline and training of this chosen nation was in accordance with the nature of man, was perfectly adapted to its purposed result, but nevertheless its *apparent* failure for a time may be expressed in the words of Isaiah : " What could have been done more to my vineyard that I have not done in it ? wherefore, when I looked that it should bring forth grapes, brought it forth wild grapes ?" The more Jehovah would favor the chosen people the more rebellious they became, the more He did for them, the harder appeared to grow their hearts, until that inborn depravity, increasing continually by a natural course of events, came to a full development in the highest crime it was within the power of man to commit,—the death of Him who came to be their Prince and Saviour. At the cross on Calvary God's infinite love and man's bitterest hatred met. There a reconciled God was manifested to sinful, rebellious men. There the middle-wall of partition which had so long stood between the Jew and the Gentile was broken down, and a way of access to the Holy of Holies, which had hitherto been approached by an earthly High Priest, and that only once a year, was opened fully to every human soul. Pardon, with all it involved, was open and free to those who would accept it. Christ, living and dying in the flesh as the Son of man, proclaimed a common salvation for all the sons of Adam, and abolished forever both the enmity and power of the law over those who received Him. By uniting them to Himself, and making them in a special sense the sons of God, He wrought out for them an elective or personal salvation different in nature, extent, and privilege from that which resulted to the entire race from His assumption of human form. The enmity of the law having been taken away by pardon, there remained nothing that would prevent the acceptance of a full and finished salvation by any human soul. Law had been conquered by Grace. Men were free to choose either, but must abide by their choice. Those who would live by the Law might gather what advantage they could from it, but judgment by that Law must be the consequent of their election.

Without any present consideration of the causes by which the chosen people were led, in spite of their long-continued course of discipline and preparation, to refuse the promised Messiah, who would at that time immediately have entered upon the fulfilment of the prophecies relating to their nation, we accept the fact that the Jews rejected Christ, and thus opened at once a way of salvation for the Gentiles, and rest in the faith that, as God in His infinite wisdom has made the wrath of man to praise Him, He will in the future latter days establish an Earthly Kingdom of Heaven, leaving to His Church the blessed work of *witnessing* for Him during the long interval existing between the apparent failure of the Legal Jewish Dispensation and the manifestation of His glory at the appearing of Christ.

As Law in all its power of restraint and penalty was the spirit of the old economy, and Grace with its absolute freedom and its happy results following from their proper cause is the moving impulse of the new economy, it is evident that the Christian dispensation must be in every respect different from that which had preceded it. The objects and motives in each being dissimilar, the process by which the end of either can be attained will have but little in common. The Jew and the Christian cannot travel on the same highway. They may indeed observe the same code of morals and be governed to a certain extent by the same eternal laws of right and wrong in all their relations with their fellow-men, but they can never stand in the same relation to God, the Father of all, until they are full participants in a common faith. The ceremonial worship, which had served so good a purpose in pointing the faith of Jewish believers to Christ, was shorn of its strength and beauty, and could no longer be of any efficiency to the worshipper, for it was displaced by that heart-worship "in spirit and in truth" of which Christ had spoken. The bloody sacrifices were unavailing, for Christ had by His own death deprived them of all power. An examination of some points in which the difference between the Law and Gospel, or the Jewish and the Christian dispensations, is strongly marked, may be of practical benefit to some Christians who are tempted to rest their hopes more on "the works of the law" than on the finished salvation through Christ so freely manifested for their acceptance in the Gospel.

The whole legal system was a result of the covenant between God and Abraham and his descendants. A covenant continues in force during a specified time or until the death of either of the parties. All the blessing and mercy promised in this covenant culminated in the gift of Jesus Christ, who, coming from the Eternal Father, stood ready to give to the chosen people just what they had long hoped for, and which would have been the fruition of all their desires. With Christ's death the covenant of works became null and void by the act of those for whose benefit it had been instituted, or rather its provisions were held in abeyance and temporarily suspended. What, then, is the position of a believer in Christ? He, by faith, becomes a participant in the blessing resulting and flowing from the Covenant of Grace between God the Father and Christ the Son of Man. Christ, by His death, becomes a Testator, and bequeaths to all believers the infinite riches of His love and grace in the New Testament of His blood. By it all believers become the sons of God and partakers of Eternal Life. They form a new creation in Christ Jesus, different in origin, in spirit, and in result from any life that had previously been in the world.

Under the Law, God was worshipped more acceptably in certain places than in others. Access to Jehovah was through the priesthood. The priests could venture to approach the Holy Place only after a process of purification and clothed in a prescribed dress. The magnificent earthly temple at Jerusalem was the one spot where the Lord was most fully manifested to those who would seek Him. An offering or a sacrifice of the best he possessed must be presented by him who would enjoy the Divine favor. The entire service was national in character, adapted to an earthly people, and restricted to localities. Gospel-worship is universal in character, spiritual in nature, reaching beyond the temporal, and finding its consummation in the eternal. Its participants serve in the newness of the Spirit, being fully delivered from the oldness of the letter. The old material worship, visible to the outward eye, brought with it no peace to the conscience, no blessed assurance of pardoned sin, but the invisible spiritual, eternal Gospel-worship brings with it the peace of God by uniting the soul to God. While it is universal, it is also individual by virtue of this union. While Christians are not a nation in the proper sense, and do not worship in a worldly temple, yet they do form a holy nation, a peculiar people, having citizenship in heaven, and a Great High Priest, who, having risen from the dead, offers up continually spiritual sacrifices acceptable to God. Christianity is in one sense a religion without a temple, an altar, or a sacrificing priest. All who are drawn by the power of the Holy Ghost become the subjects of that faith by which they receive Christ in all His fulness as their Saviour, and thus are made members of the redeemed Church, saved from the power of sin, delivered from the bondage of the law, and made partakers of the liberty of the children of God.

Of these, and these only, is the Church of Christ composed. The Church is formed of sanctified souls called from the world, made members of Christ, and members one of another. They are the members of the "one Body," of which Christ is the Head,—they are all new creatures in Christ Jesus. The Church is formed of those who, in the truest and deepest sense, are the people of God, and are such because, as Simeon declared, "God at the first visited the Gentiles, to take out of them *a people* unto His name." (Acts xv. 14.) It is the result of Christ's life-work and death, by which He hath broken down the middle-wall of partition, and made in Himself of twain *one new man,*—a new creation, different from all that had preceded it. The perfect manifestation of a reconciled God, in the person of Jesus Christ, forever abolished the Jewish Law, the Jewish temple and sacrifices, everything that was material and external, and made the faith of the individual soul the means by which the new relation between God and man was begun and continued. The religion of Jesus Christ, being spiritual in essence, swept away all that was visible save that which sprang legitimately from His own sacrifice, an outward sign for an inward grace.

A logical inference may be drawn from this scriptural view of the constitution of the Church that would relegate to their proper place among the typical ceremonies of the Jewish economy many of the practices of modern Christendom which have a tendency to make the Church nothing more than a refined Judaism. They are the result of a human mingling of what God hath forever separated,— Law and Grace. The spirit prompting them is dishonoring to God; for, denying the truth that "Christ is the end of the law for righteousness to every one that believeth," it would establish a righteousness of human effort and would cover the simple truth of the Gospel with the misty clouds of a human and false theology. It would transform the Gospel of glad tidings of great joy to all people into a system of intellectual philosophy, finding its proper home in a visible organization claiming to exercise by a Divine right the same spirit and legal force which were undoubtedly lodged with the priesthood of the ancient people while under the reign of law. The sad results are seen in the multitudes of the professed followers of Christ who are "almost, but not altogether," Christians; struggling between law and grace; having too much light to find all their satisfaction in the world, but not enough confidence in grace to come out and be separated from the world; striving to believe that they are at peace with God, but not having the peace of God dwelling in their hearts; working that they may obtain life instead of manifesting by their work the Divine life which has been implanted in their hearts.

In endeavoring to get some idea of the characteristics which mark the Jewish Dispensation, the great contrast which they offer to those of the Gospel Dispensation, as they are presented in the Old Testament and in the New, in Law and in Grace, may make them more evident. It has been truly said that "the New Testament is hidden in the Old, and the Old is opened in the New." Adam is the head of a fallen creation, Christ is the Head of a new spiritual creation. In the old creation, man belonged to death; in the new, death belongs to man. (1 Cor. iii. 22, 23.) In the old, death takes everything from man; in the new, death gives us all things. In one, death was a master, in the other, a servant,—in one, an officer to drag to justice, in the other, a messenger to carry us home to glory. To the humble saint death is not an end either to be avoided or to be desired, for when the time comes it is simply a bridge to carry him over the Jordan.

The Old Testament is temporal, literal, and national; the New is eternal, spiritual, and individual,—the law of God stamped upon the heart of each saint. The Old was a bondage in which no rest, joy, and peace could be found. It was a revelation of death involving man in a curse. (2 Cor. iii.) The New opened up to man all the blessings that his soul could long for, and is to him an instrument of life and delivery from the curse. The Old was a ministry of condemnation; the New, a ministry of righteousness.

The Old constrained to action by external force; the New incited to action by spontaneous love in perfect freedom, love, and delight, at the same time imparting the Grace by which the soul is sustained. The Law was to educe from man what he was to God; Grace was to manifest what God is to man.

THE JEWISH NATION AND ITS FUTURE DESTINY.

ASIDE from the great interest connected with the Hebrew nation as the source through which we have received a Divine Revelation, its history has a strong fascination arising from an antiquity extending farther back in the remote ages than that of any other people. In reading, we feel assured that it is an authentic history, whose records are based on substantial foundations. We have a consciousness, dear to every Christian heart, that the religion of Jesus Christ rested upon and was developed from Jewish history. This consciousness is assured not only by the indisputable facts of Revelation, but by the continued existence of the Jewish nation,—not, indeed, in the ordinary form of a nation possessing an objective government, but in the form and under the exact conditions which had been plainly revealed to the Jews by their own inspired prophets while they were inheriting their own promised land. Since the destruction of their Holy City they have lived in the world and among other nations separate and alone. At various periods of their history they have come into close contact with other nations, have mixed with them, and have lived with them in bondage, but have never become identified with them and never allowed their history to be so blended with that of their conquerors that they could not at the appointed time be again entirely separated, and by some inherent principle or power of cohesion at once form again a homogeneous nation, carrying with them it may be some of the ideas, or perhaps the vices, of their oppressors, but never to such an extent that the peculiar characteristics of their nationality were materially changed. Their principles, hopes, and faith are as strongly and apparently as unchangeably fixed in their minds as the peculiar features of countenance are marked upon their faces. Living as they do in every part of the civilized world, holding constant business communication with the people among whom they dwell, having nothing that can be recognized as a national or ecclesiastical head, apparently nothing that could cherish or maintain State and Church politics, adapting themselves, as far as may be necessary, to the laws and customs of the country where they sojourn, they do still, to-day, maintain in greater or less purity the distinctive principles of their faith and practice, and do still draw strength, comfort, and consolation from the inspired words of Isaiah and Jeremiah, and still look forward with unshaken faith to the full and literal fulfilment of the covenant which Jehovah made with their progenitor Abraham. Their continued separate existence, despite of political and national annihilation and a continuous persecution such as no other people on earth ever suffered for so long a period and in such varied, far-reaching forms, is unparalleled in human history. Other nations conquered by superior force have under similar circumstances maintained their primitive character for a few generations at most and then gradually faded away, leaving some names and words as the only memorials of their existence; but the Jews of the present age, having lived for nineteen hundred years " without a king, and without a prince, and without a sacrifice, and without an image, and without an ephod, and without teraphim," or any of the essentials of a nation and Church, do to-day stand in a position to respond to the call of any leader whose credentials would assure them of a Divine commission. Let us not say that the "age of miracles" is past, for the continued existence of the Jewish nation is an ever-present miracle. Its past, present, and future history has formed, and will continue to form, one of the most wonderful and far-extending displays of supernatural power that has ever been manifested on the earth.

Instructive and interesting as would be the consideration of the causes which led to and produced the dispersion of the Jews among the nations of the earth as they are recorded in the Old Testament and abundantly confirmed by the actual facts of history, the whole subject must take its place among the fulfilled prophecies of Scripture, and the attention be directed to their future destiny as it is predicted by the same prophets who so truly announced their degradation and suffering. The more carefully the passages of Scripture relating to the restoration of the Jews are studied, the more apparent will be the truth that the hope of the Church—the glorious appearing of the Saviour—is closely united with God's purpose of good to His ancient people, and that in the latter days when by His love they shall be turned from sin and unbelief to righteousness and faith and established in honor and glory in their own land, with Christ as their personal King, this royal people, now too generally regarded as the offscouring of the earth, will be, as was promised, a blessing to all the families of the earth, and inheritors of a glory and dignity far surpassing that of any Gentile potentates. While the declarations of Jehovah "of the things which must shortly come to pass" have great significance to the Christian who believes that the promised Messiah has once lived on the earth, to the pious Jew they must have an intensity and force of meaning far beyond our conception. They are part of his inner life, the basis of all his hopes, the consummation of all his devout desires. They may be regarded by us as types and symbols, or as records of that with which we have no personal concern, but to the Jew they are still the "oracles of God," instinct and throbbing with life, a sacred trust committed to him by the great Jehovah.

It is not the present purpose to quote all or even a large portion of the many chapters of the Old Testament which so clearly predict the future glory and happiness of the children of Israel, but to select from the many, some that more definitely than others declare the manifest intent of God.

As it is a fact that the descendants of Abraham are now scattered over all the earth, so it is plain that they shall be gathered from all lands and restored to their own country. Isaiah declares: "And it shall come to pass in that day, that the Lord shall set his hand again the second time to recover the remnant of his people which shall be left from Assyria, and from Egypt, and from Pathros, and from Cush, and from Elam, and from Shinar, and from Hamath, and from the islands of the sea. And he shall set up an ensign for the nations, and shall assemble the outcasts of Israel, and gather together the dispersed of Judah *from the four corners of the earth.*" (Chap. xi. 11, 12.) Jeremiah says: "At that time they shall call *Jerusalem the throne of the Lord.* In those days the house of Judah shall walk with the house of Israel, and they shall come together out of the land of the North *to the land* that I have *given for an inheritance unto your fathers.*" (Chap. iii. 17, 18.) And again it shall be said: "The Lord liveth, that brought up the children of Israel from the land of the North, and *from all the lands* whither he had driven them: and I will bring them again into their land that I gave unto their fathers." (Chap. xvi. 15.) "And I will gather the remnant of my flock *out of all countries* whither I have driven them, and will bring them again *to their folds,* and they shall be fruitful and increase." (Chap. xxiii. 3.) "Hear the word of the Lord, O ye nations, and declare it in the isles afar off, and say, He that scattered Israel will gather him and keep him as a shepherd his flock." (Chap. xxxi. 10.) In Zechariah we read: "And when I shall have scattered them among the people, they will remember me among the far-off countries: therefore shall they live with their children and return again, and I will bring them out of the land of Egypt, and out of Assyria will I gather them : and into the *land of Gilead* and *Lebanon* will I bring them, and it shall not be sufficient for them."* (Chap. x. 9, 10.) In these and in many other passages three facts are prominent,—that by Divine purpose and power the Jews have been scattered in all lands; that by the same power they shall again be gathered; and that they shall dwell in the land given to their fathers, Palestine. The statements are clear, plain, and literal. Any process which would spiritualize such declarations must conflict with the ordinary rules of biblical interpretation and result in disastrous confusion. In the study of this as of any other line of scriptural truth, the intent of any particular passage becomes more evident by the reading of the whole paragraph, or even book, in which the text occurs.

Strange as it may appear, those who have despised the Jews shall, at the time of their restoration, treat them with respect and bear a willing part in advancing the purpose of God. Isaiah says, "Thus saith the Lord Eternal, Be-

---

* Some of the passages are quoted from Isaac Leeser's "Twenty-four Books of the Holy Scriptures, according to the Massoretic text, after the best Jewish Authorities." This fact accounts for some slight variations from our accepted English version.

hold, I will lift up to the nation my hand, and to the people will I raise up high my standard: and they shall bring thy sons in [their] arms, and thy daughters shall be carried upon shoulders. And kings shall be thy nursing fathers, and princesses thy nursing mothers: with the face toward the earth shall they bow down to thee, and the dust of thy feet shall they lick up." (Chap. xlix. 22, 23.) When the day shall come, many will gladly share in their blessing: "For the Lord will have mercy on Jacob, and will again make choice of Israel, and replace them in their own land: and the strangers shall be joined unto them, and they shall attach themselves to the house of Jacob." (Isaiah xiv. 1.) "And it shall come to pass in the last days . . . many people shall go and say, Come ye, and let us go up to the mountain of the Lord, to the house of the God of Jacob; that He may teach us of His ways, and we may walk in His paths." (Isaiah ii. 3.) "And many people and strong nations shall come to seek the Lord of Hosts in Jerusalem, and to pray before the Lord." (Zech. viii. 22.)

While the restoration of the Jews may be in one sense the result of the natural laws of God's providential dealings with mankind, there are many passages warranting the belief that it will be attended with unusual and miraculous displays of Divine power; for Micah, in speaking of the "flock of God's heritage" feeding "in Bashan and Gilead, as in the days of old," says, "As in the days of thy coming out of the land of Egypt, *will I let them see marvellous things.*" (Chap. vii. 15.) Isaiah declares that "the Lord will utterly destroy the tongue of the Egyptian sea; and He will swing His hand over the river with His mighty wind, and will smite it into the seven streams, and render it passable with shoes; and there shall be a highway for the remnant of His people, which shall remain from Asshur; like as it was to Israel on the day that they came up from the land of Egypt." (Chap. xi. 15, 16.) They shall have a leader divinely commissioned: "Behold I send unto you Elijah the prophet before the coming of the day of the Lord, the great and the dreadful: and he shall turn back the hearts of the fathers to the children, and the hearts of the children to their fathers." (Mal. iii. 23, 24.) Isaiah gives us a record of miracles that will be coincident with the return of the ransomed to Zion: "The blind eyes shall be opened, the deaf ears unstopped, the lame leap, the dumb sing: waters break out in the wilderness, and brooks in the desert, sandy wastes be changed into pools, and thirsty lands into springs of water: all ravenous beasts will disappear; joy and gladness shall be the portion of His people, and sorrow and sighing shall flee away." (Chap. xxxv.)

A civil polity resembling the ancient *régime*, with counsellors and judges, will be established, with Christ as their personal King. In the first chapter of Isaiah, the Eternal of hosts declares that, after having taken satisfaction on their enemies and purged His people from dross, He " will restore thy judges as at the first, and thy counsellors as at the beginning" (verse 26); and in the twenty-third chapter, " And I will raise up over them shepherds who shall feed them: and they shall fear no more, nor be dismayed, and none of them shall be missing. Behold, days are coming, saith the Lord, when I will raise up unto David a righteous sprout, and he shall reign as King, and prosper, and he shall execute justice and righteousness on the earth." (Verses 4, 5.) " And they shall serve the Lord their God, and David their King, whom I will raise up unto them." (Jer. xxx. 9.) In that sublime and glowing prediction of the future glory of his nation written in chap. lx. 16, Isaiah reaches the highest point in the declaration: "And thou shalt know that I the Lord am thy Saviour, and thy Redeemer, the Mighty One of Jacob." Ezekiel, too, gives clear testimony on this point: "And my servant David shall be King over them; and one Shepherd shall be for them all: . . . and David my servant shall be Prince unto them forever." (Chap. xxxvii. 24, 25.) Hosea, also, declares that after the many days of dispersion and desolation "will the children of Israel return, and seek for the Lord their God, and David their King; and fearing will they hasten to the Lord, and to His goodness in the latter days." (iii. 5.)

If the passages already quoted do clearly set forth the facts that the Lord by His mighty power will gather the Jews again into their own land and re-establish a Theocracy of which Christ will be the head, it must follow as a natural consequence that the position of the nation among other nations of the earth will be unique and peculiar, resembling in some respects the position held by it in the ancient days, with, however, this great difference,—that in the future or "latter days" it will be the source of blessing to all people, and thus in the most complete sense fulfil God's promise to Abraham. All their high privileges of their former days shall be enjoyed again, "for I will have mercy upon them, and *they shall be as though I had never cast them off*." (Zech. x. 6.) A remarkable passage worthy of careful study is found in Zechariah (xii. 7, 8): "The Lord also will save the tents of Judah first, in order that the glory of the house of David and the glory of the inhabitants of Jerusalem shall not become boastful over Judah. On that day will the Lord be a shield around the inhabitants of Jerusalem; *and the feeblest among them shall* be on that day like David; and the house of David shall be like divine beings, like an angel of the Lord before them." The privilege of an Israelite being hereditary, a divinely-conferred birthright, all will enjoy it. It will be not only national, but *individual* and particular.

In the full favor of Jehovah they "shall be in the midst of many people like dew from the Lord, like showers upon the herbs that wait not for man, nor hope for the sons of man." Their enemies shall not be able to stand against them, for they "shall be among the nations in the midst of many people like a lion among the beasts of the forest, like a young lion among flocks of sheep: who, if he break in, both treadeth down, and teareth in pieces, while none can deliver" (Micah v. 6, 7), and even more emphatically in the succeeding verse: "High shall thy hand be lifted up above thy adversaries, and all thy enemies shall be cut off." In the day when the Lord shall save them as the flock of His people, "like the stones of a crown will they elevate themselves over His land. For how great will be the happiness of that generation and how great its beauty! Corn shall make the young men sing joyfully, and new wine the virgins." (Zech. ix. 16, 17.) "No weapon that is formed against thee shall prosper, and every tongue that will rise against thee in judgment thou shalt condemn." (Isaiah liv. 17.)

As the land on which the Jews once lived has been a partaker of the curse pronounced on its inhabitants, it will also participate in the blessing; its fertility shall return and its abundant harvests yield food to the thronging multitudes: "Lo, but yet a very little while more, and Lebanon shall be turned into a fruitful field, and the fruitful field shall be esteemed as a forest." (Isaiah xxix. 17.) "And I will make them [the wilderness and the forests] and the environs of my hill a blessing; and I will cause the rain to come down in its season; rains of blessing shall they be. And the tree of the field shall yield its fruit, and the earth shall yield her products, and they shall be on their land in safety." (Ezek. xxxiv. 26, 27.) "Then shall they say, This land, that was desolate, is become like the garden of Eden, and the cities that were ruined and desolate and broken down, are become fortified and inhabited." (xxxvi. 35.) Amos gives us a graphic picture of the fertility and abundance of the land in the day when the tabernacle of David shall be raised up and rebuilt as in days of old: "Behold, days are coming, saith the Lord, when the ploughman shall come close up to the harvester, and the treader of the grapes to the one that scattereth the seed; and the mountains shall drop with new sweet wine, and all the hills shall melt away. And I will bring back the captivity of my people Israel, and they shall build the wasted cities, and dwell therein; and they shall plant vineyards, and drink their wine; and they shall lay out gardens, and eat their fruit. And I will plant them upon their own soil, and they shall not be pulled up any more out of their land which I have given unto them, saith the Lord thy God." (Chap. ix. 13–15.) Joel also says, "Fear not, O land; be glad and rejoice; for the pastures of the wilderness have become green; for the tree beareth its fruit, and the fig-tree and the vine yield their strength. And the threshing-floors are full of corn, and the vats overflow with young wine and oil." (ii. 21, 22, 24.)

It may be claimed that as these prophecies are essentially Jewish in character, referring to and embracing only the descendants of Abraham, they are not of general interest to the Church of Christ or the world at large. To the Church the fulfilment of these prophecies will be the fruition of all her hopes,—the coming of the Lord. To the nations of the world their fulfilment will be the beginning of the terrible things that are to come upon the earth in the latter days. Everywhere in the Old Testament the conversion of the Jews and their restoration to their own land are closely connected with great wars and confusion among the nations, and widespread desolation through all the earth. Read carefully the thirty-fourth chapter of Isaiah, with its parallel passages in both the Old and New Testaments, and learn what is involved in "the day of vengeance unto the Lord, and the year of recompense for the controversy of Zion. . . . Inquire out of the book of the Lord and read" what will take place when He calls all nations and people and the earth itself to hearken and hear. Joel, too, is clear and explicit in his declarations of what shall take place "in those days and in that time when I will cause to return the captivity of Judah and Jerusalem," when the Lord " will assemble all nations, and hold judgment with them because of my people and my heritage Israel, whom they have scattered among the nations, and for my land which they have divided out." (iv. 1, 2.) Zephaniah also reveals the Divine purpose: "Therefore wait but for me, saith the Lord, for the day that I rise up to the prey, for my judgment cometh to gather the nations, for me to assemble the kingdoms, to pour over them my indignation, all the fierceness of my anger; for through the fire of my jealousy shall all the earth be devoured." (Chap. iii. 8.) The restoration of the Jews will be an evident and public fact, claiming the attention of other nations, and attended with punishment on those who have oppressed them: "Thus saith the Lord Eternal, When I gather the house of Israel from the people among whom they are scattered, and shall be sanctified on them *before the eyes of the nations*, then shall they dwell in the land that I have given to my servant Jacob; they shall dwell thereupon in safety . . . when I execute judgments on all those that despoiled them." (Ezek. xxviii. 25, 26.)

The bright picture of peace, prosperity, and happiness which the prophets present of the future of the chosen people is not without dark and ominous clouds. It does not fully appear that their restoration to their own land and their conversion are either synonymous or identical. On the other hand, some of the prophetic declarations seem to refer to a period between the *return*, or at least a partial restoration and their *conversion*, during which they will undergo a process of discipline and purification resembling in its severity the refining of gold and silver. While in many cases the promises of the regathering of Israel would at first glance seem to be wholly for their comfort and peace, yet in others the context seems to connect it closely with a time of dreadful distress, corresponding in some respects with the terrors which are to come on other and less-favored nations of the earth. In the thirtieth chapter of Jeremiah, so full of rich promises to the Jews, and of threatenings to their oppressors, after a statement of bringing "again the captivity of my people Israel and Judah" to the land of their fathers, the Lord speaks concerning them: "A voice of terror have we heard, dread, and no peace. Ask ye now, and see whether a male doth give birth to a child? wherefore do I see every man with his hands on his loins, as a woman in giving birth? and why are all faces turned pale? Alas! for that day is great, there is none like it; and a time of distress it is unto Jacob; yet out of it shall he be saved." Of similar import is the passage in the twenty-second chapter of Ezekiel where God speaks of the nation as "copper and tin and iron and lead in the midst of the furnace; the dross of silver are they become;" and declares, "*Because* ye are all become dross, *therefore* will I gather you into the midst of Jerusalem, and blow upon them with the fire of His wrath, will melt them *there* as silver is melted in a furnace, and they shall know that the Lord has poured out His fury upon them." But even more remarkable is the passage in the fourth chapter of Michah, where, after the beautiful picture of " the mountain of the Lord's house firmly established on the top of the mountains," the nations joining restored Israel, the prevalence of universal peace, when "they shall sit every man under his own vine and fig-tree, with none to make them afraid," the dark cloud, the time of Jacob's trouble, suddenly appears, and we read, "Now why dost thou cry aloud? is there no king in thee? is thy counsellor lost? that pangs have seized on thee as on a woman with child? Be in pain and labor to bring forth, O daughter of Zion, like a woman in travail: for now shalt thou go forth out of the town, and thou shalt dwell in the field, and thou shalt go as far as Babylon; there shalt thou be delivered." Another direct reference to the same time of trouble is found in Zech. xiii. 8, 9 : " And it shall come to pass that in all the land, saith the Lord, two parts therein shall be cut off, shall perish; but the third part shall be left therein. And I will bring the third part into the fire, and I will refine them as one refineth silver, and will probe them as gold is probed." On this very important part of Israel's future destiny the reader is advised to read Isaiah li. 17–23; lix. 1–18; Ezek. xx. 32–37; Joel ii.; Zeph. i. It would appear that this trial of Israel will be sharp, fearful, and decisive, an infliction of a terrible and final judgment before their acceptance of Christ. In the same connection a careful study of one of the most comprehensive discourses of Christ, as it is given by Matthew (xxiv. 1–44), may throw some light on prophecies that otherwise might be obscure. If, as Lightfoot says, the New Testament was written "among Jews, by Jews, for Jews," and therefore cannot but speak the language of the time, both as to form and to contents, let it be borne in mind that Matthew, above all his fellow-apostles, was the Jew of Jews, having a mind that seemed not to possess the power of receiving, comprehending, or imparting truth unless it was closely related to the destiny of his nation. It must also be remembered that while this wonderful discourse takes in the destiny of the Jewish remnant, the general history of Christendom, and the judgment of the nations, it does not include or refer to the Church. The great truth of a Divine Church—one body composed of Jews and Gentiles—could not have been and was not announced at this time, because the Messiah had not yet left the earth, and God, in the Person of the Holy Ghost, without whose presence there could be no Church, had not descended upon the earth. If, therefore, we attempt to apply the teaching of our Lord to the Church of the present dispensation, we fail to grasp the truth He intended to convey, and introduce an element of confusion that will make its reconcilement with many other passages difficult, and with some impossible. The Gospel Dispensation, with its resulting Church, finds no place in the prophetic records, for it is an interval, a break, a parenthesis, between the rejection of Christ and His Second Coming to the earth to receive His people to Himself. The time for the development of the Christian Church had not yet arrived, neither was its existence essential or in any way necessary to the full accomplishment of all that Christ here revealed. An examination of the teachings of Christ in the context—the record of which is greatly marred by the unfortunate division into chapters—may make evident the fact that in answer to the question of His disciples, "Tell us when these things shall be?" Christ sketched for them in outline the future history of the Jews; or, to state it more particularly, the experience, the trials and destiny, of the faithful remnant of Israel that will be left on the earth during the interval between the departure of the Church from the world and the final consummation of all things. Having made His final appeal to the apostate nation of Israel, He "went out and departed from the temple," never again to enter it, and, withdrawing to the Mount of Olives with His disciples, left the chosen people to that long period of darkness and desolation just about to close in upon them. Away from the multitudes, in confidential discourse with the disciples, He foretold the trials coming upon them, and taught them that although He would be rejected by the Jews as a nation, yet He would in the last times gather about Him a portion of His "brethren according to the flesh," who would be the successors and representatives of the few faithful ones who listened to His words on the mountain. They listened to His words, but they did not comprehend them. They came to Jesus "for to show Him the buildings of the temple." Their minds were filled with what was dear to every Jewish heart, and occupied with hopes of an immediate restoration of the earthly kingdom. The warnings they had already received that their leader should be delivered to the Gentiles, should be mocked, scourged, and crucified, had been unheeded because they had been incomprehensible. The quotation from Daniel, in the fifteenth verse, with which they were familiar, is very specific, and makes it clear that His reference was not to the destination of their holy city, but to the time of the end, when, as Daniel declares, "Thy people shall be delivered, every one that shall be found written in the book." (Chap. xii. 1.) The persons, therefore, addressed were Jewish believers, those who accepted Christ when He was with them in personal form on the earth, and those who in the long years after—the pious remnant of Israel—should accept the Messiah whom their fathers had rejected. To these only could the words of Christ have any possible application. Believers under the Grace dispensation have no part in this discourse. "This Gospel of the Kingdom," to be "preached in all the world for a witness to all nations," is something very different from "the Glorious Gospel of the Grace of God," which the apostles preached after Christ had ascended to heaven and the Holy Ghost had taken up its abode in human hearts. *This distinction must be made or confusion is inevitable.*

After this digressive examination of our Lord's statement of the future history of the faithful portion of the Jewish people, corresponding so exactly with the words of the ancient prophets, it would be well to learn what the Old Testament declares with reference to Christ and the restoration of the Jews. Take the eleventh chapter of Isaiah (still quoting from the accepted English translation of the Hebrew by Isaac Leeser), beginning, "And there shall come forth a shoot out of the stem of Jesse, and a sprout shall spring out of his roots: and there shall rest upon him the spirit of the Lord," etc., and the tenth verse, "And it shall happen on that day, that He of the root of Jesse, who shall stand as an ensign of the people, to Him shall nations come to inquire: and His resting-place shall be glorious,"— and we have a description of Christ as He was on the earth, and of what He shall be when He "puts forth His hand again the second time to acquire the remnant of His people." Consult also Zech. xiv. 1–21, Ezek. xxxvii., and Zech. xii., and the passages already quoted, with their parallel texts, and there will be found abundant evidence that Christ will come to His own people to deliver them from all oppressors, lead them into paths of truth and righteousness, unite and establish all the tribes in their own land, make the city of Jerusalem the seat of universal empire, in which He will rule as their Personal King, and make the Jews to be a blessing to all the nations of the earth.

While basing the restoration of the Jews to their own land on the fact that it will be the result of special Divine agency attended with miraculous power, it is yet germane to the question to examine the present situation of the Jews with reference to their return to Palestine, and discover the causes, should any exist, which may tend to the fulfilment of prophecy by the ordinary and natural operations of God's providence. Believing firmly in and insisting strongly on the truth that the dispersion of the Jews, their wonderful preservation during a long interval, and their ultimate restoration are only the separate parts of a revealed purpose and plan of Jehovah, carried on in a manner different from His general overruling and guidance of the nations, it may yet be profitable to consider some events which have transpired during the last ten years that have beyond a doubt influenced the return of many Jews from all parts of the world, but more especially from the great empire of Russia.

Rev. James Neil, whose residence for some years as incumbent of Christ Church in the city of Jerusalem gave him an intimate acquaintance with what has happened in the Holy Land and grounds for an intelligent opinion, declares in the most positive terms that there are now to be discerned very definite signs of the beginning of this momentous movement in the return of the Jews before their conversion in very considerable numbers to their own land. He gives as his opinion, based not only upon his own observations on the spot, but also upon the result of careful inquiries made of many unprejudiced Jews, that the Hebrew population of Palestine proper, one-half of which resides in Jerusalem, now numbers thirty thousand, to which must be added seven to eight thousand in Sidon, Beyrout, and Damascus,—all cities within the Land of Promise. If this be a correct calculation, there are at present in the Holy Land a considerably larger number of Jews than of any other civilized nation. The three causes which Mr. Neil believes "have in the providence of God mainly contributed to bring about this marked return to the Land of Promise are, first, a new land law affecting Palestine; secondly, new laws of military service in Russia; thirdly, new civilization throughout the East." Until very recently a Jew, or indeed any foreigner, could not have a valid title to Real Estate unless he became a Turkish subject. Above all things such a course would be repugnant to the Jews. In June, 1867, an Imperial Rescript gave to any subjects of foreign powers the liberty of purchasing and holding landed property in their own names. As a natural result of this new and liberal legislation, many Jews availed themselves of the privilege, and purchased land in and about the larger cities. In a short time there sprang up numerous little villages or communities composed exclusively of Jews. Their remarkable industry, thrift, and economy, combined with consular protection, soon placed these people in positions of considerable importance in the districts where they settled. The great bulk of the resident inhabitants of Palestine being Moslem Arabs, ignorant and in every way unfitted to be the dominant power in a province, must inevitably yield to the superior intelligence and patient persistence of the former possessors of the land. Every year the increase of wealth and the constant additions to their numbers add to their power. It is, therefore, not an extravagant hope—it may, indeed, be regarded as an inevitable fact resulting from the operations of simple natural laws—that within a few years the Jewish inhabitants of Palestine will have attained such wealth and power that the province will be virtually, if not in name, in their full possession, and so within their control that they may be able to dictate terms to the nominal owners.

It is said by those who have made the most careful computations that at least one-third of the Jewish nation (supposed to number in all about eight millions) lives within the Russian dominions. For many years, although the constant victims of oppression and persecution, the Jews have been practically exempt from military service in Russia, the number impressed having been only five to each thousand. In 1874, Russia adopted the German system, and all Jews throughout the empire were required to be enrolled and drilled in the army at the age of twenty-one. Whatever may be the reason, it is a fact that the Jews in all parts of the world are singularly averse to military service. With a vivid recollection of the many grievous wrongs they had suffered at the hands of Russia, it is not surprising that they should manifest a strong reluctance to fight on the side of their oppressors, or that they should take immediate steps to leave the country in spite of the most despotic laws to prevent such departure.

In addition to the facilities for acquiring land in Palestine and the dread of enforced military service in Russia, the movement of a new civilization in Syria presents some attractions that will exert some influence on European Jews. Mr. Neil regards the labors of missionaries from England, Germany, and the United States, with the presence of their wives and families, as a potent element in ameliorating the condition of the people, and thus making it possible for the Jews to share in the religious toleration and freedom which have from time to time been conceded by the Turkish government. He also claims that the establishment of good schools and the promotion of education among all classes by the missionaries have compelled the bigoted Jews to open and maintain schools for Jewish girls in order to keep the young people away from the missionary institutions, and thus the younger generation is being prepared for the great work before it.

The establishment in Syria of Consulates of various civilized nations, whose representatives are intrusted with important powers, while extending protection to their own people, has also prevented those outbreaks of Moslem fanaticism and cruelty to which the Jews had been so long exposed; for a Jew residing in Palestine who is or has been a subject of any foreign power now has the privilege of demanding trial before the consul of the country where he had lived.

Another civilizing element worthy of notice is the large and constantly-increasing number of visitors travelling in Palestine during the pleasant six months of the year, for whose comfort, convenience, and safety the various European governments have made ample arrangements. These tourists expend large amounts of money, so that their presence is regarded as a favor, not an intrusion, as formerly. All of these influences combined have compelled the abandonment of many annoying regulations formerly rigidly enforced by the Turks, so that the whole character of life in

Palestine has been greatly modified, the populace brought more directly under refining measures, and the country rendered more tolerable,—at least as a place of residence for Europeans. All the advantages resulting from the power and influences of the leading nations of Europe are open to and participated in by Jews.

One remarkable circumstance mentioned by Sir Moses Montefiore in his "Narrative of a Sojourn in the Holy Land," in 1875, would seem to indicate a steady and growing demand for dwelling-places by Jews. He states that while at Jerusalem he received from the Building Committee of a little colony called *Meah Shearim* (Hundred Gates) an invitation to participate in the ceremony of laying the corner-stone of a row of houses. The object of the association, numbering one hundred and twenty members, is to build each year not less than ten dwelling-houses, which, on completion, are allotted to ten members. On inquiry, he learned that there were then among the Jews at Jerusalem two other similar Building Associations, the practical combined result of which would be, that "in a very few years two hundred and thirty-five Hebrew families would be the owners of most comfortable houses in a very salubrious locality outside the city limits."

Even more significant is the fact that the Governments of England and the United States have, within a few years, sent expeditions to explore the Holy Land and obtain detailed and authentic information of its topography and present condition. Such expenditures of money on the part of associations of private individuals would seem to offer some return in definitely fixing the localities of the Sacred Text, and gaining the information that would enable reverent seekers to enjoy the results of scientific search. But an Ordnance Survey, largely assisted by governmental aid, is an unusual proceeding, for which a very clear reason cannot be assigned. These things are all evidences of a great and revived interest in the Holy Land and the Jews, that at present seems to be pervading the minds of many in all Christian lands, and, taking, as it does, a practical form, may with great reason be accepted as the precursor of the restoration, so far as this extraordinary prophetic event may be the result of natural causes. As has been said, "those who assent to the true laws of language and symbols will no more deny or doubt that the prophecies teach that the Israelites are to be restored, than those who assent to the definitions and axioms of geometry will deny the demonstrations that are founded upon them. There is not a proposition in the whole circle of human knowledge of more perfect certainty than that God has revealed the purpose of regathering that scattered nation, establishing them as His chosen people, and reappointing a temple-worship at Jerusalem that is to embrace some of their ancient rites. It is not merely certain, but is taught with a frequency, an emphasis, and an amplitude, and invested with a dignity and grandeur, that are proportionable to the vastness and wonderfulness of the measure in the great scheme of His administration over the world."

Even though the prophets had been silent concerning the future of their nation, the consideration of Jewish history during the last nineteen centuries, an examination of the indestructible and unsurmountable barriers which have so completely separated the Jews from all other people on the earth, the fact that they have retained all of their original characteristics wherever they have been scattered through the world, and have, under all circumstances, maintained the spirit of a religion that was local in its character, the rites of which could only be properly celebrated in the city of Jerusalem,—all combine to give reasons for the belief that in God's providential dealings with the nations the Jews are reserved to take a place and perform a high duty, worthy, in all respects, of the people of whom, "according to the flesh," Christ came. The natural principles which have attended the development and decay of other nations utterly fail to account for their wonderful continuance. The factors of destruction in the history of another nation, which would have destroyed every trace of national existence in a very few centuries,—conquest, abrogation of civil and ecclesiastical government, slavery, forcible removal from their native land, dispersion through the entire world, bitter and relentless persecution,—all have failed to accomplish the results which to human view seemed both natural and inevitable. The causes which have disintegrated other nations and in time scattered the fragments beyond a possibility of recognition, seem only to have strengthened the invisible but potent influence binding the Jews in one compact, homogeneous mass. On simply natural grounds the mysteries and problems clustering around Jewish history are beyond solution. Accepting what we believe to be a scripturally-demonstrated conclusion, that from the time of Abraham, the Jews have been the chosen people of the Lord,—the subjects of a miraculous guidance and care so steady and uniform in manifestation that they seem to take a place among the ordinary operations or developments of a natural law,—we find the principle which underlies all Jewish history, and explains what would otherwise be so perplexing. Accepting this fact, with all its involved consequences, we can confidently look to that bright future of the nation on which their own inspired men have so delighted to dwell. We look for a literal, personal, and national restoration of the ancient people, a re-establishment of their former glory, an exact fulfilment of promises of peace, plenty, and earthly prosperity,—in short, the full culmination of the earthly kingdom of Heaven predicted by the prophets and assured by the words of Christ.

It is passing strange that so many Christians will read the Divine declarations of a complete dispersion of the Jews in their literal sense, will even find in the history of the race facts strengthening their faith in the authenticity of the Old Testament, but yet, at the same time, put a spiritual interpretation upon the connected promises immediately following in terms no less literal. This singular and most unreasonable perversion of Scripture truth, has not escaped the notice of that acute critic and profound Jewish theologian, J. Cohen, of Paris, who says, "And when Christianity, at a later period, abandoning Judea and Jerusalem for the Rome of the Cæsars, became the conqueror over ancient society, and assumed the organization and development which seemed unto it fit,—when Christianity was no longer able to apply literally to the new religion the predictions of the prophets, the promises of the Holy Book, and the textual expressions of the Old Testament,—it nevertheless preserved and combined them in its dogmatic phraseology and was content to set them forth in symbols. Thus, though the throne of David, Jerusalem, and the nationality of Israel were engulphed by the wars of Roman invasion and have totally disappeared, the Christian Church maintains that they still exist, but transfigured and raised to the dignity of a supernatural myth. The name of Israel has been symbolically given to the assembly of the faithful of the new creed; a heavenly Jerusalem has replaced, in the hopes of Christians, the earthly Jerusalem, which, according to the Jewish faith, is yet to become the centre of the moral world, and the throne of

David has become idealized in the universal empire of Christianity." He then forcibly remarks, "But, whether symbol or reality, it is not the less true that the whole world has existed subject to the influence of these ideas and words of essentially Jewish origin." While willingly admitting his claims that the entire domain of religion has been much influenced by Judaism, that Christianity has made known to the world and everywhere taught the admirable Psalms of his nation, that Christian ritual has been largely borrowed from the Old Testament, that the names of the patriarchs, Moses and Aaron, and of the great Hebrew prophets, are everywhere cited amid the rites and services of the Christian Church, and that all these facts do inseparably connect modern times with the imperishable remembrance of the exodus from Egypt, yet we cannot allow the inference based upon them, that the Christian Church owes "its splendor, its power, and universal dominion to Judaism." Believers in Christ have appropriated much that is eternal and true in Judaism, and rightfully, for it is our common inheritance through the promised Messiah, who hath broken down the wall of partition and given us a just title to the inestimable privileges and truths which hitherto had been the peculiar possession of the favored nation. Surely the Jews will not complain because Christians have taken hold of the sublime truths and great moral principles revealed to them by Jehovah, and made them means of blessing to all nations. The day will come when they themselves will be the missionaries to "the isles afar off which have not heard my name," and shall preach these same truths with a power and success probably far exceeding any that has hitherto been granted to the Christian Church. The Christian Church has taken from Judaism some features and ideas not in accordance with the fuller revelation of truth received from its Founder and Head. It has so accepted the Law given to the Jews while under tutorage and training, that it has failed to appreciate the blessing, the freedom, the full justification, belonging and extended to all who by faith in Christ would "be partakers of the Divine nature." Its devotion to the Law has been so constant that its "whole life has been enwrapped in a network of prescriptions governing every moment, every impulse, every action." It has substituted the Law, a series of mechanical commands and prohibitions, lifeless and useless in themselves, for that love of Christ and indwelling of the Holy Spirit constraining us to crucify the flesh with its lusts and affections, and thus, by a Divine power and ever-present impulse, not only fulfilling the Law in its true meaning and broadest scope, but going far beyond the requirements involved in a fixed and arbitrary rule. For the Jews—those who rejected Christ—the Mosaic Law has not been abrogated. To it they still cling, and for them it may have rich blessings in store. But it is their heritage, and there may be lodged in it a hidden meaning and abundant excellence which will be manifested only during the personal reign of the Messiah on earth, when He shall have gathered His own into their Holy City. May there not be in the sacrifices and ceremonials, which in former days so significantly pointed forward to the life, sufferings, and death of the Messiah, a secret spirit and reserved force, by which they may in the future point back to the finished work, and thus equally serve two purposes,—prophetic and commemorative? While there will be no more offering for sin, yet the words of Isaiah, "that all the flocks of Kedar shall be assembled unto Thee, the rams of Nebaijoth shall minister unto Thee: they shall come for a favorable acceptance upon my altar, and the house of my glory will I glorify" (lx. 7), point directly both to a Temple and a ritual of sacrifice akin to those of the former days, and give abundant evidence that Christ will come to His own people, be joyfully accepted as their King, and lead them into the full possession of promised blessing.

Considering that the words of the prophets were almost exclusively devoted to the future destiny of the Jewish nation,—that anything relating to other nations came in incidentally, as it were,—and divesting the mind of the mistaken idea that these bright pictures have any reference to the Church of Christ existing under the present Grace dispensation, let us endeavor, even at the risk of repetition, to gain some definite and literal idea of the future in store for the chosen people. With these two principles in view, the reader of the Old Testament may well be astonished at the multiplicity of promises that are scattered on every page, and amazed at the minuteness and exactness of detail which characterize them. While there are many pointed texts in Leviticus, Numbers, and Deuteronomy declaring God's love for and care over Israel, with intimations, more or less clear, of the high position the nation will take "in the latter days," the same truths are more fully developed by the Prophets and the authors of the first three Gospels, and are abundantly confirmed and verified in all their far-reaching influences in the Apocalypse. Although the Apostles, after the resurrection and ascension of Christ, wrote with special reference to the Church which He established, yet in the Epistles we find hints of the close connection between the future of Israel and the coming of the King,—that coming of the Lord for His saints previous to those remarkable and stupendous events which are subjects of prophecy.

In St. Paul's clear and logical presentation of the condition and future of his brethren, as affected by the Gospel which he preached, recorded in the tenth and eleventh chapters of the Epistle to the Romans, the expression in the fifteenth verse, " For if the casting away of them be the reconciling of the world, what shall the receiving of them be but life from the dead ?" is replete with vital meaning, and opens up a resurrection which will be a cause of rejoicing to all who love the Lord Jesus Christ. Looking at the Jews as the " brethren" of the Lord, it may be a question whether the love and devotion which the Christian Church has professed for the Master have been genuine when unaccompanied by a corresponding love and affection for those to whom His heart went out with such tender sympathy. It is surely a most favorable sign that within the last twenty-five years many thoughtful men in all parts of Christendom have awakened to the consciousness that the fruition of the hope of the Church is closely related to the future of the elect people of God.

The prophecies of Daniel, who, above all others, was the prophet of the Jews, give the general outline of future events on the earth as far as they relate to kingdoms and nations, for to him the Lord declared, "Now I am come to make thee understand what shall befall *thy people* in the latter days," and, that it was not for the immediate time, the statement is added, "For the vision is yet for the coming time." (Daniel x. 14.)

While the future was opened to him, he does not enter upon the reign of glory of his people. He only comes, as it were, to the threshold, to that time when "Michael the great Prince shall stand forth for the children of His people." He sees in vision the "time of distress, such as hath never been since the existence of any nation, until that same time;" he has the assurance that "at that time his people shall be delivered, every one that shall be found written in the book;" he learns that some of his brethren "shall awake to everlasting life and some to disgrace and everlasting abhorrence;" and he catches some glimpses of the glory that is to be their portion when "the intelligent shall shine brilliantly like the brilliance of the expanse of the sky," and of the mission in which they will be employed, for "they that bring many to righteousness shall be like the stars for ever and ever." (Daniel, chap. xii.) Seeing and learning so much of the future of his people, the prophet naturally cries out, "O my Lord, what shall be the *end* of these things?" but the only response is, "Go thy way, Daniel! for the words are closed up and sealed till the end of the time," with the final injunction and promise, "But thou, go thy way toward the end; and thou shalt rest, and arise again for thy lot at the end of the days."

In whatever may have been revealed to Daniel and Matthew of the future of their beloved nation, there is no evidence that either had any conception of a future spiritual Gospel dispensation. The range of their prophetic vision passed over that elective dispensation of God's Grace during which, for a specific purpose connected with His ultimate glory, God would gather a people for His name, and fixed upon that point when Messiah would rule over the house of Jacob and the glory of their nation would be manifested on the earth, when Israel would be central sun of all nations. Everywere in the Old Testament we find prophecies of the King who is to rule over the Jews, under whose sway the nation shall prosper abundantly and bear dominion over all the nations of the earth, but it was not revealed to the Jews that during the long period of their shame, following the advent of the Messiah and their rejection of Him, that a people would be taken from among the Gentiles who should reign with Christ in His spiritual kingdom. This was the mystery hidden until the Spirit revealed it by the Apostles.

While there can be no doubt of the fact that a glorious future is in store for the Jews, it would not be the part of wisdom to endeavor to fix the time when, as a nation, they will enter upon it or, even with the specific details recorded in Scripture, to attempt to forecast its conditions. The book is sealed, and so it must remain until the time of the end. But our faith in the future of the saints is not more surely or more scripturally based, than our faith in the future glory and happiness of God's chosen people,—the Jews.

THE COMING OF CHRIST.

In every system of religion, even in those which are the products of unenlightened human reason, there may be found one grand central idea or truth, with which all the others are so intimately connected, that its comprehension and acceptance are essential to the understanding of the whole philosophy. It is the pivotal point about which the subordinate truths revolve, the key which opens many confusing mysteries, the foundation-principle without which there can be no logical consistency. When it is firmly established all the other dogmas, with their practical results, rest securely upon it. If it be based upon the shifting sands of falsehood, the superstructure, however fair and substantial in appearance, must topple and fall into ruins.

Such a broad, wide-reaching, and well-defined principle we find in the Gospel of Grace, in the simple fact plainly stated by Christ, and fully expanded by His Apostles, that the Lord Jesus Christ *will come again*,—that at some future period He will leave the Father's Throne and come in the clouds of heaven to receive His people to Himself, to execute judgment on all evil, and to establish His own universal and everlasting Kingdom.

This *coming of the Lord* is placed before the Christian as an object of faith and hope, closely bound up with and powerfully influencing all that concerns his life on earth. It is not placed before him as an idea with which he has no personal practical interest, but it is constantly assumed and referred to in Scripture as an encouragement to duty and an incentive to perseverance in the Christian life. While the fact itself must take its place in unfulfilled prophecy, our faith in the second coming of Christ rests upon the same solid foundation that it has for accepting the predictions and the accomplishment of His incarnation and crucifixion, or for the descent and continued presence of the Holy Ghost. The recorded facts of the life, death, resurrection, and ascension of our Lord are not sustained by more indubitable proofs, or more worthy of our hearty acceptance than is the cognate fact that He will personally, actually, and literally come from Heaven to earth, and take to Himself the power and glory promised by the Father. The testimony concerning it is so abundant that it may be found on almost every page of the New Testament. It is so clear and distinct, that the neglect or indifference with which the blessed truth is regarded at this present, is one of the saddest signs of the times for Christendom. The great importance and value of the truth which God has revealed for the comfort and consolation of His chosen ones, and which He has placed so prominently on the pages of His word, can be evaded only by a criminal carelessness that passes it by as a matter of little moment, or by a natural perversity of heart and mind that wilfully refuses it. The simple statement given to men by supernatural witnesses, that "this same Jesus which is taken up from you into heaven, shall so come in like manner as you have seen him go into heaven," followed by the universal prayer of the Church, as spoken by the last surviving Apostle, "Even so, come Lord Jesus," reveal a truth which was coincident with the birth of the Church, closed the canon of inspiration, and in its manifestation will be to the Church an entrance to its highest glory.

A full belief in the appearing of Christ was so prevalent

in the Primitive Church that Christians lived in almost daily expectation of it. When the Apostle wrote of "*waiting for the coming of our Lord Jesus Christ,*" or of "*our conversation in heaven, from whence also we look for the Saviour,*" or of "*waiting for His Son from heaven,*" or of "*looking for that blessed hope* and the *glorious appearing* of the great God and our Saviour Jesus Christ," they accepted the words as a literal statement of a fact which would surely take place and of which they hoped to be witnesses. Their hope was not that they would go to Christ, but a belief that He should one day come for them. They expected the coming, they desired it, and *waited* for it. This belief exerted more or less influence on the visible Church until the ninth century, when it seemed to culminate and disappear in the fanatical delusion that Christ would appear and the world be suddenly destroyed. After the reaction following the dashing of that idea and the utter failure of the many predictions concerning the dreaded catastrophe, traces of a genuine belief in the scriptural declaration could be found scattered through the Church up to the time of the Reformation. While the Reformation yielded precious fruits in the opening of a sealed Bible, and in the delivering of the people from the tyranny of a corrupt Church, and a cruel priesthood, it also resulted in the formation of many belligerent sects, each one retaining the main elements of the Jewish legal system, and struggling bitterly for the possession and retention of temporal power, forgetful of the fact that Christ's kingdom is not of this world. In the strife thus engendered, the precious truth of Christ's appearance was either discarded or treated with indifference as a mystical fancy of unpractical dreamers. The prevailing belief came at last to be that when the world was converted by the active labors of the Church, Christ would come and the earth enjoy its promised Millennium. It must be confessed that since the Reformation to the present time, the majority of those who compose the visible Church have not been looking for the coming of Christ, and have not, except in a general and crude manner, made the belief in it an article in their theoretical and intellectual creeds. Absolutely shut out as the Church of the present dispensation is from any participation in the prophecies of a glorious future, except as they may be connected with or dependent upon the appearance of Christ, the indifference and often aversion which so many of her members manifest to this truth, can only be accounted for by the prevalence of false ideas concerning this period of God's dispensational dealings with the Church, when its head is hidden in the heavens, and the Holy Ghost is working in the hearts of men forming that body which is to be the Heavenly Bride. It is a lamentable fact, that the Church does not cherish a lively hope that Christ will personally come to the earth to remove the curse, to destroy the works of the devil, and to rule as King of the Jews and King of nations. A consideration of some of the causes producing this widespread unbelief of one of the most vital Gospel facts, may place the truth more definitely before the mind and make evident the folly of its rejection.

A *spirit of materialism* resulting from the insidious temptations of Satan, has so permeated the visible Church that Christians have made their personal future safety a primary object of solicitude, while their interest in that which relates to Christ's future glory has become secondary. When the peace and rest which the covenant of Grace has provided and made sure for all who accept the gift of the Son of God, has been allowed to usurp that place in the desires and affections of the heart which should be occupied by earnest hopes for, and deep interest in, Christ's glory, both in Heaven and on the earth, the fact is sad evidence of but slight progress in the Divine life, and of a state of contentment with privileges far below those which are, or might be, the present possession of every Christian. If by reason of misty and uncertain views, springing from careless or indifferent study of the truth God has revealed in His word, our aspirations do not reach forward beyond the changing and evanescent scenes of this mortal life, our religion, which, like its source, should be wide-reaching as the universe, becomes contracted and narrow, and degenerates into a species of selfishness, a form of self-righteousness which accepts the results of a "life hid with Christ in God" as a reward for service rendered, a merit for active effort, or wages for labor performed. The "glorious liberty" vouchsafed by the Gospel is transformed into legalism, and the infinite love of God is measured by the amount of earthly good granted, or the delights of Heaven promised, rather than by the glory to be manifested in His Son, at whose coming all who are united to Him by faith, will be made the full and honored participants. The almost irresistible temptation to Christians, of the false ideas thus formed, is to regard this present dispensation as the last, or "the end of days," and to believe that the Church is to be the means of the conversion of the world under this system of Grace. Very naturally, then, more dependence is placed on human effort for the accomplishment of the supposed plans of God, than upon the influence and power of the Holy Ghost, who leads into all truth and duty. An activity springing from a voluntary act of the human will, and a misdirected zeal prompted and guided by the forces of human organization—elements which never can accord with the supernatural influences of the Holy Spirit—have been fully developed in the history of Christendom, and are still working out their disastrous results in the schisms, disputes, and errors that so sorely afflict the visible Church, and make her so often, and too universally, the weak and feeble witness of her absent Lord. There are, certainly, here and there many Christians who cherish a true though cloudy view that Christ *may* come and reign on the earth; but the preaching of a worldly gospel paralyzes even that dull hope, and deprives it of the little power it might otherwise exert.

There is another error into which many fall that is worthy of remark, viz., the confounding of two facts altogether different in character and results,—the *coming of Christ* and *the death of the Christian*. The statement is often heard from the pulpit to the effect that the natural death of the body is to the individual soul the coming of Christ, and its immediate entrance into the conditions of its final and everlasting destiny. Without entering upon any discussion of that intermediate state of souls existing between the death of the body and its resurrection, we would call attention to the four passages of the New Testament referring to the natural death of the Christian, assured that their examination will most conclusively prove that the coming of Christ so explicitly foretold is not in any sense connected with natural death. The words of Christ to the penitent thief, "This day shalt thou be with me in paradise" (Luke xxiii. 43); the last words of the martyr Stephen, "Lord Jesus, receive my spirit" (Acts vii. 59); Paul's expression of willingness "rather to be absent from the body and to be present with the Lord" (2 Cor. v. 8), and his "desire to depart and to be with Christ" (Phil. i. 23), are all we have. While these passages do most certainly teach that the souls of believers will in some sense be present with

Christ in that "paradise" into which Paul was caught up and "heard unspeakable words which it is not lawful for man to utter," yet they give no warrant for the idea that Christ comes to us at death, or that His reception of our souls is in any sense that coming of which the Apostles speak. On the eve of His departure Christ plainly said to the disciples, " I go to prepare a place for you, and if I go and prepare a place for you, *I will come* again and receive you unto myself,"—a promise that can have no reference to the death of believers. Our going to Him, and His coming for us, are different facts in every respect. In Scripture they are never confounded, and it becomes us, if we would fully comprehend the truth, to carefully observe the wide space which separates them.*

Another fruitful source of confusion, existing in the minds of Christians concerning the unfulfilled prophecies of the New Testament, is the acceptance of the "coming of Christ" and "the day of the Lord," as one and the same thing. The times themselves are frequently regarded as synonymous, and the events as identical. The one is, or should be, the hope and expectation of the Church; the other is the fulfilment of the words of prophecy contained in the Old as well as the New Testament. The one has special and direct reference to the Church only, those who are called out from the world by the Grace of God; the other embraces the Jewish nation and all people that may be dwelling on the face of the earth at the time of its manifestation. By an examination of a few of the passages of frequent occurrence in Scripture, we may arrive at some definite conclusion as to what is involved in that terrible phrase, "the day of the Lord." Joel says, in second chapter, "Let all the inhabi-

---

* See them contrasted, John xxi. 23.

tants of the land tremble: for *the day of the Lord* cometh, for it is nigh at hand; a day of darkness and of gloominess, a day of clouds and thick darkness, as the morning spread upon the mountains; . . . the earth shall quake before them, the heavens shall tremble, the sun and the moon shall be dark, and the stars shall withdraw their shining, and the Lord shall utter His voice before His army, . . . for *the day of the Lord* is great and terrible, and who can abide it? . . . And I will show wonders in the heavens and in the earth, blood and fire and pillars of smoke. The sun shall be turned into darkness and the moon into blood, before that great and terrible *day of the Lord* come." Compare these words, spoken to and primarily intended for Jews, with the words of Christ as recorded by Matthew, the Jewish apostle, whose mind, more than that of any other disciple, received and comprehended the utterances of the Master that had the closest relation to the national hope and destiny, in twenty-fourth chapter, twenty-ninth verse: "Immediately after the tribulation of those days shall the sun be darkened, and the moon shall not give her light, and the stars shall fall from heaven, and the powers of the heavens shall be shaken, and then shall appear the sign of the Son of man in heaven, and then shall all the tribes of the earth mourn." Isaiah says, in the thirteenth chapter, "Howl ye, for *the day of the Lord* is at hand: it shall come as a destruction from the Almighty. Therefore shall all hands be faint, and every man's heart shall melt, and they shall be afraid. . . . Behold *the day of the Lord* cometh, cruel both with wrath and fierce anger." And again, in chapter thirty-fourth, after predicting great and fearful changes in the ordinary course of the heavenly bodies, and the falling of the hosts of heaven as the leaf falleth from the vine and the fig-tree, he says:

" For it is the day of the Lord's vengeance, and the year of recompense for the controversy of Zion." Compare these, and many other similar predictions of all the Jewish prophets, with the words of Christ, as given by Luke in the twenty-first chapter of his Gospel: "And there shall be signs in the sun, and in the moon, and in the stars: and upon the earth distress of nations, with perplexity; the sea and the waves roaring; men's hearts failing them for fear, and for looking after those things which are coming upon the earth; for the powers of heaven shall be shaken." From all that is recorded of this great and terrible day of the Lord, we learn, that while it will be a period of wonderful changes in the course of nature, of terror and distress to all men, a time of judgment upon the world, a day of reckoning with Gentiles and apostate Jews, it will not be the day of the coming of Christ,—that it has nothing in common with that day of peace and joy, that day of rapture and glory, when Christ shall have been forever and inseparably united with his people.

A study of the passages where "*the day of the*" Lord is predicted by the Jewish prophets, and spoken of with still greater emphasis by the Lord Himself, will divest the mind of the reader of many false or confused ideas, and assure him that "the day" and "the coming" are not one and the same thing. While there may be an interval of time between them, which cannot be fixed with precision, yet Scripture teaches that they are not simultaneous. The "coming of Christ" will *precede* "the day of the Lord," and, as a result, the deliverance of the Church from judgment will have been manifested, for the Church, ere that day arrives, will have been taken to Heaven, and made joyful in the presence of the Lord. The four-and-twenty crowned elders, representing the redeemed saints, shall be gathered around the Lamb in glory, before the seals shall be broken, or the vials poured out, or any portion of the terrible scenes which were opened to John's prophetic vision shall take place. The one will be the fulfilment of John's prophecies given to and intended for those who have accepted Christ; the other is the culmination and final completion of God's purpose with His chosen people, and the entire race of men, those " that know not God, and that obey not the Gospel of our Lord Jesus Christ."

The practical influence of a clear comprehension of this important distinction can scarcely be overestimated. The present comfort of a Christian is in some measure dependent upon, and governed by, his hopes of the future, which spring from, and are influenced by, true or false conceptions of revealed truth. Not in possession of the key which only can open the mystery, or failing to grasp the first principle of truth on which all depends, the mind is filled with vague or fearful ideas of the future, and the soul takes to itself all the tribulations and anguish, the judgment and terrors, which are so certainly to be the accompaniments of "the day of the Lord," and loses sight of the heavenly glory, the quiet peace and rich comfort that are the promised portion of Christ's people when He shall come for them. The utter failure to make the proper distinction between Christ's descent into the air to receive all His people to Himself, and His appearing in a glory visible to all, to set up His Kingdom and to enter upon the inheritance promised by the Father, takes away from the Christian any deep interest in, and earnest desire for, participation in the answer to the universal prayer of the Church, "Amen: even so, come Lord Jesus."

An inference may properly be drawn from the very different manner in which the two great facts are always presented to us in Scripture. With all the Apostles it is assumed that believers are looking, and waiting for the coming of Christ. It is placed before the heart and affections as a bright and blessed hope that may be realized any moment. There is no reason revealed, no cause given why it might not take place this day. The coming is not awaiting the fulfilment of any prophecy, is not dependent on any preparation that can be made, or any labor that can be performed. We rest safely on the scriptural ground that when God's purpose of love to His children in this world is completed, when all who are the elect of God have been united to Christ by faith, then "He will come." The "day of the Lord," its sudden coming with attendant darkness and destruction, are used by Paul as a strong argument to press home upon the consciousness of the Thessalonians, the necessity of soberness, watchfulness, and the constant exercise of faith, love, and hope in those who are to stand as witnesses of their absent Lord.

There is present in the minds of many well-meaning and intelligent Christians a lurking fear, based unfortunately on reasons of certain force, that a belief in the second coming of Christ is associated with and will inevitably lead to unauthorized speculations and absurd conclusions which should be reprobated rather than encouraged by thoughtful pious men. It cannot be denied that some men have allowed this truth to gain such exclusive possession of the mind that it has produced in them and their followers, an extravagance of language and conduct, a spirit of intolerance and uncharitableness towards those who may not be able to agree with them, a feeling of self-satisfaction and spiritual pride, accompanied by vain imaginings and fanatical expectations, that these obnoxious features have been regarded as the legitimate fruits of the doctrine rather than as the results of intemperate zeal. There may be such an overwhelming persuasion of the truth of any particular doctrine, especially if it relates to something in the future, that the subject may become oblivious to the claim of ordinary daily Christian duty, and yield himself to the fascinating but useless labor of reconciling the events of social or political life with the details of his preconceived notions of prophecy. To all such, an outbreak among the nations, or a treaty of peace, the advent of a remarkable man, or the death of an earthly potentate, or the thousand other facts of human history that seem to have more than an ordinary importance, are claimed as the immediate precursors of the coming of the Lord, and made the foundation of the most absurd expectations. These things may, or may not, have some connection with the event; they may appear very plausible or exceedingly foolish; but they do not in the slightest degree affect the substantial evidence in our possession that the Lord will return to the earth. They should not be permitted to influence in any way the settled and practical hope cherished by the Christian. It may also be remarked that a true and genuine faith in the fact itself, may subsist in company with gross errors that do not spring from it or bear any relation to it.

The belief in, and expectation of the return of Christ, is based wholly upon a Divine revelation. It is a matter of faith throughout,—faith in testimony abundantly sustained. It rests on the declarations of Christ and His Apostles. The fact that it has not been a lively hope in the consciousness of the Church, and has occupied but a secondary position in the formulated confessions of the various sects of Christendom, is only an evidence of strange carelessness and prevailing materialism. It is not the present purpose to examine in detail the many plain declarations of the fact which meet the Christian whenever he opens the New Testament, but simply, if it be possible, to remove a few of the misconceptions that have gathered about the whole subject, and endeavor to break up, in some measure, the indifference which would pass by this important truth, as something which could not have any immediate practical connection with the individual life and destiny.

In the consideration of this, as of any other fact of revelation, we must come to the record with an earnest and sincere desire to learn just what the Holy Spirit has communicated through the medium of His servants, and what the Lord Himself hath spoken. The ordinary rules governing transmitted records may be applied here with full force. If the language of any particular passage is symbolical in character, it must be interpreted in accordance with the rules generally accepted in biblical exposition. But, when the language is simple, plain, and literal, when it is a strong declaration and prophecy of what shall be, it should be accepted as the truth which the Lord God would make known. Human reasoning and arguments may remove some of the obstacles standing in the way of an apprehension of Divine truth, but the revelation itself, impressed on the heart and mind by the indwelling of the Holy Spirit, alone can make the truth effective, and so incorporate it into the very soul of the Christian that it will become a living and constant impulse of the life. Trusting that a careful study of the fact, as it is revealed in Scriptures,* may bring it home to the heart and con-

---

* Texts referring generally to the coming of Christ: Psalms ii. 8, 9; Isaiah xxiv. 23; Jer. xxiii. 5–8; xxxiii. 14–17; Ezek. xxi. 26, 27; xliii. 4; Acts i. 11; Matt. xxiv. 27, 37, 39; xxvi. 64.

Texts referring specially to the appearing of Christ to meet the Gospel Church for the purposes of completing their redemption, of

science of believers, we would note some correlative facts, inferences, and practical results, that seem to be associated with the truth.

We have claimed that the second coming of Christ is a *central truth* of Christian doctrine, that its importance is manifested in the reconciliation it effects between points of belief which would otherwise stand in direct opposition to each other, as well as in the correct interpretation which it places upon all related passages of Scripture. In it we may

---

calling the bodies of believers from the grave, and the changing of those who may be living on the earth, and, finally, of receiving them unto Himself, and fulfilling to them all promises of dominion, power, and glory: Luke xxi. 27. 28; Eph. iv. 30; Heb. ix. 28; 1st Cor. xv. 42–44, 51–54; 1st Thes. iv. 14–17; Phil. iii. 20, 21; John xiv. 3; 1st John iii. 2; 1st Cor. iv. 5; vi. 2, 3; Rev. ii. 26, 27; 2d Tim. iv. 8.

Texts referring to the influence which the belief in, and hope of the coming of Christ should have on Christians: 1st Cor. i. 8; Phil. vi. 1, 10; Heb. x. 25: 1st Peter i. 7; 1st Thes. v. 23; 2d Thes. i. 10; 1st Tim. vi. 14; Heb. x. 25; 1st John ii. 28; James v. 7; Matt. xxiv. 44; Mark xiii. 33, 36; Luke xii. 35, 36, 40; xxi. 34; Rom. xiii. 11–14; Rev. xvi. 15.

Texts setting forth the appearing of Christ as the highest hope of the Church: Titus ii. 13; 1st Peter i. 13; 2d Tim. iv. 8.

For many clear statements as to the relation between Christ's coming and the restoration of the Jews, the reader is referred to the passages, and their contexts, quoted in essay on the Jewish nation, pages 65–72. Nothing but careful study of the Scriptures setting forth the manner in which Christ will come, first for His Church, and then for judgment, with the attendent consequences to the Church, to His ancient chosen people, to unbelievers, to Antichrist, and to the world at large, will make evident to the mind the importance of that tremendous event which has been regarded, even by believers, as a matter of little moment, or as a revelation of that which could have but slight connection with, or influence upon, the daily life of God's children.

see all the diverse lines of prophecy meeting, all the promises of good converging, all the Divine purposes of glory, both for time and eternity, approaching culmination. Following out the idea as it has been revealed in Scripture, we soon meet statements that bear very strongly against the prevalent belief that there will be a promiscuous resurrection at the same time of all who have lived on the earth. The belief is so prevalent and so apparently based on scriptural authority, that many are startled, indeed, rather shocked, by the claim that there will be *two resurrections*, different in character and widely separated in points of time. But yet this fact of two resurrections, following from and involved in the second coming of Christ, cannot be classed among those which are but dimly foreshadowed. John, in the fifth chapter of his Gospel, distinctly makes mention of "the resurrection of life" and "the resurrection of evil." He does not, it is true, in this passage make the distinction of *time*, but the difference in *character* of the two resurrections is so emphatically marked, that there is good ground for the conclusion that "the resurrection of life" is the one which will take place when Christ shall call the bodies of His sleeping saints to Himself.

The Apostle Paul, who cherished so deeply in his own soul and so frequently and earnestly enforced the glorious truth of the coming of Christ, when speaking out his own feelings to the brethren at Philippi, "if by any means I may attain unto the resurrection from among the dead," clearly and evidently refers to a resurrection of those who had known Christ "and the power of His resurrection and the fellowship of His sufferings, being made conformable unto His death." His hope was not for a part in a general awakening of the dead, but for a participation in an elective special resurrection, like unto that of his Master, based upon the revelation to him by the Holy Spirit of the future coming of Christ. It was a hope in something above the ordinary belief of the multitude gathered in the judgment-hall of Felix, that there would be "a resurrection of the dead, both of the just and unjust."

While we have ground for assurance that there will be two resurrections, in the circumstances connected with the second coming of Christ, and while they give logical and irresistible reasons that the "coming" and the "first resurrection" will be simultaneous, we have positive testimony of the fact in the twentieth chapter of Revelation. Whatever difficulties may gather about the correct interpretation of this most interesting chapter, the fifth verse, "but the rest of the dead lived not again until the thousand years were finished. This is the first resurrection," should remove any doubt that may have been felt by Christians on this important truth. Two points are absolutely fixed,—there will be two resurrections, and there will be an interval between them. Let the term "thousand years" be literal or mystical, it certainly denotes a period of time extending from the occurrence of a stated fact until another period when the fixed appointed time shall have been completed. This, being only a matter of degree and detail, does not in any manner affect the general truth, that at the coming of Christ the bodies of those who have believed on Him "will arise from among the dead," be reunited with their glorified souls, and in company with the saints who may then be living on the earth, who have been suddenly changed, enter upon their perfected eternal condition, "be priests of God and of Christ," ready "to reign with Him a thousand years."

The fact of a first resurrection of the saints, dependent as it is on the coming of Christ with Divine power to raise them from the sleep of death to meet Him in the air, is in correspondence with the principle of God's plan of salvation by Grace. Called to Christ by a special elective work of the Holy Spirit, called out of the world to be the witnesses of their absent Lord, separated from the world and formed into that mystical Body which is to be the first fruits of Christ's sacrifice,—a separation from among the dead and a glorious uniting with Christ the Head,—would seem to be in perfect accordance with God's plans with His saints, as they have been revealed in Scripture and by providence.

There is another of the generally received opinions of Christendom that will be greatly modified, and, in many individual cases, entirely changed, by the acceptance of the fact of Christ's second coming and a consequent first resurrection of the saints,—viz., a belief in a general judgment at one time of all who have lived on the earth, and a final decision of the eternal destiny of all. Aside from the statement of Christ (John v. 24), that he who heareth His word and believeth on Him that sent Him, "hath everlasting life, and shall not come into condemnation," putting all believers beyond the fact of judgment, their participation in the first resurrection, the union with Christ, render it impossible that the saints should have any part in a judgment which includes rejecters of Christ. Whatever may be involved in the fact, it is very evident from Scripture that the "saints" are not represented as being judged *with* the world, but, on the contrary, will stand in the responsible and honorable position of *judges of the world*, rulers in spiritual over the earth with Christ,—stations for which they have been prepared by training and education on the earth. In reading such statements as are found in 1 Cor. vi. 2, 3; Jude 14, 15; Rev. ii. 26, 27; iii. 21; v. 10, it is difficult to understand or in any manner account for the prevalent belief, that the saints who were redeemed to God by the blood of Christ "out of every kindred, and tongue, and people, and nation," and thus "made kings and priests," and who are represented as saying in the "new song," "*We shall reign on the earth,*" must, in some imagined future day of judgment, take their place with those who had rejected the love of the Lord as it was manifested in Jesus Christ. When they accepted Christ they "passed from death into life." The burden of their sin had been borne by Christ on the cross; their guilt had been washed away by His blood; there can be "no condemnation to them which are in Christ Jesus." They are the "blessed and holy" that will have "part in the first resurrection," upon whom "the second death hath no power," who will have been reigning with Christ before the "dead, small and great, stand before God," before the books are opened and the dead "judged out of those things which were written in the books, according to their works."

From among the many passages that abound in the New Testament setting forth by statement, by exhortation and encouragement, the practical results connected with a right apprehension and hearty acceptance of the fact of the Lord's coming, it is a difficult task to select any one, or even a few, that do perfectly and fully manifest the true position of the waiting Church of the present dispensation, for there is no special grace entering into a completely developed Christian character that is not urged upon or presented to the believer by the consideration of the appearing of his Saviour. In the exhortation of James (chap. v. 7–8), "Be patient therefore, brethren, *unto the coming of the Lord.* Behold, the husbandman waiteth for the precious fruit of the earth, and hath long patience for it, until he receive the early and latter rain. Be ye also patient; establish your hearts, for *the coming* of the Lord draweth nigh," perhaps more clearly than many, exhibits two of the characteristics which spring from faith in the promise,—viz., *patience* and *steadfastness*. Believers have been "turned from idols to serve the living and true God, and to *wait for His Son from heaven*,"—they are to have "their loins girded about and their lamps burning," because they are "like unto men that *wait for their Lord*,"—they are to "come behind in no good gift, *waiting for the coming of our Lord Jesus Christ*," by whom they shall be "confirmed unto the end, blameless in the day of our Lord Jesus Christ,"—their conversation is in heaven, "from whence also they look for the Saviour,—"denying themselves ungodliness and worldly lusts," they are to "live soberly, righteously, and godly in this present world, *looking for that blessed hope* and the *glorious appearing* of the great God,"—they are to be "sober and hope to the end for the grace that is to be brought unto them *at the revelation of Jesus Christ*,"—they are to be so fully influenced by this hope of His appearing, and their consequent transformation into His likeness, that its result will be purification, "even as He (Christ) is pure,"—they are to avoid indulgence in worldly pleasure that is so strong a temptation when the idea creeps over the mind that "the Lord delayeth His coming,"—they are to be constantly in the expectant attitude of those who are waiting for the cry, "Behold, the Bridegroom cometh,"—they are the subjects of the prayer of Paul when he asks that their "whole spirit and soul and body be preserved blameless *unto the coming of our Lord Jesus Christ*,"—they are the "blessed and holy," having "part in the first resurrection," upon whom "the second death hath no power,"—they are those who shall be "accounted worthy to escape all those things that shall come to pass, and to stand before the Son of man." Indeed, the second coming of Christ forms so large a portion of Scripture, that holiness, purity, diligence, faith, prayer, separation from the world, love for brethren, patience under difficulties and suffering, courage, hopefulness, contentment, firm assurance, and every Christian grace in this life, as well as every future glory with which the saint is to be crowned, is connected and closely bound up with it. If the faith and hope of the Christians of the Apostolic age were animated by the thought of the nearness of the Lord's coming, and if the literal coming of Christ was an impulse of such mighty power in their souls, how much more power and influence should the fact exert on us, who, by the lapse of time, are brought so much nearer to the glorious culmination of the Divine purpose? Has not the Church lost much of its power for "witnessing" by allowing a mere hope of individual salvation immediately after natural death, to take precedence of that glorious hope so clearly held up to it in the Gospel of Grace?

Aside from the practical influence exerted upon the daily Christian life by a hearty belief in the second coming of Christ, it is important as the *fact* which gives unity and coherence to all the prophecies of Scripture, however diverse and even opposite they may appear in character and result. As Scripture is mainly a revelation of God's purposes towards men, not only as to their final destiny as individuals, but nations as well; and as God's own ultimate glory is to be fully manifested in His procedure with the human race, and the earth as its dwelling-place, we are not crossing the boundaries which limit lawfully our investigations when we search for that *fact* which gathers up in itself all the lines of prophecy vouchsafed to us by Infinite Wisdom, and are not rashly intruding on forbidden ground when we strive to find in that relation the *point* where all the Divine plans will centre. Such a fact, fully comprehended and followed out in all its proper relations, will reveal order and symmetry where all seemed to be confusion and perplexity. The dark problems of human history and experience, if not solved, will at least assume a very different appearance when viewed in the clear light of God's revealed purpose.

Among the many comprehensive groupings of scriptural truth which have been made by learned pious men, we are indebted to Rev. Horatius Bonar, D.D., for one that combines the merits of completeness and simplicity. He claims that there are lines of prophetic truth running throughout all Scripture, with more or less distinctness, for the most part parallel to each other, sometimes coming into contact, sometimes crossing, and at every short distance sending out lateral branches partaking of the nature of the main one; that at no time are they wholly independent of each other, yet they are separate and distinct, so that each may be traced singly, while viewed at the same time in its relation to kindred and collateral lines. He classifies these main lines of prophecy under the following heads, leaving out the subordinate ones under each:

1. "One takes up God's purpose regarding Creation, —viz., the material globe,—tracing it from its first calling out of nothing down through its present ruin to its final restitution."

2. "Another exhibits God's purpose respecting His Son, the Christ of God, from the first promise of the woman's seed to the vision of His kingly glory."

3. "Another reveals to us God's purpose concerning the Church, as the chosen of the Father and the Bride of the Son, from her first beginnings to her glorious completion and blessedness."

4. "Another follows out the history of Israel, from the calling of Abraham to the time of their resettlement in Canaan in the latter day."

5. "Another is occupied with the history of 'the world,' —that world that lieth in wickedness,—making known to us its true character as the Church's enemy, and its doom because of its overflowing ungodliness."

6. "Another traces out Antichrist in all his varied aspects of evil downwards to his last overwhelming ruin."

7. "Another fixes our eyes on Satan himself, the old serpent, the great deceiver of the race, pointing him out to us in Eden, and never losing sight of him till he is cast into the lake of fire."

Placing, then, clearly before the mind these seven main lines of prophecy, running through Scripture like the great mountain ridges of a continent,—Creation, the Christ, the Church, the selected nation, the world, the Antichrist, and Satan,—the careful Bible student may find, in the many passages announcing the second coming of Christ, statements which connect the fact closely with each and every one of them. Taking any of the single prophecies of the Scriptures, under any or all of these general divisions, and the second coming of Christ will be its perfect culmination as a separate truth, its point of union with all other revealed truths, and, we may even claim, the reason why, and the purpose for which, the special truth was revealed. We see the material world in its perfection and beauty; then as the dwelling place of man, suffering the curse which followed the advent of sin; but when the Lord comes the earth will partake of the gladness, its curse will be replaced by blessing, and it will be an abode worthy of its Creator. We trace Christ through all His period of earthly humiliation, His death of suffering, His triumphant resurrection, but only in His second coming do we see the promises of His glory fulfilled in connection with the Church, the chosen nation, with the earth itself, and in His conquest of sin and Satan. We see the Church, the little flock, the pilgrims and strangers on the earth, the faithful witnesses of her Lord, passing through the long period of shame, persecution and suffering, waiting patiently for the time when the appearance of her Lord shall end her sorrows, begin her joys, and put her in possession of her promised glory. We trace the history of Israel—as we can trace the history of no other nation on the earth—from the time of the promise to Abraham up to the present hour, and can find no hope of the fulfilment of the promises of peace, joy, and happiness, to the outcast people until her Messiah "shall stand in that day upon the Mount of Olives." In the history of the world—that portion of the human race not included in the Jewish nation, or in the Church of Christ—we can see nothing but increasing sin and wickedness until the time when Christ will come and introduce His own kingdom upon the earth. The Antichrist, be it a power or a person, the opposition to God and His Christ, which was visible to Paul and to John, will conduct his rebellion with greater power and larger success until the destruction which shall result from the brightness of the Lord's coming. We see Satan, the usurper, the enemy of man, ruling with power until the time when the Lord appears and binds him forever. The point, then, where all the lines of truth embracing the life of men on the earth meet and unite, is the arrival of Christ, the coming of the Son of man, "the glorious appearing of the great God."

PERVERSIONS OF SCRIPTURE.

When it is remembered that the Bible, as we now possess it, is a book made up of the writings of different men living sixteen hundred years apart, prepared without concert, containing history, law, poetry, and personal experience, many things typical, much that is prophetical, and all relating to modes of life and conditions of society entirely different from our own, it would seem at first sight as though a full comprehension of its contents was beyond the power of human attainment. Well might we shrink from the attempt, were not the main purposes of the Bible to be discerned on its own pages, and assured by our own experience and that of those who have lived before us. Briefly stated, the purposes of the Bible are to enlighten us as to our true relation to our Creator; as to our duties in this world; and as to our destiny in the world to come. Filled as it is with unfathomable mysteries, and treating of matters of which nothing can be known certainly by personal experience, as we are at present constituted, there are two fundamental principles concerning its study, thus stated by Ruskin: "That, without seeking, truth cannot be known at all, and that, by seeking, it may be discovered by the simplest. Without seeking it cannot be known at all. It can neither be declared from pulpits, nor set down in Articles, nor in any wise 'prepared and sold' in packages ready for use. Truth must be ground for every man for himself out of its husk, with such help as he can get, indeed, but not without stern labor of his own. As surely as we live, this truth of truths can only be so discerned: to those who act on what they know, more shall be revealed; and thus, if any man will do His will, he shall know of the doctrine whether it be of God. Any man,—not the man who has the most means of knowing, who has the subtlest brains, or sits under the most orthodox preacher, or who has his library fullest of orthodox books, but the man who strives to know, who takes God at His word, and sets himself to dig up the heavenly mystery, roots and all, before sunset, and the night come, when no man can work. Beside such a man, God stands in more and more visible presence as he toils, and teaches him that which no preacher can teach,—no earthly authority gainsay."

It is of primary importance to the profitable reading of the Scriptures, that any declaration of either fact or doctrine, should be received and interpreted naturally in connection with the context and free from the influence of any previously accepted system of theology or preconceived notions. While it may be difficult to receive the Bible as a *new* book, and read it with a mind absolutely free from associations and ideas springing from early education, or the influence which the prevailing thought and preaching of the former or present time have thrown around it, yet a diligent study of the Scriptures, with a constant reference to the object of the writer, the circumstances of those to whom the special writing was directed, and a definite idea of the time or dispensation to which the particular truth under consideration belonged, will save us from that ignorant or wilful perversion of Revelation which has so long been the bane of the Church. Many of the carefully elaborated inferences in the sermons of the present day, although closely connected with, and perhaps essential to, the accepted systems of theology, are not warranted by, and cannot be deduced from, the isolated passages upon which they are based. While the Bible is a Revelation of *facts* and *truths*, the *inferences* drawn from them have in many cases covered the fact itself with the rubbish of human reason, and sometimes have so distorted the truth that to an unprejudiced mind it appears as a hideous caricature. This use of fact and truth is particularly marked in that preaching which would use external constraint to aid the work of the Holy Spirit,—that would supplant the glorious liberty of the Gospel by the fetters of the ancient legalism,—that would operate on the senses of the body and the fears of the mind in the hope of saving the soul. The evil results of such teaching may be found in the coldness and formality in the visible Church, now so prevalent that the few Gospel Christians whose hearts are withdrawn from the world, and who are patiently waiting for the coming of their Lord, are regarded as "righteous overmuch" and branded as fanatics.

Among the many detached texts from Scripture that have thus been falsely construed, and made to do a service for which they were never intended, is that expression of the Psalmist, "The wicked shall be turned into hell, and all nations that forget God." (Psalm ix. 17.) In the long-continued controversy whether or not the truths of a future life and the immortality of the soul have been revealed in the Old Testament, it has always been claimed by one side that this text had direct reference to the final doom of the ungodly, while it has nothing to do with the doctrine, but simply refers to the fact that all are swept from the earth by death. As there are no "nations" in the future world, the words can have no application to the eternal condition of either of the two classes of men. Those who are most competent to decide these philological questions, upon which so much depends, assure us that the word which is here translated "hell" invariably means the *grave* or the invisible state of spirits,—that *intermediate state* of souls between the death and the final resurrection. The word here rendered "hell" is the very same used by Jacob when he cried, "Then shall ye bring down my gray hairs with sorrow to *the grave*" (Gen. xlii. 38), and by David again, in a passage subject to the same misconception, when he was speaking of his enemies, "Let death seize upon them, and let them go down quick into *hell*" (Psalm lv. 15), or, as it is correctly rendered in the marginal reading, "the grave," or, as it is literally given in Leeser's version, "Let them go down alive in the nether world." The same word was also used by Jonah when he spoke of his burial in the body of the fish, "Out of the belly of *hell* cried I," or, as it is literally translated in Leeser's Jewish Bible, "Out of the depths of the *grave* I have cried." The "hades" spoken of in these and many other passages, is the place of disembodied spirits, which, doing neither good nor evil, are awaiting the last judgment. The Church, generally, teaches that sinners do immediately after death enter into an eternal destiny of torment, and the saints into their glory,—that is, *before* the time when Christ will come to take His Church to Heaven, and His saints shall receive their glorified bodies,—a doctrine which, whether true or false, is certainly not established by texts of this character.

There is a clause in the twelfth verse of the fourth chapter of Amos, "Prepare to meet thy God," that is almost invariably used in a wrong sense. The reading of the whole chapter makes it apparent that the words were primarily and only intended for God's chosen people, Israel, warning them that continued persistence in their course of disobedience would cause Him to bring upon them, in a fatherly spirit, a course of discipline of a temporal nature, in the destruction of crops and vineyards, that would insure their return and submission to Him. This phrase is frequently, if not always, used to intimidate sinners by awakening a slavish fear of future eternal punishment at the hands of an angry God, with the mistaken idea that the emotions thus produced will be the means of leading them to Christ and converting their souls. Such glaring perversions of the truth work only injury to the Church, and have a tendency to make the "almost" but not "altogether" Christians, such as are neither hot nor cold, and who are no honor to Christ and His cause.

How often have we heard exhortations to immediate repentance based upon, or enforced by, the words of Solomon, "And if the tree fall toward the south, or toward the north, in the place where the tree falleth, there it shall be"! Torn from their connection, these words of the wise man are used to prove the statement, that as death overtakes you, so will judgment find you,—as though judgment had not been passing on man since the fall of Adam, or as though death was not the effect following close upon the cause. Solomon was not alluding to anything of a spiritual or eternal nature, but was speaking of "the things done under the sun," of the wisdom needed by men in the ordinary transactions and social intercourse of human life on the earth. If there be in the Old Testament any clear declarations of the future life, this passage is not one of them. At first sight the abrupt injection of this clause in a short discourse concerning the duties of charity may be slightly perplexing, but, following closely after a beautiful example of bounteous giving taken from the course of nature,—the clouds full of rain emptying upon the earth,— the natural and most satisfactory interpretation is that which regards the words in question as a warning against delay in the performance of those charitable duties which seem to be imperative. What follows in the next and the succeeding verses, is not only in harmony with this interpretation, but seems to be strongly confirmatory.

In the twenty-fifth chapter of Matthew, at the thirty-first verse, there is the thrilling description of the coming of the Son of man in His glory, when He will judge the Gentile nations. The "sheep" and the "goats," the believers and the unbelievers, " all nations," are gathered before Christ on His throne. Careless readers of the Word infer from this passage, that there are but two classes into which *all* men are divided. But where are the Jews,—God's chosen, peculiar people? Where are those of whom the Lord said by the mouth of Balaam, "the people shall *dwell alone,* and shall *not be reckoned among the nations,*" and are spoken of by Hosea as "abiding many days" without " King, sacrifice, ephod, or teraphim,"—all those strongly-marked characteristics of national and church life which had been the glory of the children of Israel,—but who would return to seek and " fear the Lord and His goodness in the *latter days*"? They are *not included* among those gathered before the throne; they are *not reckoned* among "all nations;" but they are the third party referred to by the words, "*my brethren.*" In this connection it may be remarked that scattered all through the prophecies, the first three Gospels, and the Apocalypse are many statements of truths and declarations of facts, closely related to and coinciding with each other, which do not concern the grace-saint in any other than a *typical* sense, but have a direct reference to the *future perfected Jewish dispensation* which is to find place on the earth in " the latter days," the glory of which is so graphically portrayed in the fourteenth chapter of

Zechariah, and in the sixtieth to the sixty-fifth chapters, inclusive, of Isaiah.

One of the most unaccountable misapplications of Scripture truth may be found in the manner which many Christians and some commentators use certain passages in Isaiah. That passage beginning at seventeenth verse of forty-second chapter, ending with the chapter, is supposed to refer to Jacob,—the Jews,—while the first eight verses of the succeeding chapter are appropriated to the Gospel Church; and, again, from the twenty-first verse of forty-third chapter to the close, is applied to Jacob, while the first nine verses of the forty-fourth chapter are taken for the Gospel Church. The absurdity of giving all the threatening and reproofs to others, and appropriating to ourselves all their comfort and blessing, becomes very evident on a consecutive reading of the whole chapters. The entire portion is exclusively intended for and addressed to the Jews,—one people. Doubtless, in these instances, as in many others, the confusion arising in the mind of the ordinary reader is caused by the untrustworthy and often false headings of the chapters by which many of our English Bibles are disfigured. In both cases referred to the headline of the forty-third and forty-fourth chapters reads, "The Lord comforteth the *church* with His promises." It is difficult, from the force of habit, to read the Bible without regard to the arbitrary divisions of chapters and uninfluenced by the perverse headings; yet those who would seriously study the Word, and gain its true meaning, must pass these by as a human contrivance valuable only for convenience.

The seven parables of our Lord recorded in the thirteenth chapter of Matthew, exhibiting the entire development of the Kingdom of God in its general outlines from its beginning to its final consummation, have been the subjects of misconception, and have been strangely wrested from their true purpose. It has been assumed that the "grain of mustard-seed" grown into a tree represents the true Church of God, when in fact it is only the outward church-form of the Kingdom in the branches of which "the birds of the air"—the false doctrines and human inventions of Christendom—find lodging. The beasts of the field and the birds of the air, in the Old Testament and in Revelation, are symbols of the masses of corrupt human nature. Christ, in His explanation of the parable of the sower, speaks of the devil as the bird of the air that takes the Word or good seed out of the heart. Isaiah speaks of the way in which the "fowls of the mountain and beasts of the earth" have fed upon and trodden down God's chosen people.

In considering the meaning of these wonderful parables of our Lord, it must be remembered that although spoken about the same time, and referring to the same general subject, the *first four* were spoken to the multitudes from the ship, but the *last three* to His own chosen disciples in the house, so that the persons *to* whom they were addressed must have an important bearing on the interpretation. In the first parable, to the disciples alone "the kingdom of Heaven" is likened "unto treasure hid in the field; the which when a man hath found, he hideth, and for joy thereof goeth and selleth all that he hath, and buyeth that field." A popular interpretation of this parable among Christians, frequently heard from the pulpit and met on the pages of biblical exposition, but for which it is difficult to find any basis in the text, is that Christ is the "treasure," and that for "joy" at this discovery the *sinner* "goeth and selleth all that he hath" to buy the treasure,— as though Christ or His truth ever were or could be "hid," or the unrenewed soul should, as it were, stumble on Christ and joyfully give up all to gain Him. Of the many perversions of scriptural truth, this seems the most amazing. The hid " treasure" is Christ's *redeemed Church*,—those for whom He died, who in every age by faith accept Him. He saw His " treasure" covered with the rubbish of a sin-cursed world, He gave up all He possessed for it, ransomed it with His blood, He left His purchased possession in the world, but will come again to claim it. In the mean time its true life is " hid with Christ in God," and its glory will not be fully manifested until He who is its " life shall appear, when it shall also appear with Him in glory." The " pearl of great price" is an emblem of the Church as it appears to the Redeemer, pure, spotless, and entire. The concluding parable of the net is one that to the Jews, to whom so many kinds of fish were an abomination by the Mosaic law, had a peculiar force. The net is the drag-net of the Gospel, passing through all nations, gathering within its folds both good and bad. The fish having neither fins nor scales, living in the mire and filth at the bottom of the sea, will, when the net is dragged to the shore, be separated from the fish that by aid of fins live in the clear water in the light of the sun.

There has been, and there now is, prevalent in the visible Church an idea that it is in full possession of all the truth of Revelation,—that the researches of great theologians and the labors of men of mighty intellect have so thoroughly explored the dark recesses of the deep mine, that there remains but little to reward the diligent student of God's Word. The strong temptation is to rely more for the elucidation and understanding of the sacred text upon the archæological, philological, and scientific discoveries of learned men, which usually have more direct reference to the literal signification of the record, than to the revealed truth of which it is simply the expression or means of communication, than upon the personal exhaustive study of the truth itself, regarded as a revelation of God's eternal glory and His will concerning man's life on earth and his future destiny. These discoveries of science are of profound interest and great value to all who will make the proper use of them, and find in them the evidences of harmony and agreement between the records of God as shown in Scripture, in the whole constitution of man, and in the realm of nature, even though the scientist had prosecuted his researches with other and far different purposes. But the faith in and personal profit to be derived from searching the Scriptures as for hid treasures are not dependent upon, while they may be aided by, the results and discoveries of human wisdom. Neither are they the product of a special illumination of the natural mind by the supernatural influence of the Holy Spirit, an enlightenment of defective reason, or an enlargement of the mental faculties. There is, however, as Henry Dunn remarks, "A blessed indwelling of the Holy Spirit,—the only influence we are authorized to seek and pray for,—which is not *intellectual*, but moral; which is inseparable from candor, love of truth, and obedience generally; which manifests itself in growing sympathy with the Divine character; and which, *therefore*, involves clearer perceptions of, and a deeper insight into, the Divine mind and will, as exhibited in the Bible, than can be obtained in any other way." This is a purely natural process,—natural in the sense that it works in perfect accordance not only with the moral and mental powers of humanity as a race, but with special adaptation to the particular individual. The influence of the revealed truth of God, entering into human life from a supernatural point indeed, yet like any other force in human progress, works organically and naturally in its development, first, in each individual soul, and then, as a result, through the entire Church. Accepted and yielded to by each soul, it becomes a corrective of those pernicious delusions of enthusiastic minds, which seem ever ready to break out in the Church and make its record one of tyranny and violence.

By this "indwelling of the Spirit" the revelation given to an ancient people remains to us an ever new and vital force, constantly enlarging the sphere of human thought and bringing it into closer sympathy and union with its Divine Source. The Scripture thus vitalized, is not and cannot be a dead letter to the Church of the present or the future age. We have all that was embraced in the revelation to the prophets and apostles, and vastly more, for we have seen the truth adapting itself not only to the development of God's purposes, but to the increasing experience of Christian consciousness. While it is exceedingly difficult to state clearly in words just what that "blessed indwelling of the Holy Spirit" is, or to accurately define the modes of its operations in diverse hearts and minds, yet it is an actual and real fact in the experience of each Christian, a something which can be appealed to in his own consciousness, the results of which are perfectly satisfactory to his own mind, and the guidance and powers of which in his daily life he frankly and gratefully acknowledges. There are but few Christians who will not say with S. T. Coleridge, after he had read all the books of the Old and New Testaments, each book as a whole and also as an integral part, that he has found everywhere "copious sources of truth and power and purifying impulses,—found words for my inmost thoughts, songs for my joys, utterances for my hidden griefs, and pleadings for my shame and feebleness. In short, whatever *finds* me bears witness for itself that it has proceeded from a Holy Spirit, even from the same Spirit which, remaining in itself, yet regenerateth all other powers, and, in all ages entering into holy souls, maketh them friends of God and prophets." There have been those who claimed to be so fully under the influence of the "indwelling of the Spirit" that they have received communications of Divine truth separate from or even independent of the scriptural record. This is a dangerous perversion of truth, a delusion of vain human wisdom.

There is for some minds a peculiar fascination in the study of the unfulfilled prophecies of the Bible, while others regard the same portion of Scripture truth with a feeling akin to fear. It cannot be denied that there is some ground for fear, for, while there is probably in the knowledge of every reader, instances where men and women have been carried into insanity by exclusive devotion to some form of prophetic interpretation, there are also periods in the history of the Church when the wild fanaticism of dogmatic and confident interpretation of mystic utterances, has wellnigh destroyed, not only the common sense but the piety of the multitudes infected by it. Admitting fully the difficulties and the dangers that may beset the path, the fact remains that the prophecies form a large part of the Divine revelation, and are therefore proper subjects for diligent, careful study. The benefits to be derived are of great value. An assurance of faith, a fixity of purpose, and an unwavering trust in the wisdom and power of God may be gained from the study of the many prophecies which have already been accomplished. We will lose a part of our rightful portion if we neglect that "sure word of prophecy to which we *do well* to take heed." We have a positive exhortation to the study of unfulfilled prophecy in the words of John, when he would "show the things which must shortly come to pass" in the blessing promised to him "that readeth, and they that hear the words of this prophecy, and keep these things which are written therein." Here, then, in the Apocalypse, where is prophetically recorded the history of the Church between the death and the return of its Lord, may be found a region where believers may study the Divine purposes with interest and profit. The ingenious inventions and conflicting conclusions of learned commentators greatly increase the difficulty of gaining the real meaning of the symbolical language; but, read in proper connection with parallel passages, and in humble dependence upon "the blessed indwelling of the Holy Spirit," the Revelation of St. John will yield a rich harvest to every Christian.

It would be impossible to note the many perversions that cluster about the scriptural prophecies. One source, however, from which they spring is worthy of attention. Among the unfulfilled prophecies of Scripture there may be found a large class which, while having a direct reference to events of the national Jewish life, do yet stretch forward to a period in the future, reaching from the hour when they were uttered to the time when the purpose of Divine Providence shall be completed. Abrupt transitions so break up their continuity that the path cannot be clearly traced,—ages of time intervene between events that to human sight should follow each other in rapid succession. Accurately and very definitely predicting events which have happened to the nation, the prophecies are sometimes expressed in language that, seeming to bear a double meaning, connects them with other events still in the future. In any endeavor to catch the truth which may be hidden under these symbolical and mystical words, the first questions, upon the answer to which depends our proper knowledge, must be,—"To whom, and for what purpose, were these prophecies of futurity given?" In reply, we would make the general observation that the prophecies of the Old Testament, including promises of good for well-doing, threatenings of evil for breach of moral law, and fierce denunciations of wrath for departures from Jehovah, were spoken to the Jewish nation, with special and primary application to it only, and that when the course and destiny of any other nation come into view, it is by reason of some immediate connection with the chosen people and the declared purpose to be wrought out by them. The prerogatives divinely granted to the children of Abraham, the fruitful land given to them for an inheritance by Jehovah, the future happiness and welfare of the human race, inseparably connected in some mysterious manner with the life and continuance of their nation, are the subjects which underlie and influence every prediction of future events. Resting upon the secure foundation built for them, as they believed, by the authoritative promises and declarations of their God, the Hebrew Seers could not, without violence to their faith, predict that which would be contrary to any prior statements of Jehovah, or take any special cognizance of matters distinct from their national history. From the remote period when the first promise was given to Abraham, up to the hour when the whole series shall have culminated in the covenanted ingathering and restoration of the chosen people, there is not embraced in the Old-Testament prophecies a single one that did not find its source in Jewish national or ecclesiastical life, having primary reference to the Jewish nation, and applying incidentally to other nations only as they were in some measure connected with the Israelites. If this be the correct theory of the ancient Jewish prophecies, their true purport can never be gained by any mere compilation of detached proof passages, or by deductions and inferences from scattered texts. It must be reached, if at all, by a living and sympathetic insight into the true spirit and thought which were the moving impulses in the mind and heart of the prophet at the time of utterance. In pursuance of this idea, let an examination be made of the Book of Isaiah, which has well been said " to embrace and to comprehend and, in one sense, at once to recapitulate the revelations of all preceding ages, and to foreshow the revelations that were yet to come." The canons of the moral law are clearly enunciated, and with them is combined the essence of the Gospel of the Messiah. The rules of morality governing the relations of man with his fellow, find place in the earnest protests for truth, justice, and mercy, in the scathing denunciations of oppression and cruelty, and in the tender exhortations to the care of the widows, the fatherless, and the afflicted. The emotions and aspirations of the spiritual life, yearning for the satisfaction springing only from communion with the Infinite Father, are voiced more distinctly by Isaiah than by any other writer of the Old Testament, excepting, perhaps, the authors of some of the Psalms. A pure theology, and a code of ethics unsurpassed by any other than that announced by Christ, may be found in these pages. These strongly-marked characteristics of the teachings of Isaiah, in which more nearly than any other Jewish writer he approaches the perfection of Christ, combined with the fact that he has predicted a future state of earthly peace and happiness for all men, perhaps give the reason why so many Christians of this age, misled by an apparent coincidence between that era predicted by the prophet, and that which they have fondly hoped would result from the proclamation of the Gospel of Grace, have, with violence to the whole spirit and import of the author, and with utter disregard to the preceding causes and conditions of this future happy condition of human affairs, wrested his words from their proper connection with the nation for whom they were intended, and applied them to the Church of the present Dispensation. Broad and catholic as Isaiah is in his declarations, they are all limited by clear references to Jacob, Israel, Jerusalem, and Zion,—are qualified by the authoritative statement of Jehovah, "*This people* have I formed for myself; *they* shall show forth my praise." Many of the bright pictures of peaceful rural life, addressed to "Jacob my servant, and Israel whom I have chosen," which conveyed to the minds of the Jews very definite ideas of the earthly prosperity and happiness which were always associated with the prevalence and triumph of their religion, have been torn from their appropriate position and accepted as prophecies of a supposed condition of human affairs resulting from the preaching of the Gospel and the diffusion of the knowledge of Christ. So, indeed, they may be in a certain restricted sense, but will become such only by and through God's ancient people. The "singing of the heavens" and the "breaking forth into singing" of the mountains, the forests, and the trees, the gladness of the wilderness and the solitary places, the rejoicing of the desert and its blossoming as the rose, have been, and will be again, " because the Lord hath redeemed Jacob and glorified Himself in Israel." The time when nations shall not "learn war any more," when "swords shall be beaten into ploughshares, and spears into pruning-hooks," will be when the people shall say, " Let us go up to the house of the Lord, to the house of the God of Jacob." Partly through ignorance and carelessness, sometimes from the misleading head-lines of many editions of our Bibles, but oftener, perhaps, from the unconscious belief that just what the prophet predicts should, under ordinary circumstances, be the legitimate fruits of Gospel truth, Christians read these prophecies of future events that are to take place when Israel shall have accepted her Messiah, as statements of that which relates to the Christian Church of the present Dispensation. They take that which was given to an earthly Church, to which immortality had not been clearly revealed, and by a spiritualizing process, for which there is no scriptural warrant, apply it to a Church redeemed by the blood of Christ, spiritual in birth and life,—a body belonging not to time, but to eternity; not to earth, but to heaven. Forgetting the truth that the Church of Christ has no part in the ways of God with Israel and the earth, ignoring the fact that there is a great break, a long interval, between the rejection and crucifixion of the Messiah by the Jews and His coming to the earth for His redeemed saints, which is not referred to by the Jewish prophets,—a period of time important as it may be to both Jew and Gentile, but which yet does not form any subject of prophecy,—Christians plunge themselves into inextricable confusion, and fail to enjoy that calm confidence and firm assurance which they should have in contemplating the unfolding of the plans of Divine Providence, by appropriating to a spiritual and, while on the earth, a subjective Church, that which was intended for, and given to, a material and objective Church under a legal economy.

ORGANIZATION.

WHEREVER the word *church* is used in the New Testament, its primary meaning is an assembly or congregation of men. At times it certainly signifies all of the human race who have been, are, or will be the subjects of God's special love,—the entire number of the elect,—those who at the appearing of Christ will compose the Bride, the Lamb's wife. Again, it has a wider signification, including all those who are professed believers in Christ. When thus used it embraces good and bad, wheat and tares, sheep and goats, clean fish and unclean. It is in this broad sense that we now employ the term in considering the "*organization*," which by reason of its close connection with the Church is too often supposed to be a part of it, and regarded as essential to its existence.

If one would carefully study all the words of Christ and the directions of the Apostles relative to the formation and government of the congregations or assemblies of men, and then endeavor to discover in them even the germs of that stupendous organization commonly called the *Church*, he would be forced to the conclusion that the Apostles had no adequate idea of the importance of their mission, else they would have given more specific directions concerning the visible manifestation of the truth they were preaching, or that the mind of man, gathering wisdom by the experience of years, had devised and put into operation a more excellent method of accomplishing the desired result. A review of the history of the Church from the Apostolic age to the period of the Reformation, reveals a growth of organization and an expansion of machinery for the conversion of the world, but with these a constant increase of error with a corresponding retrogression in morals. In the early centuries of the Christian era, the Church had fallen into a sad condition of ignorance, decay, and delusion. Heart-sick with the contemplation of the Church record of this period, we may well say with Isaac Taylor, "The history of Christianity! Alas, the ominous words, which sink like a mortal chill into the heart! Christianity has absolutely no difficulties, or none that ought for a moment to stagger a sound and well-informed mind,—none excepting such as attach to its history; but these, although clearly separable from the question of its own divine origin, yet how serious and disheartening they are! The Christian, if he would enjoy any serenity, should either know nothing of the history of his religion, or he should be acquainted with it so profoundly as to have satisfied himself that the dark surmises, which had tormented his solitary meditations, have no substantial bearing upon the principles of his faith." The character and specific quality of the course of events in the ancient Church was the "perpetual superposition of materials upon the apostolic foundation, at the capricious bidding of superstition, enthusiasm, fanaticism, spiritual tyranny, craft, and hypocrisy." A suspicion, growing at times to a conviction, comes into the mind that we of the modern Church are following in the course of the ancient, employing the same methods and attaining similar results, modified only by the circumstances of the age and the progress of the sciences.

While we admit that the general aspect of the Gospel economy might seem to warrant a condition of human affairs far different from that which history has recorded, and that there would seem to be some substantial basis in the predictions of the Jewish prophets for our hopes of the prevalence of that era of peace, purity, and happiness that was to succeed the advent of the Messiah, yet the Christian's faith, in contemplating the seasons of deep darkness that have passed, the coldness, depression, and formality, which seem to envelop the Church of the present, or the " perilous times" that must come on the earth in the future, may be sustained by two facts of Revelation,—the repeated announcements, made by Christ to His followers, of persecution, universal hatred, and cruel death, as far as they were personally concerned, and a widespread, deep-seated corruption of the pure faith once delivered to the saints; and, as the Jews waited long for the advent of the predicted Messiah, so, in the development of God's providential plans, may His *own Church*, in its true sense, wait long for His promised reappearance to receive it to Himself, learning in the mean while by painful experience that with her Lord " a thousand years is as one day."

A primitive Church, as we find it in Scripture and the imperfect records of that age, was a simple association of men and women having faith in Jesus Christ as the Son of God, impelled by a desire to follow His precepts and to obey His last words by " being witnesses unto Him unto the uttermost parts of the earth." The strong personal love which each had for a common Saviour formed a band of union that persecution could not sever. By the word of Christ no form of organization was declared. Those present at the ascension of Christ were told " to wait for the promise," the " power" which was to follow the baptism of the Holy Ghost " not many days hence." When this supernatural power—the gifts of tongues and of healing—came upon the three thousand that gladly received the words of Peter, "they continued steadfastly in the apostles' doctrine and fellowship, in breaking of bread, and in prayers." The primitive Church, under the immediate ministry of the Apostles, and perhaps for a short time after their death, enjoyed a "power" of the Spirit far beyond and above that which has been granted to the Church for many centuries. From the repeated references in the Epistles to the "coming of Christ," and the exhortations that abound to all to be in readiness for that "coming," it is evident that there was in the minds of the early Christians an expectation that "this same Jesus," who had been so suddenly and supernaturally taken from them, would "so come in like manner" again from the clouds of heaven. The early records make apparent the fact that the gradual disappearance of the supernatural power conferred upon believers, was followed by the waning and beclouding of the hope of Christ's reappearance to take full possession of the earth. It is very probable that even before Peter died he had heard of some who scoffingly asked, "Where is the promise of His coming?" and sustained the scoff by appeals to the continuance of all things as they were from the beginning. The faith of the Church in the speedy advent of Christ on earth, which had doubtless been a strong element in the success of the early preaching, having been weakened by unexpected delay and the dashing of many ardent hopes, was succeeded by the idea that, as the supernatural powers hitherto exercised were then but feebly manifested or entirely withdrawn, it was possible that they had mistaken the purpose of God concerning the Church and its mission in the world. At all events, as early as the third century, the fixed and settled conviction of the Church seemed to have been that the world was to be converted from paganism

ORGANIZATION.

and idolatry by what we would now term the ordinary operations of the Holy Spirit upon the individual mind and heart, in distinction from those wonderful Pentecostal displays of supernatural power no longer vouchsafed.

It does not come within our present purpose to consider the *cause* of the withdrawal from the world of the miraculous power which had been so effective on the hearts of men,—whether the influence was phenomenal, essential to a specific purpose for a limited time, or whether it was a great blessing which might have been permanently retained, but which was lost to men by their failure to appreciate its value and depend upon its agency,—but rather the *fact* that the Church has not now in its possession, and has not had for many centuries, the gift so largely exercised by the early believers. The statement in Acts ii. 39, "For the promise is unto you and your children, as many as the Lord shall call," would seem to imply that this "power" might have been one of the ever-present forces in the mission of the Church, but, like many other divinely-proffered blessings, lost by want of faith on the part of Christians. In the results following the withdrawal of the "power" we think we can discover some of the causes which led to the formation of, and subsequent accretions to, that stupendous form of *organization* which has so heavily burdened the Church and made its efforts for the eighteen hundred years of comparatively so little avail.

That we have departed from the example of the Apostolic Church is evident. That a return in all particulars would be best, even if it were practicable, may well be questioned. Living under a system of Church government and procedure received by inheritance from the fathers, it is exceedingly difficult to form any correct idea of the primitive simplicity and unbounded liberty which characterized the Apostolic assemblies. The fundamental idea of our social economy—itself the product of human worldly selfishness—causes us to shrink in terror from the ordinary custom of those who received the "power of the Holy Ghost," of "selling their possessions and goods," parting them to all as every man had need, and having all things in common. While this practice is only incidentally referred to by Luke, as part of the ordinary routine of their social life, yet it is spoken of in connection with the "signs and wonders done by the Apostles," with the "gladness and singleness of heart," and with "praising God." It is possible that some of the conceptions of Christ and His Gospel closely allied to the spirituality of religion held by these primitive saints, would be as shocking to our modern theology as their ancient communism is to our present political economy. But none of us would venture to deny that these men were under a most specific and particular dispensation of the Holy Spirit.

If asked to state what we accepted as the underlying idea of the vast organization termed "The Church," believed by so many to be the power of Christ present in visible form in the world, we would say that the followers of Christ, having given up as an active principle of their faith and life the belief in, and hope of, the speedy coming of the Lord Jesus, assumed that their obligations to Him involved, as far as it could be accomplished by human means, the conversion of the world to Christianity by active measures and aggressive assaults. Forgetting that they were to be "witnesses" for Christ, they were soon transformed into violent propagandists. The assumption—for as such we regard it—that the conversion of the world was dependent on the Church, involved an aggregation of resources, a combination of energy, and a massing of effort which took form first in a system of belief, and then in an organized government. The love and affection for a personal Saviour, which had been the main-spring of Christian life, was gradually displaced by a faith *about* Him, and dogmatic conceptions concerning His teaching, which were made the basis and tests of fellowship. The attracting and assimilating influence of a perfect personal moral ideal manifested in the life of Christ, made potential not only by the force of its Divine origin, but by the peculiar energy of the Holy Spirit, was thought to be of less importance in the progress of Christianity than the inculcation of a logical system of theology. Religion then took forms in Creeds and Symbols. Acceptance of, and adherence to these creeds being imperatively demanded, societies were at once formed different in their features from the Apostolic assemblies. The guidance and direction of these bodies was slowly, perhaps, but surely taken from the Holy Spirit by the wisdom of men. In the fourth century, we find in the visible organization of the Church those germs of evil whose future development has so clearly manifested the depravity of the human heart. This view is confirmed by the history of the Church. As an English layman remarks, " The errors and superstitions of ancient Christianity; the crimes of ecclesiastics; the miseries of the Inquisition; the no less brutal superstitions and cruelties of Puritanism towards persons suspected of witchcraft; the exaltation of satanic powers; the absence of all tenderness in religion; the ever-present terror; the moral element in Christianity superseded by the dogmatic; doctrine taking the place of rectitude; faith determined neither by Scripture nor by reason, but by the intellectual influences of the time; improvement produced only by advancing rationalism; past errors unatoned, and existing falsities still cherished and fought for,—all united, render it almost a mockery to speak of the last eighteen hundred years as the period of the dispensation of the Spirit."

The sources from which the evils of organization flow are, first, the natural depravity of the human heart,—that disposition which prompts man to follow any path but that marked out by Divine wisdom and love; second, the exclusion of the Holy Spirit,—taking His position as the Guide and Teacher of all believers, and thus placing something between God and the individual soul; third, a perversion of Scripture,—which, ignoring its natural and proper signification, employing the Word in sustaining a worldly gospel, limited by time and in agreement with the desires of the human heart, would establish a Church or community where a line could not be drawn between a professing Christian and an intelligent, cultivated, worldly man; fourth, that the majority of those constituting the visible Church, being more under the influence of the "letter" which is human, than of the "Spirit" which is Divine, will in life and action place confidence in measures prompted by short-sighted human wisdom rather than in the promised power of the Holy Ghost. The truth that the Holy Ghost is ever present in the Church of Christ as a reality to all believers—instructing in all truth, guiding in all duty, uniting and binding in one those who have in Christ died unto the law—seems to have been systematically ignored, and regarded as one of the elements of an effete mysticism.

But leaving in the background the principles which govern the questions involved, a cursory consideration of some of the practical results of the organization to be seen in every-day life, will give proof of departure from primitive ideas, and consciousness of this may be a first step in reform. The doctrine that "Might makes Right," while not openly professed by church organizations, or by governments of those countries that are nominally Christian, is often assumed and acted upon by either. Our treatment of the Indians is sad evidence that, in spite of Bibles, churches, and clergy, we have as a nation yielded to a temptation arising from the possession of mere brute force, —a power that we could exercise almost with impunity on rational human beings, destitute of light and culture. The forcible removal of the Indians from the land we now occupy cannot be indorsed by justice or equity,—the sanction of the Holy Spirit certainly cannot be claimed for a course of action dictated solely by a spirit of covetousness. When they refused to give up their land, and relinquish their natural rights for a trifling remuneration, we surrounded them by emigration, introduced among them the vices of our civilization, drove them off by main force, and took their lands without any recompense. We have broken solemn treaties, and when the oppressed have stood up for their assured rights, we have called them "Indian dogs," and wellnigh exterminated them. The day of God's justice is steadily advancing, when as a nominally Christian nation we must answer for our national sin.

England—the most enlightened nation on the earth—acquired possession of India by might and in a way that cannot be sanctioned by justice and equity. Having obtained control of so vast a dominion, her whole procedure in the political and commercial economy of its government has not been influenced by Gospel principles. As a Christian nation, she has suffered, and must continue to suffer, from the evils that inevitably follow a breach of moral law.

In 1847 an eminent jurist of our own country, an elder in a Presbyterian church, openly advanced the idea that the United States government would be right in entering upon Mexico, and subduing it by force of arms, on the ground that a people so richly favored with a beautiful country and fertile soil had abused the gifts of God by their gross superstition and wicked priestcraft. And this theory found many bold and outspoken advocates within the bounds of the visible organization. A Christian nation, entering upon a war of conquest on a heathen nation, appoints by its civil and ecclesiastical authorities a day of fasting and prayer, asking the Lord to prosper its arms in a wicked enterprise. When a bloody victory has been obtained a day of thanksgiving and praise is proclaimed. Such facts occurring among the most learned and enlightened nations betray a most lamentable ignorance of the true spirit of the Gospel.

There is pervading the entire country, in civil and ecclesiastical societies, in corporations and associations of all kinds, extending from the national government down to the most inferior municipality, an abuse of power, springing from or aided by organization, that places heavy burdens of taxation upon all, but which press most heavily on the ignorant, the poor, and the laboring classes. It is not, indeed, openly asserted that "might makes right,"—physical external force is not employed,—but shrewd, calculating men, using the power of intellect, wealth, and position, aided by the force of combination and organization, in a delicate and refined, but none the less cruel manner, do accomplish ends that are grossly selfish and bitterly oppressive to the community. By these schemes of combined capital and cunning brains the power escapes from the many to the few; the rich are made richer and the poor poorer. By this indirect but powerful oppression many a worthy and honest citizen feels that his means of livelihood are gradually being taken from him, and a fatal blow, from a source of which he is ignorant, is being aimed at his prosperity. As the pressure bears more heavily upon him, he comes to the consciousness that he must be crushed or take part with the oppressor and in turn press down on those below him. Occasionally the details of some such scheme are providentially exposed to the public gaze. Could the whole series of robbery, corruption, falsehood and crime, be fully revealed, it would show a state of society unequalled in deformity by that of a Mohammedan or heathen nation. But the saddest fact of all, is that when these astounding revelations burst upon us, many who have occupied high positions in government or associations, have been most deeply engaged in these nefarious schemes, when at the same time they held correspondingly high positions among the sects of the visible Church. Yet the means employed are not gross in nature, but on the contrary are plausible in outward appearance,—indeed, but seldom require anything that would be outwardly inconsistent with a "profession of religion" in any of the denominations.

This same spirit which is so prevalent in the government and worldly corporations is plainly to be discerned in the churches. Within the century a change has taken place in the policy and usage of the Church which is not an improvement on the old ways. It is a change for which the clergy are no more relieved from responsibility than are the laymen. In the olden time of our fathers, a clergyman would remain in one pastorate for a quarter of a century, or during a lifetime, performing his duties with fidelity, and seeking the reward of his labors in a happy and contented society gathered about him. Now, worldly prosperity and a desire for ease and comfort tempt pastors to such frequent changes that a ten years' settlement is rather remarkable. Some wealthy, influential city congregation learns of a good man settled in a quiet, retired place. It sends a committee to "feel" him, or, in plain words, to tempt him, by the promise of increased salary and greater worldly advantages, to desert the position assigned him by the Holy Ghost. Loving his people, and in turn loved and respected by them, reverenced by the children and indorsed by the community, he at first gives no heed to the charmers who place before him in such glowing colors the greater privileges of a metropolitan residence, the advantages enjoyed by the pastor of a cultivated, intelligent congregation, the increased educational facilities within reach for his children. They flatter his latent vanity by an intimation that "one of the most important churches of the denomination, the very stronghold of orthodoxy in the region," demands and must have a pastor of just his peculiar fitness and qualifications, and skilfully sustain the plea by the presentation of a far "wider field of usefulness in the vineyard of the Lord," where his talent and ability will insure a tenfold harvest of souls. The larger salary, the longer vacations for rest, the occasional voyage to Europe or the Holy Land, are quietly referred to, but of course not strongly urged, as reasons for a change, for worldly prudence would not thus defeat its own ends by too bald a statement. The worldly temptation having entered into his soul, the shrinking pastor begins to consider the case in his own mind,—his present circumstances shrink into nothing compared with those he might obtain,—his wife's health assumes an importance it never had before,—his limited locality never seemed so small and confining or its disadvantages so apparent,—and "the wider field of usefulness" opened before him is accepted as an intimation of the will of the Holy Spirit. Usually without consultation with his people, the call is accepted, a useful and pleasant relation is severed, and a precious assembly of saints is robbed of a beloved pastor by a sister organization professing to believe that there is but "One Church" where the unity of the Spirit is to be kept in the bonds of peace, and where all should seek the edification of the Body of Christ. On the other hand, the church seeking a minister, in its public and social services has been praying that the Spirit would guide them in all their deliberations, that God would in His own time send them a man after His own heart, while in their own mind they have already determined to call one whose eloquent preaching will fill the pews and draw into the fold those learned and wealthy persons in the community who will pay off the burdensome church-debt, increase the contributions to the Boards, and thus make the particular church popular in the denomination and the world. To gain this end they are ready to pursue a course that in the ordinary business transaction of life among worldly men, would not only be considered an aggressive intrusion on private interests, but a procedure that no honorable merchant would approve or consent to adopt. This is not an exceptional case occurring at long intervals, for its frequency and its truth will at once be acknowledged by those who have been connected with the inner machinery which is supposed to be essential to the judicious management and wise control of a church organization.

The question, "How shall we secure a pastor?" asked by a company of professed believers that may be without one, and the means so often used to obtain one, are evidences that the present form of organization is not from God, but from men, and the consequent difficulties arising in the case are the inherent evils of the system. When a congregation regards the oratorical power, the intellectual ability, the scriptural knowledge, or the genuine piety of the minister, as so many talents to be bid for and obtained by the payment of so much money, and when the congregation is regarded by the minister as a number of people gathered to listen to and enjoy his scientific, philosophical, or metaphysical discourses, or the means by which he may acquire reputation as a scholar, rather than a proclaimer of the Gospel of his Master, then are we experiencing the most deadening and fatal results of organization.

It is an undoubted proposition "that they which preach the Gospel should live of the Gospel." (1 Cor. ix. 14.) It is the duty of believers to contribute of their substance for the support of those whom the Spirit of the Lord hath called to instruct and edify saints, so that their minds, being free from earthly cares, may be given entirely to the discharge of the high and holy office. But this duty, which should be regarded as a privilege, is often sadly neglected by those who claim to regard the Gospel as above all price. The true Gospel spirit does not solicit, implore, or beg anything spiritual or material. What is given for the support of the Gospel must be the gift of a willing heart, must bear the seal of Divine approbation and have God's blessing on it, or it will accomplish no good. While I would not solicit anything from an unbeliever for the support of the Gospel, and would have no right to refuse it if freely offered, yet I cannot but believe that the offerings of Christian believers, prompted by the Holy Ghost, are the most effective material means of doing good. If the method used to support public worship should be by *pew-rent*,—the propriety and wisdom of which may well be questioned,—the prompt meeting of the obligation should never be neglected. Strange as it may appear, many are derelict in this respect. There is nothing sadder in the record of the organization than the sufferings of worthy pastors and their families from the failure of their people to pay what had been promised.

No one whose soul is influenced by love to Christ will fail in giving a due proportion of his means for the maintenance of the ordinances of the Gospel. There are, however, associated with the Church organization many schemes of human devising which have no essential relation to Gospel truth, and yet would make a claim for support on the ground of religious obligation. These schemes may not include that which is absolutely wrong, the funds gathered by the eloquent appeals of agents may be honestly appropriated to the specified object, but after all they have no practical utility, effect nothing in the promotion of vital personal piety, and are too often only the devices by which some, who cannot dig and are ashamed to beg, may have a comparatively easy means of subsistence. There are some men who, regarding themselves as stewards, responsible for a wise and proper use of the means placed in their hands, will not encourage or contribute to these multiplied organizations. Such must expect to be stigmatized as miserly, and be prepared to meet the frowns of many who cannot perceive, and are unable to believe, that such action is governed by a well-settled and clearly-defined sense of duty.

Similar feelings and reproaches are often awakened by, and manifested to, those who, from honest convictions, do not care to participate in many forms of bustling church activity upon which in these days so much dependence seems to be placed. There are doubtless in every congregation many thoughtful men and women, who, fully assured by Revelation and their own experience that the presentation of Christ as a Saviour from sin and death, is the one means by which men may be made Christians, cannot have sympathy with or take any part in those plans of social entertainment and amusement, carried on with the express purpose of promoting religion, which transform the house of worship into a theatre, a concert-hall, or a restaurant, and change what should be an assembly of professed followers of Christ, seeking each other's good by Christian fellowship, into a gathering of frivolous triflers seeking the pleasures which come from esthetical, intellectual, or animal gratification. When the Church, as a Church, enters into rivalry with the world in providing entertainment and amusement for its members, it will soon be discovered that the world can furnish a better article at a lower price. The world's amusements cost only time and money, but the *amusements of the Church*—the phrase has a grating sound on Christian ears—are provided at a cost that must be measured by a widespread loss of spirituality, by the increase of the worldliness so congenial to the human heart, and too often by the contempt of the worldly, who justly look for something higher and purer than mere frivolities from those who profess to be intrusted with a message of life to lost and condemned sinners. Were it not for the serious results, it might be amusing to read the accounts, in the daily papers, of the fairs and festivals, the dinners and tea-parties, the musical and dramatic entertainments given by church organizations for some avowedly religious object. These are occasions where Christ may be taken as a visitor, but not as a life—places where the conversation may perchance for a few moments be about and around Christ and *our* Church, but not in Christ or His *one* Church. In truth, it requires a stronger and more enlightened faith to meet and resist the seductions of Satan when thus presented in the guise of religious worldliness, than it did when he brandished the fagot and fire. Only by constant and firm reliance on Divine power can the Christian keep his heart free from the entanglements of the world and his garments unspotted.

But it may be asked whether these multiplied agencies and all this complicated machinery of organization have not resulted in good. While not denying that some good may have been done by these means, it might still be shown that the good results have been not gained by, but in spite of, the system, and that had the Church called to her aid the mighty power of the Holy Ghost, submitting herself to the Divine guidance promised by the Father, her history of nearly two thousand years would not have been a record of comparative failure. A pious English layman, after an impartial survey of the meagre and unsatisfactory results of active effort at home and abroad, says to his Christian brethren that " Our call is to *be*, rather than *to do;* that *being* what we ought to be, there will be little danger of our failing *to do* what we are called upon to perform; that truth rather than triumph should be the great object of our ambition; that God loves His creatures far better than we can do; that *acquiescence* in His dispensations, founded on implicit confidence in the revelation He has been pleased to make of Himself to us, is far more acceptable than restless zeal for the promotion of His kingdom; that the simple acceptance of that great body of FACTS which it has pleased Him to give for our learning, is far better than any amount of theological deduction that may be drawn therefrom; that all noise and clamor on behalf of One who when on earth did neither strive nor cry, nor make His voice to be heard in the streets, is out of place; that all pandering to human vanity, all love of notoriety, all planning and directing, and governing of machinery, all greed of money for God's service, all excitement and publicity, all faith in mere oratory, all silencing of witness lest it should interfere with our projects,—*everything*, in short, which is contrary to childlike faith, to the silent and loving operations of the Spirit,—'is not of the Father, but of the world.'"

No intelligent Christian doubts that the hearty recognition of these truths, and their persistent, quiet following on the part of individuals, would do much to purify the Church, to renovate society, and promote genuine heart-piety, and prove by blessed results that it was a plan in accordance with the Divine method as given in the Word. The following extract from an Epistle to Diognetus, written at the beginning of the second century, only a few years after the death of the Apostle John, by some primitive Christian whose name has perished, presents so beautiful and truthful a picture of the early Christians, and of the manifestation of Christ in men, that we quote at length :

"Christians pass their days on earth, but they are citizens of heaven. They obey the prescribed laws, and at the same time surpass the laws by their lives; they love all men, and are persecuted by all; they are unknown and condemned; they are put to death and restored to life; they are poor, yet make many rich; they are in lack of all things, and yet abound in all; they are dishonored, and yet in their very dishonor are glorified; they are evil spoken of, and yet are justified; they are reviled, and bless; they are insulted, and repay the insult with honor; they do good, yet are punished as evil-doers; when punished, they rejoice as if quickened into life; they are assailed by the Jews as foreigners, and are persecuted by the Greeks, yet those who hate them are unable to assign any reason for their hatred. To sum up all in one word, what the soul is in the body that are Christians in the world. The soul is dispersed through all the members of the body, and Christians are scattered through all the cities of the world. The soul dwells in the body, yet is not of the body, and Christians dwell in the world, yet are not of the world. The invisible soul is guarded by the visible body, and Christians are known indeed to be in the world, but their godliness remains invisible. The flesh hates the soul and wars against it, though itself suffering no injury, because it is prevented from enjoying pleasures; the world also hates the Christians, though in nowise injured [by them], because they abjure pleasures. The soul loves the flesh that hates it, and also the members; Christians likewise love those that hate them. The soul is imprisoned in the body, yet preserves that very body; and Christians are confined in this world as in a prison, and yet they are the preservers of the world. The immortal soul dwells in a mortal tabernacle, and Christians dwell as sojourners in corruptible bodies, looking for an incorruptible body in the heavens. The soul, when but ill provided with food and drink, becomes better; in like manner the Christians, though subjected day by day to punishment, increase the more in number. God has assigned them this illustrious position, which it were unlawful for them to forsake. Do you not see that the more of them that are punished, the greater becomes the number of the rest? This does not seem to be the work of man: this is the power of God,—these are the evidences of His manifestations.

"How will you love Him who has first so loved you? And if you love Him, you will be an imitator of His kindness. And do not wonder that a man may become an imitator of God. He can, if he is willing. For it is not by ruling over his neighbors, or by seeking to hold the supremacy over those that are weaker, or by being rich and showing violence towards those that are inferior, that happiness is found; nor can any one by these things become an imitator of God. But these things do not at all constitute his majesty. On the contrary, he who takes upon himself the burden of his neighbors; he who, in whatsoever respect he may be superior, is ready to benefit another who is deficient; he who, whatsoever things he has received from God, by distributing these to the needy becomes a god to those who receive his benefits,—he is an imitator of God. Then thou shalt see, while still on earth, that God in the heavens rules over the universe; then thou shalt both love and admire those that suffer punishment because they will not deny God; then thou shalt begin to speak the mysteries of God; then shalt thou condemn the deceit and error of the world when thou shalt know what it is to live truly in heaven; when thou shalt despise that which is here esteemed to be death; when thou shalt fear what is truly death, which shall afflict those even to the end that are committed to it."

PARDON OF SIN.

THERE is not, perhaps, within the entire range of human emotions, any feeling more satisfactory in character or more productive of peace, than the personal belief in and assurance of pardon and forgiveness of sin through the Lord Jesus Christ. No article in the Creed enters so fully into our consciousness, or touches so closely our individual lives, as that by which we express our faith in "the forgiveness of sin." Although to the natural mind the *process* by which the righteousness of God is manifested, the *way* in which "He might be just" and at the same time "the Justifier of him which believeth in Jesus," may be an inscrutable mystery, yet the simplicity of the Gospel is such, that among the first experiences of a soul led by the Holy Spirit, is a full persuasion of the power and willingness of God to pardon all sin, and remove forever both its pollution and its consequences. At the very entrance upon the Divine life, the Christian finds a new and personal meaning in the words of David, "Blessed is he whose transgression is forgiven, whose sin is covered. Blessed is the man unto whom the Lord imputeth not iniquity, and in whose spirit there is no guile," that he had no conception of before. After the consciousness of sin has entered into the soul, after it has experienced the "sinfulness of sin," there can be no peace without the assurance of pardon,— there can be no sure and steady hope without the belief, based on the word of Jehovah, that the awful debt has been paid. We cannot conceive an idea of Christian life without faith in the promise of pardon,—not only for past sin, but for that which intertwines itself with daily experience. It is the foundation of all hope, an essential of peace, a requisite to union with God. It is a blessed privilege granted to all who are led by the Spirit. The promises of pardon in the Word are so full and free, the conditions on which it is granted are so simple, the recorded instances are so remarkable and clear, that there should not only be no doubt of the general fact of pardon through faith in Christ, but of its possible personal appropriation by each individual by the exercise of faith. The instances of pardon rendered in Scripture are not special or extraordinary, but run in the ordinary course of human experience, and may therefore be accepted as general cases and precedents given for our encouragement. Let it be marked that the only condition of pardon for sinners is plainly given by Peter: "That through His name, whosoever believeth in Him shall receive remission of sins."

There are, perhaps, few Christians who either doubt or deny the truth that God, in His infinite mercy, through the life and death of Christ, does pardon all the sins of those who are truly united to His Son by the Holy Spirit. As a dogma, an article in their creed, all accept it, but yet there are but few who take it in all that it involves, making it an essential part of their Christian experience, and drawing from it the comfort and strength which follow its possession. Pardon, being a prerogative of God only,—a gift of grace, which no work or wealth of man can purchase,—must be accepted as such. Its source is found in the sovereign grace and mercy of God. On no other foundation can any human hope be based. As a right, it cannot be claimed. Christ has died, and we have the promise that by faith in Him we shall receive remission of sin. It may be that this gracious act far transcends human comprehension, but Scripture assures us that in the blood of Christ the justice of God is satisfied, and the sins of all who are united to Him are forgiven, blotted out, taken away, covered up, imputed no more. It would seem that God in His infinite mercy had taken special pains to convince men that sin might be pardoned through faith in His Son; that remission of sin was a logical and necessary result of faith in Christ; that a hearty and honest *confession* of sin would be immediately followed by pardon.

Now while the truth of pardon of sin may be accepted theoretically by the majority of Christians,—may be insisted upon as a cardinal axiom of faith, and in the heat of argument advanced as a pivotal point,—we claim that the almost universal custom of concluding a social or private prayer with the phrase "Pardon all our sins" is a sad evidence of ignorance of the *spirituality* of the Grace dispensation, and a proof that many are striving to work out a righteousness by the Law. This petition takes its place with others of similar character. It is a request for a blessing which has already been granted,—a prayer for that which the soul has already in possession, if the promises of God are fully accepted. It is a petition that will bear a very careful examination by every Gospel saint, and, regarded in the light thrown upon it by the Word, may seem to be one that he would hesitate to offer. In that part of the New Testament—from the beginning of John's Gospel to the close of Revelation—which embraces all that God through the Holy Spirit has revealed to men of His dispensation of Grace in Jesus Christ, there is no injunction to pray for the pardon of sin, or any recorded example that would influence a child of God to offer such a petition. When John declares that if "we *confess* our sins, He is faithful and just to forgive us our sins," he places before us the condition on which pardon will be granted, and gives us the warrant for believing that honest, hearty *confession* of sin is the pardon of sin; that, by the Grace of God, *confession* of sin and *pardon* of sin are inseparably connected; that if any burdened soul, conscious of guilt, and realizing the true nature of sin, sincerely and fully confesses the same, pardon is assured by the promise of God.

There are several motives and influences, always present in the Church organization, giving impulse to the petition for pardon of sin, none of which, however, can be surely based on Scripture. The spirit of legalism, the force of habit, the power of conscience separated from grace in the heart, the absence of faith in plain promises of God, the strange longing of the human heart to gain peace by works of the law, all combine to lead Christians into a form of prayer which, carefully analyzed, reveals the fact that they who above all others should feel that in Christ they are delivered from condemnation, and enjoy the liberty which God has given to His children, are held in a bondage like to that of Mount Sinai which enthralled the Israelites. We are no longer children or slaves. We are heirs of God,—can plead His promises,—can claim by the word of the Father that by the death of Christ on the cross the sin of all who trust in Him is washed away in the blood of Calvary, and therefore there can be no condemnation. If we cannot accept the clear scriptural declaration of God concerning the free and absolute pardon of the sins of all believers, we must give up all hope, for the promise of pardon rests surely and entirely on the same foundation upon which we base our hope of immortality. If, like the Jews, we had no Divine warrant for immortality,—if that blessed reality, assured to us by the resurrection of Christ, took its place only as an object of hope and desire,—the pardon of sin would not be a question of more than ordinary import. The consequences involved would be of little personal moment, for the human mind, with the rapidity of a lightning-flash, would reach the conclusion that if there is no immortality,—no conscious continuation of individual existence,—*sin*, with all it involves, is an evil connected only with the brief life on earth, the consequences of which do not pass beyond our present knowledge and experience. Without any desire to enter upon the discussion of the influence of a belief in a future life, on the morality of the present, we would yet endeavor to make evident the fact that a belief in pardon rests upon, and, in the mind of a believer, must be inseparably joined with, the same scriptural promises and assurances which lead him to think he is an "heir of immortality." Throwing aside all controversy, giving no heed to the utterances of human wisdom which would cloud faith, receiving the Scripture and the results of the operation of the Holy Spirit on the individual soul of the believer as the truth God would reveal to men, no reason is apparent why a full belief in the absolute pardon of sin should not be as heartily embraced and thankfully rejoiced in, as the assurance that the appearance of Christ "hath brought life and immortality to light through the Gospel."

But the question remains, *Why* should a Christian who has received the word of the Master, exercised faith on Him, and based all hopes in Him, have the faintest desire to pray for a blessing which the Father, the Son, and the Holy Ghost have combined to assure him *has been granted*, and is even now, and will be forever, in his own possession?

There are in Scripture—reference is made only to the New Testament—a few isolated texts which, taken without regard to the time, place, and circumstances of their utterance or record, might at first sight, to some minds, seem to give a warrant for a prayer for pardon of sin. Prominent among these, and one that is always placed in the front,—not only as an example, but as an example which, considering its source, is claimed to be equivalent to a positive injunction,—is the petition in the Lord's Prayer, "Forgive us our debts as we forgive our debtors." Now this phrase is so definite that taken alone it would appear like an authoritative sanction the force of which none would deny. But when we remember that those who received this formula from the lips of the Blessed Master were Jewish believers in the Messiah gaining the first intimations of the wealth of blessing He was soon to lavish on them,—who were then in a transition state, passing from a system of works into one of Grace, in bondage to a legal dispensation and having no clear ideas of the new freedom which was to be their portion when redemption should have been completed by the sacrifice on Calvary,—having no conceptions of the spiritual enlightenment and gracious power that would follow the advent of the Holy Spirit,—estimating all truth that came to them by the conditions of tutorage and discipline under which they lived, and thus incapable by reason of ignorance of any real comprehension of the spiritual import of Christ's teachings,—giving to all these facts their due consideration, it is not a matter of wonder that the Jews accepted the petition in a strictly literal sense, and believed their "debts" would be forgiven, *because* they had forgiven their debtors.

Such an idea was the natural result of Jewish legalism, but cannot consistently find place where Grace reigns. It is in direct opposition to the first principles of the Grace system. The Gospel saint who believes in his own heart that he has been taken out of the world by God's free and sovereign Grace, who "walks not after the flesh, but after the Spirit," because God's law has been written upon his heart, who has been crucified with Christ, has been buried and has risen with Him, been baptized by the Holy Ghost and thus made an heir of all the blessed privileges of the children of God, who knows that Christ has worked out a full, perfect, and complete salvation for all who trust in Him, *has,* or *should have,* an absolute assurance that all his sin, past, present, and future, is borne by, and atoned for, by his Substitute and Sin-bearer. He rests his faith on the word of Paul, that the Son, before "taking His place on the right hand of the Majesty on high," "*had by Himself purged our sins*" (Heb. i. 3), and "that the worshippers *once purged* should have had no more conscience of sins" (Heb. x. 2); and recalling the reproof of Peter to those who "had forgotten that they were purged from all their old sins" (2 Pet. i. 9), takes the comfort these declarations of truth were certainly intended to give. By the Grace of God being delivered from the conscience of all past sins by the new life or the new creation in Christ Jesus, the believer hates sin and cannot hold or cherish the least sin in his own heart. The Holy Spirit dwelling within him, he is inclined to and desires to be conformed to the image of his Lord. He cannot sin, for he is born of God, and the seed of God remaineth in him. He is sanctified through the offering of the body of Jesus Christ once for all, by which he is perfectly sanctified. (Heb. x. 10 and 14.)

During the centuries that have passed since our Lord was on the earth, myriads of redeemed souls, loving and trusting Him, have found in these words an expression of the inmost desire of their hearts,—an earnest desire for deliverance from the power of sin. Few of these, with a true consciousness of the inherent wickedness of the human heart, would venture to say, "Forgive us our debts, *as we forgive our debtors.*" In the light poured upon early Christians by the succeeding utterances of Christ, and by the inspired revelations of the Apostles, we can perhaps discover that which has transfused a Jewish prayer with the spirit of Grace and put into it a meaning far beyond the comprehension of those who first heard it. The truth hidden in this petition seems to be that a Christian, trusting only to the guidance of the Holy Spirit, will always be in such a state of mind and heart that he naturally and truly forgives all his debtors, and like his Master loves those who are his enemies. But this forgiveness which he so freely extends, is the genuine fruit of the indwelling of the Spirit in his heart, and is not, and cannot be the ground on which he believes that his own sin has been pardoned. He knows that in Christ sin has been condemned, justice satisfied, the law of God magnified, and believers saved from the consequences of a departure from the source of light and love. He cannot have the presumption or hardihood to cherish the thought for a moment, that his own pardon is dependent on or in any way the result of the forgiveness he may extend to others.

Simple, plain, and clear as are the promises of God to pardon sin on confession, the fact that so many prayers include a petition for pardon, is an evidence that the professed Christians of this age either *do not believe* the statements of revelation or that they have failed to *comprehend* their real meaning. Absence of faith or careless ignorance must be the impulse of a prayer for which there is no warrant in the Grace dispensation. Holding fast to the declarations of truth in the Old Testament,—perfectly adapted and invaluable to those for whom they were intended and to whom they were given,—many Christians, not appreciating the blessing of freedom and full justification extended to them in Christ, are continually striving to *do* something in the line of the law that will recommend them to God,— seeking for that which may be offered as an equivalent for the blessing promised and given to them,—working out a righteousness which they can offer to God. Would it not be more rational to follow the Divine injunction, "Believe on the Lord Jesus Christ,"—accept heartily that which God, "faithful and just to forgive us our sins and to cleanse us from all unrighteousness," offers to us, and yield ourselves to the guidance and teaching of the Holy Spirit? Believing that "Christ is the end of the law for righteousness to every one that believeth," accepting the declaration that "He hath chosen us in Him before the foundation of the world that we should be holy and without blame before Him in love,"—assured that "we are His workmanship, created in Christ Jesus unto good works which God hath before ordained we should walk in,"—satisfied that the Father "hath made Him to be sin for us, who knew no sin, that we might be made the righteousness of God in Him," —having a consciousness of "the liberty wherewith Christ hath made us free,"—trusting in the word of St. John that we "have an unction from the Holy One and know all things" essential to salvation,—being "fully persuaded that what God has promised He is able also to perform,"—we rest on the word of St. Paul that "if we believe on Him that raised up Jesus our Lord from the dead, who was delivered for our offences and was raised again for our justification, *therefore*, being justified by faith, we *have peace with God* through our Lord Jesus Christ, by whom also we have access by faith into this *grace* wherein we stand and rejoice in hope of the glory of God." Considering the richness and fulness of the promises of God to pardon sin, and the fact that "He is faithful and just to forgive us our sins," is there any reason for doubting that *all the sins* of *all believers* were laid upon and atoned for by the Sin-bearer,—that Christ by His death on Calvary laid an eternal foundation for the pardon of sins, that any human soul feeling the burden and guilt of sin might surely rest upon?

• In the daily intercourse with the world, in the ordinary walks of life, the Christian will fall into sin, and do that which his own conscience tells him is contrary to the holiness of the Law of God. With the confidence of a loving child he confesses his sins, pours out his heart before the Father in humble acknowledgment of his transgression, trusting in the Great High Priest at the right hand of God who intercedes for him, and thus throws off the burden which human strength cannot bear. Knowing so well by personal experience the weakness and infirmity of the flesh, the evil dwelling in his natural heart, the power of the temptations and blandishments of the world, and the force of the fiery darts of Satan, the Christian is always in a praying and confessing mood, and is continually judging himself that he "should not be condemned with the world." He does not approach a throne of grace with any slavish fear, or with any desire to gain a reward for obedience, or with the hope of avoiding an evil. His one earnest wish is for deliverance from the power and guilt of sin. Knowing that the Father has an infinite hatred of sin, that for his sins Christ was crucified, he will not deliberately hold the least sin upon his conscience, would not crucify his Lord afresh, or grieve the Holy Spirit, or prove a stumbling-block in the pathway of other human souls; he simply accepts God's word, humbly and penitently confesses his sin, believes that true confession is pardon, and trusts in the grace of God to deliver him from the power and temptation of his spiritual enemies. Knowing so well the weakness of his faith, conscious of the faint appreciation he has of the infinite worth of the sacrifice of Christ, finding within himself a spirit of selfishness, and a disposition to settle himself in a state of carnal ease, the devoted saint will always be mourning over his sins and humbly confessing them.

THE ABIDING COMFORTER.

Among the most precious privileges given to believers by the Heavenly Father are the assurance of pardoned sin and the consciousness of entire acceptance with God. The lamentable fact that so many pass through their earthly pilgrimage without experiencing the fulness of blessing to be enjoyed by their possession, is no evidence against the existence of a very definite, scripturally-based assurance of pardon and salvation wrought into the soul by the Holy Spirit. It is, however, a sad proof that many Christians, from the want of a strict and prayerful examination of the word of God, remain in doubt of that which would most conduce to their happiness and usefulness, and fail to appropriate the blessed privilege which has been provided for every believer. On this most important point of Christian experience, where there should be calm, settled conviction, causing constant joy and peace in the soul, there are too often uneasy questionings and chronic doubtings which have in them all the essential elements of unbelief.

Believing that this precious boon is one of the results of faith wrought into the soul by the Holy Spirit, we think the absence of assurance may be traced, in many cases, to an ignorance or a misconception of the nature and offices of the Abiding Comforter, or to a doubt of the indwelling influence. Before Christ left His disciples He told them He must go away or the Comforter could not come,—that He would pray the Father to send the Comforter to "abide with them forever," to dwell with them and be in them, to teach them all things, and bring all things to their remembrance that He had spoken unto them, to testify of Him, to guide them unto all truth, and to show them things to come. Paul, in the clearest and most emphatic manner, tells the Corinthian believers that they "are the temple of God," that "the Spirit of God dwelleth in them," even in their bodies. All the hopes, the desires, the very life of a Christian are but the inspiration of the Holy Ghost. God the Holy Spirit, doing the work of God the Son on earth, silently and without observation takes up His abode in the heart of every believer, and seals every saint as an heir of salvation. Thus the Church is sustained by one Divine Life, Christ poured into each heart. Where the unity of the Spirit is kept in the bonds of peace there is one body, one temple. All are heirs of the same blessing, all are influenced by the same Spirit. Partakers of the one life, all who love Christ are one, and therefore brethren, children of the One Heavenly Father.

How often do we hear in prayers the petition, "Send down the Holy Spirit into our hearts, and upon the Church"! Although from frequent and almost constant use this phrase has become so fixed and incorporated in prayer that it is regarded as an expression of humble dependence on the influence of the Third Person of the Trinity, and an earnest desire that the soul may be led into the right path by Divine direction, yet, in the face of the many positive declarations of Scripture that the Spirit dwells in the heart of every saint, does not the use of such a petition immediately betray a want of faith in God's promises that the soul is sealed forever? Does it not manifest a doubt whether the personal salvation has been secured? Is it not an admission that the Spirit is not in possession of the heart? Is it not a confession that the Spirit is recognized as an "influence" rather than as a Person, equal with the Father and Son? While nothing, perhaps, could be farther from the minds of many who use these and similar petitions, yet they do contain an element of unbelief that is inconsistent with simple Christian faith. No one of Christ's redeemed children, however sadly he may have grieved and quenched it, is ever without the Holy Spirit; neither can he resist the Spirit as a finally impenitent soul. If a Christian supposes he can think a good thought, speak a good word, or do a good act by any inherent or natural virtue, he is simply trusting to his own righteousness. He prays for the gift of the Holy Spirit, and negatively confesses that he has departed from and is not walking in God's holy ways, and that he can retrace his steps or regain the right road by asking for the Holy Spirit. If one could be holy to-day and sinful to-morrow there would be some propriety in praying for the "gift of the Spirit" to be holy to-day, and on the morrow to follow the flesh and the world. The influence of the Holy Spirit upon the human heart is not like that of the sun upon vegetation, or of the moon upon the tides. It is a new creation, beginning at the centre of man's being and working out to the circumference. The old heart remaining in the old nature, grace does not change the character of a man, but by the inworking power of the Spirit the man is more and more conformed to the image of Christ, and thus is changed.

When our Christian graces do not shine, when the soul is discouraged and despondency hangs heavy over the affections, it is natural, and proper that we should seek relief and gain new strength from the Divine source, and pray that the Spirit within us might awaken our dull affections, quicken our desires, and open our spiritual eyes that we may behold wondrous things in God's word. Such a petition implies no doubt of the gracious presence of the Holy Spirit in the heart, according to the promise. It may be said that one who has the Comforter constantly abiding in the soul ought not to fall into such a condition, which is certainly one of the forms by which the Spirit is grieved. Granting this, the experience of the weakness of our faith, and the appreciation of the power of our wicked hearts, the temptations of the world, and the fiery darts of the evil one by which we are so continually assailed, should work in us the conviction that without the ever-abiding presence of the Divine Spirit, exerting supernatural power, the Christian faith and life are beyond our capacity of retaining and manifesting.

We fear that the Church of the present age has a very faint and inadequate conception of the mission and office of the Holy Ghost, and that individual Christians do not realize the infinite worth and power of the indwelling Spirit. Fighting against principalities, powers, and spiritual wickednesses in high places, and unable to contend successfully against the least of his spiritual enemies, the weakest Christian, by simply giving up his own strength and fully opening the heart to the Holy Spirit, may draw to his aid all the Divine powers of the Godhead, and find ever within his own soul the Comforter who will guide into all good, shield from all spiritual danger, strengthen against all temptation, and protect from all enemies. When no thought or purpose is permitted to take root in the heart, and no design or act is allowed to find manifestation in the outward life, unless fully convinced that they are sanctioned by the Almighty Friend, Counsellor, and Guide, then is the human soul being brought into union with God and

Jesus Christ by the blessed influence of the Spirit. The Christian cannot attain this happy condition by effort. It is the result of simple yielding to the operations of the Holy Spirit as they manifest themselves in the soul. Cardinal Manning, in his book on "The Internal Mission of the Holy Ghost," uses the following illustration of the grace of God working upon the heart by the Spirit: "You have seen a lock in a river, and you have watched how, when the lock is shut, the water rises against the gate. It presses with its full weight against the gate until a hand—it may be the hand of a child, with such facility is it accomplished —opens the gate of the lock; at once the flood pours in, the level of the water rises, the stream runs strong and carries forward those that float upon it without effort of their own. The grace of God—that is, the power of the Holy Ghost—is always pressing against our will, always in contact with our heart, moving us onward towards God, impelling us to good. And this pressure of the Holy Ghost against our will waits only for our will to open: 'Behold, I stand at the door and knock. If any man hear My voice, and open the door, I will come in and sup with him and he with Me.' The Holy Spirit of God is waiting at the door all the day long; in every action we do He is pressing upon our will to make us do good, and when we are doing good, to make us do better. But He waits for our will to correspond. He never forces it. The will must be willing. If we only open the gate the full tide of His grace will flow in, and uniting itself with our powers will elevate our personal will above itself, strengthen it with supernatural force, and carry it onward with facility and speed."

Nothing is more certain and invariable in Christian experience than the fact that a man cannot attain this state of union with God except by an entire renunciation and perfect denial of self, a casting out of all self-love, and such an entire surrender and submission of his own will and whole nature to the Holy Spirit that it would seem as if the Holy Spirit Himself were the man's will and desire. The all-pervading, powerful influence of the Holy Spirit in human hearts by which the thought and life are guided, may to the mind of the natural man seem unreal and mystical, a force that cannot easily be distinguished or separated from the inherent qualities of the soul, the guidance of which cannot be intelligently discerned and therefore implicitly followed, but in all ages and in every country there have been many who could say with Tauler that " what the Spirit works in the souls of those with whom He holds direct converse none can say, nor can any man give account of it to another, but he only who has felt what it is; and even he can tell thee nothing of it, *save only that God in very truth hath possessed the ground of his soul.*" But is it unreasonable that the operations of the Divine Spirit of God upon the heart and soul of man should be mysterious? Is it surprising that a process so supernatural in origin, so powerful in its influence, so widereaching and diverse in its developments, should lie beyond the reach of finite limited human comprehension? But, thanks to the Father, who hath in all ages manifested Himself by the Spirit, each soul has within itself a faculty by which it may discern the leadings of the Spirit, and recognize for itself the Divine truth which He would open to the spiritual vision; it can see what God commands inwardly without means, as well as outwardly by the help of means; it can, with the confidence of assured faith, submit itself to the direction of the Spirit to follow any path along which the Lord may lead without murmuring or questioning. Not only is it the privilege of a Christian to always live in such a condition that he will at once accept the leadings of the Spirit in everything that may be related to the outward life as well as in the inner experience of his soul,—that interior life which is known only to himself and his God,—but he may, by faith and prayer and by entire renunciation of self, have such an indwelling of the Holy Ghost, that all desires, emotions, and affections, will seem to be but the constant and instantaneous results of the Divine Will, working in such perfect harmony with his own will, that the two cannot be separated or distinguished. He will not then be conscious of any disagreement between his own desires, and the will of God as it is revealed to his mind by the written Word and clearly manifested to his soul by the Holy Spirit. Then will he be receiving and enjoying, as far as it is possible to experience in his earthly life, a full and abundant answer to that all-embracing petition of the Lord's Prayer, "Thy will be done on earth as it is in Heaven,"—not, surely, in the sense which connects the petition with the current events of the "earth," but in that personal and real sense in which the soul is given up in rightful allegiance and full trust to the will of God, continually made evident by the supernatural power of the Spirit,—a power and influence differing only by reason of earthly and material conditions from that which bears sway in Heaven.

It may be said that this phase of high Christian experience, which is claimed to be the result of the Holy Ghost's abiding in human souls, is a condition far beyond the attainment of the majority of those who believe themselves to be, and are recognized by others as, believers in Christ and children of God. It may be regarded as a point in the Christian course which can only be attained when the soul shall have cast off its trammels of flesh and blood,—the sources, surely, of the many temptations that vex the spirit and throw such a blight over godly graces, —a point from which the soul, after its deliverance from the "natural body," may start exultingly forward on an endless course of love and service under the immediate and conscious inspiration of the heavenly life; but a careful study of all the truth concerning the office and power of the Holy Spirit, given to men by Himself in the written Word, accompanied by a careful examination of the operations of the same Spirit in his own soul, will convince a Christian, beyond any doubt, that a surrender of his entire nature to the overpowering influence, a constant watchfulness to receive and act upon any intimations of the Divine Will that may come to his consciousness, will naturally and inevitably lead his mind and soul, and therefore his rebellious body, into more and more entire accord with the Will of God. None would dare presumptuously to draw a line and declare that beyond it no soul could pass in its divine experience, when the Holy Ghost, dwelling within it, is constantly impelling it to make wider attainments in spiritual knowledge, to rise to a still closer union with its source of spiritual life, which, at the same time, is sustaining it in all that it has before acquired. Such a one acts from pure grace, and not alone from conscience. The old conscience from the law caused only a slavish fear and dread, but the new conscience from the Spirit, assuring of acceptance and pardon, is followed by ever-increasing joy and peace.

It may seem anomalous and paradoxical, but nevertheless it is true, that if a Christian who has been made a willing subject of the influence of the Holy Spirit, and thus enabled to make progress far in advance of many, was asked to relate some of his inner personal experience, the first point would be grievous complaints of the great power of his spiritual enemies, and of the constant temptation from the old heart to rest upon the works of the law, rather than on the finished salvation of Christ, applied personally to his soul by the Holy Spirit. Conscious that he should, like Christ, walk on the top of the water (the world), he confesses that, owing to the weakness of faith, he can scarcely keep his head above the waves. This tumult of suffering and humiliation, springing from ever-present fears within and assaults without, does not, however, in the least affect the constancy of his hope, break up his confidence in the power and love of God, disturb the intimate communion subsisting between his own soul and the gracious Spirit, or turn aside that overflowing flood of richness and sweetness of grace always pouring into the heart ready to receive it. With perfect assurance of faith, he says, with Job, "I *know* that my Redeemer liveth," and with Paul, "I *know* whom I have believed, and am *persuaded* He is able to keep that which I have committed to Him." Humility and self-renunciation mark every phase of his inward experience and outward action. Not conscious of the fact himself, it is yet patent to every beholder that he is being transformed into the image of Christ by the Spirit of the Lord.

It is passing strange that "the full assurance of faith," the enjoyment of which is a precious privilege that may and should be attained by every believer, should be so generally regarded as a special heritage of a favored few. There is nothing special or extraordinary about it, for all may have it. It is a condition of heart and soul that inevitably follows the free and unrestricted operations of God's Spirit. It is not presumption to believe clearly and definitely on this point, but it is a false and spurious humility that would lead one to live in perpetual doubt and hopeless perplexity. With the Bible in hand, opening so clearly the work of the Holy Spirit, it would seem the height of presumption to doubt that any Christian might not live in the conscious enjoyment of the heavenly gift. The soul has been quickened to a new life by the Spirit, has passed from death unto life, has been made partaker of a new creation, has received a new heart and a new spirit, has been "saved by the washing of regeneration and the renewing of the Holy Ghost." Every believer in Christ has been made the subject of these operations of the Spirit. The sanctifying grace of the Spirit has entered into and pervaded the whole nature. If not resisted,—and the power of a strong resistance dwells in every human breast, —the Holy Ghost will enlighten the mind, revealing wondrous things in the Word of God, will implant and sustain a true faith in Christ, will lead the soul to an entire submission to the will of God, will strengthen for the performance of every duty and the patient endurance of all suffering that may lie along the pathway, will cherish and brighten all Christian graces,—the outward evidence of the hidden working,—and will, not as a result of what He has already wrought, but at the same time, and in connection with it, give the blessedness of those whose sin is pardoned, whose transgression is covered, and work in the soul the humble yet confident assurance that "He which hath begun a good work in you will perform it until the day of Jesus Christ." Only when we can believe that the Holy Spirit has ceased to strive with sinners, to create souls anew, to intercede for saints, to comfort them and guide them into all truth, to shed abroad the love of God, and to seal souls unto the day of Redemption, can we reasonably doubt the privilege of a blessed and full assurance of faith.

PRAYER.

> "Prayer is the simplest form of speech
> That infant lips can try;
> Prayer the sublimest strains that reach
> The Majesty on High."

PRAYER is simplicity itself, yet its exercise involves all the powers which God has granted to the human soul. On the true and scriptural idea of Prayer, depends in a great measure the whole course of the Christian life. Prayer is the main channel through which the Infinite Father communicates His fulness of blessing to His dependent children,—the medium by which they express to the Source of life and blessing those feelings of dependence, emotions of love and gratitude, which spring up in the soul when it is in harmony with the Divine Will. From the depths of a broken heart, possessed and influenced by the Holy Spirit, our desires go up to God as the pleadings of that Spirit, which God has promised to answer.

While it may not be within the power of the human mind to form, or of human speech to express, the true idea of Prayer, in all its characteristics and far-reaching influence, yet the child of God may consciously experience in his own heart all the blessings flowing from *the effectual fervent prayer of faith.* The effectual fervent prayer of faith is not a mere act or position of the body, even though it be in apparent accord with, or an expression of the thoughts of the mind and emotions of the soul. It is not a confession of sins, an expression of thanksgiving, or a statement of our wants in a certain form, in a fixed time and place. It is not a duty commanded by God, which we dare not neglect for fear of consequences. It is not a delight of the natural senses or a self-complacent pleasure of the intellect. It is not pleading with heartfelt earnestness and unusual solicitude in times of anticipated or present disaster and fear, or when we are sorely touched by the loss of some temporal good, or in deep distress at the removal of dear friends. It is not calling earnestly on the Creator and Dispenser of all events when the storm is raging about us, and forgetting in the sunshine that the Creator is ours only as the Father of our Lord Jesus Christ. It is not eloquent language, or appropriate, well-adjusted scriptural language spoken to God. While the effectual fervent prayer of faith includes all this, it is something far higher and deeper and purer. It is God's own prayer; it is the Holy Spirit holding communication with Himself through the sanctified human soul. When the Spirit has entered into and taken full possession of the soul, that soul is absorbed in God, and all its desires are in full accord with the will of God, for they spring from it and find their satisfaction only in it. We *pray*, only when the Holy Spirit takes such entire possession of the heart that the desires expressed are the "groanings that cannot be uttered;" when the deep longings for freedom from sin and the enjoyment of God's love spring up spontaneously from the soul; when, without any human effort or design, we yield ourselves to the influence of that gracious Guest whom the Father grants to all His children; when, guided by this mysterious, yet real presence, we are so inwardly united with God in will and purpose, that our desires are simply the expressions of the Divine will. We *pray*, when we feel that God is our Father, that we are members of His family through

Christ the Son, and prove our sonship by trusting the promises God has given us in His Word. We pray, when our wills are so perfectly united to and lost in the will of God that we give up all selfish love and can say in sincerity, "Not my will, but Thine be done."

Let it be carefully noted that the prayer of faith cannot be offered if any sin remains on the conscience. If there should be any guilt unrepented of, any darling sin cherished in the heart, conscience, the inward monitor, asserting its sway, will prove a barrier to the familiar intercourse which should always exist between the Father and the child. It must be removed by true confession, must be cast into that flood from Calvary's cross, ere the soul can find peace. Only when the soul is free from the alloy of unconfessed and unrepented sin can it find the blessed peace which is the gift of the Holy Spirit.

It is of primary importance that the Christian should know what are the prayers God has promised to answer,—should gather from Revelation some definite idea of the range of petitions which may be offered in the assurance of faith. That there are certain limitations is evident, not only from Scripture, but from the experience of each individual Christian. While we would not dare to assert that it is wrong to ask for temporal good, or that prayers for such gifts are not answered, yet a consideration of the character of God and the whole plan of providence and redemption, as revealed in Scripture, and most clearly in the person and work of Jesus Christ, has led us to the conviction that it is not necessary for a redeemed child of God to pray for temporal blessings in detail, and that in the New Testament there is no encouragement to believe, or promise given, that such petitions will be granted. Rich and full as are the promises of God, infinite as are the blessings revealed for our appropriation by faith, both must be to a certain degree limited by the general truth that an Omniscient Father desiring the eternal welfare of His children, will not grant those things which may be for their harm. Our ignorance must be subject to His wisdom and love.

Traced to their source, prayers for temporal good and worldly advantages are prompted by a covetous desire for something not in possession that will supply an imaginary want, or by an undefined fear of natural trouble or future disaster from which we would shield ourselves by the power which we imagine is connected with earthly possessions. The one element of faith essential to true prayer cannot govern such petitions, for it seems impossible for an intelligent Christian to ask for these things and believe as if he had them in possession. All that God requires of those who are His children is faith in His love. If their prayers spring from mistrust, it is not probable that, by answering them, God would encourage such a feeling in their hearts.

A promise to answer prayers prompted by the natural heart would militate against that principle manifested by God in creation and providence by which He brings to pass all His divine purposes; for such petitions, not being indited by the Holy Ghost, and therefore not in accordance with God's plans, could be answered only by a miracle or by a change in His own great laws.

As often, perhaps, as from any other cause, prayers for temporal good, spring from a desire to evade or escape from suffering. In the present material, mental, and spiritual worlds an ordeal of suffering must ordinarily be passed before the highest good can be attained. The Captain of our salvation was made perfect through suffering, so that none of His disciples may hope to attain unto salvation without undergoing the same. The Christian believes that, in God's plan of grace to his soul, all the trials and afflictions that come to him in this life, are the means by which he may be purified from sin, and prepared for the glory placed before him. Theoretically he accepts the apostolic declaration, that "all things work together for good," but practically he ignores it by asking for deliverance from some form of natural evil by which alone, perhaps, that "good" embraced in the Divine purpose could be received. Be thankful, rather, that as Christians we are not required to pray directly for those temporal evils which may be the channels through which only we may gain the spiritual blessing. Is it not as reasonable to pray for temporal evils as to pray for what we consider temporal good? Are not both the means to an end, and is not that end "holiness"? We may quietly rest in the conclusion that, as we may not pray for the temporal evil which will result in our good, neither may we ask for that temporal thing which, although it may appear to be a present good, will result in eternal spiritual injury to the soul.

In truth, what are usually termed evils become such in reality by the rebellion and murmuring of the human heart. In God's hands and under His direction they are transformed into blessings, and become means of grace, without which the soul would not be prepared and fully equipped for entrance on its high destiny. God's eternal laws are perfect, and by their full, completed operation will bring those who are willingly exercised by them into entire union with their Divine Source. The Christian, fully trusting God, believes that no real evil can come upon him, for all things, by promise, will work together for his good, so that even "his enemies will be at peace with him" when "his ways please the Lord." Assured that God's ways are higher than man's ways, he is not troubled by seeming mystery, but rests quietly in the faith that all will be for the best and be fully manifested in the proper time. His main idea is not to discover the easiest and most comfortable route to the heavenly city, but to find that path in which God would lead him. Believing that *holiness*, not happiness, is the object placed before him, worthy of the exercise of all his powers, he seeks not his own life, but yields it up, and by the very act of self-renunciation gains all that is promised. But, let it be marked, this end is not obtained *for* humility, but "by humility;" just as the Israelites were saved, not *for* the looking, but *by* the looking at the brazen serpent. It must be an act of the heart, and not the result of any ascetic spirit that would perform a required duty. It must spring from the influence of the Holy Spirit, and thus caused will be in accordance with the will of God.

There are in the New Testament many passages which, at first sight, taken from their true and proper connection, would seem to give a warrant or encouragement for prayer for temporal good. A careful examination of any or all of them will show that these promises are general, not special and particular. It will not be claimed by any Christian that passages of this character have exclusive reference to temporal things, but the claim may be justly made that if the *spiritual* be the legitimate end of prayer, these promises must have a close connection with that which is spiritual.*

Each and every one of the passages is qualified with believing, faith, and thanksgiving before the blessing craved can be granted. This at once makes the prayer one of

---

* Matt. xvii. 20; xviii. 19; xxi. 22; Mark xi. 24; Luke xi. 24; John xiv. 13 and 14; xvi. 23 and 24; xv. 7; Phil. iv. 6, 7; 1 John v. 14 and 15; iii. 22.

faith indited by the Holy Spirit. This can only be for that which will promote growth in Christian grace, or for protection from that which may impede the progress of the soul in holiness. This, and this alone, can be a " good and perfect gift," even though it be opposed to the inherent, selfish desires of the human heart, and should come only by means of trial, trouble, and temporal afflictions. Such a view limits the free construction that is often placed on the words " anything," " everything," and " whatsoever," for it brings them all within a circle bounded by the words " according to His will." The saint would not be willing to accept them in the literal sense, for he would pray only for those things which would be for the highest good. He prays in full faith that God who knows his heart, and knoweth all things, will grant him just those mercies that will result in his eternal good, although they should not be exactly what he had asked for.

A careful reading of the first part of the eleventh chapter of Luke will show that the point of the whole passage has a clear reference to those spiritual graces or blessings which the Father is always willing to grant " to those who ask Him." They are, for our clearer comprehension of the truth, placed under the figure of the temporal; but when we read the conclusion of the whole passage, " How much more shall your Heavenly Father give the Holy Spirit?" (verse 13), have we not ground for the belief that the "asking," the "seeking," and the " knocking" have reference to these higher and purer needs of man, which God only can supply by the communication of His Spirit? Again, in the eighteenth chapter of Matthew, from the fifteenth to twentieth verses, it will be found that the whole matter refers to the Church—the body of Christ—and to individuals, only as they are connected with the Church. Read the context in 1 John iii. 18–24, and chapter v., fourteenth verse to the last,—passages just quoted,—and it will be seen that all relates to spiritual blessings. In Phil. iv. 6, 7, the reference is to Christian graces, and in particular to Paul's gladness at their manifestation of Christian benevolence. The sentence, " Be careful for nothing," is an independent one, a preface, a general exhortation, a sermon in itself, inculcating entire freedom from any fear of the future, or covetous desire for that which is not in possession. It is an expression of full faith in God. It may, with the same propriety, be used as a preface to such exhortations as " to know God, whom to know aright is life eternal ;" or " to press forward to the mark ;" or " to lay aside every weight and the sin that doth so easily beset us," and many others of a similar import.

If we would have a simple and consistent plan of interpretation of scriptural truth, it must necessarily be one that will not come into conflict with other declarations that seem apparently to teach truths contrary to these under examination. If the foregoing texts be accepted as exhortations to prayer for the things that may be desirable for temporal ease or comfort, we shall find great difficulty and confusion when we meet the many plain and simple directions to " take no thought for the morrow," and numerous other texts teaching the same doctrine of trust in God for the supply of such temporal good as may be best for us. The principle announced by Christ is, that if you ask blessings in faith, believing as though you had them in possession, such blessings will be granted. Now, if you ask spiritual prosperity will He give you earthly prosperity if it should be the means of preventing your advancing in the divine life? He certainly will not. If you ask any temporal mercies in detail, severed from their connection with a higher spiritual good, you cannot, neither can any saint, believe as though they were in actual possession, and without this element the prayer is not one of faith. What we term our wants are usually the imaginary desires of the old natural heart, and are not those things that may be necessary for us. The word "want" should not be used by the Christian. It is a word destitute of comfort, for it supposes a painful vacuum, and implies a fear that nothing will be given to fill it. The saint may lack more grace to make him perfect in Christ Jesus, but he has the conviction that the covenant is well ordered and sure, and in it his bread and his water are included. God has never said He will give wealth, honor, or pleasure, but He has bound Himself to give grace and glory,—the best gifts,—and, in addition, has said that no good thing shall be withheld from those who walk uprightly. All things are yours, ye are Christ's, and Christ is God's. Our Saviour has given us a perfect word in "need," which signifies all things that may be spiritual, both for time present and time to come. You may, in your heart, want wealth or honor, while in God's mind you may need grace, although you may not feel it; but when you desire grace it is a need, and is immediately supplied. True desire is love in motion, delight is love at rest. The desire for a spiritual mercy is always in accordance with God's plan, for it is a blessing that tends to make us more like Himself. God has given us the privilege of praying for spiritual blessings without bounds. Indeed, He declares that He is honored by our large petitions. The more we need the more He is ready to give. His free promises are not given as conditions of rewards, but their fulfilment is a result. If we had the promise that our petitions for temporal good would be answered, our reception of the things asked might rob others of what is really necessary to them, so that the imaginary wants of our hearts might be supplied. This cannot be the case when we ask largely for spiritual gifts, for all the children of God cannot exhaust the magazine of God's rich grace. From this we may draw without stint, but He reserves to Himself the prerogative to judge and supply as may be best the temporal good needed, and this He grants in answer to a petition for it, made in subservience to and in connection with prayer for spiritual things. As an example, we take the petition in the Lord's Prayer, "Give us this day our daily bread." All Christians, when using this form, believe that they are asking for the spiritual food to nourish the soul, and with that greater good are asking that sustenance needful for the body. The needs of the soul are primary, those of the body secondary; the lesser is included in the greater. How it limits and confines the signification of that glorious petition to make it refer specially to the bread that perishes! How much more consistent to regard it as a general petition for all those things, either for the soul, the mind, or the body, that may better enable us to glorify God by living a life of faith in Him! The qualifying words "this day" make the petition parallel with the words of Christ, "Sufficient unto the day is the evil thereof."

In the history of the earthly life of Christ we find many incidents related from which we may draw logical inferences, and, by careful study, gain a knowledge of the doctrines he announced for the government of the lives of all those who formed His kingdom. Among the many instances where the disciples or others came to Christ asking for temporal good and were met with a gentle reprimand, or the words of stern rebuke, the following are selected: The mother of Zebedee's children, who would have her sons sit on the right and left hand of Christ in

His kingdom; the disciple who would first go and bury his father; the disciples whose anticipation of future evil awoke their Master in the storm; the man who would have Christ speak to his brother to divide the inheritance with him; Peter when he was sinking in the waves; Martha when she was "encumbered about much serving;" the disciples when they "had forgotten to take bread;" the apostles who, just before Christ's ascension, asked Him, "Wilt Thou at this time restore again the kingdom to Israel?"—make evident Christ's method of treating all desires for earthly good or avoidance of anticipated evil. Another indirect rebuke—the more powerful because it was indirect—may be found in Luke xii. 30. After Christ had told His disciples what they should *not* care for—the things that perish with the using, such as nourishment and clothing for the body—He said, "For all these things do the nations of the world seek after." He told His disciples to take no thought for their lives or that which was necessary for the body, because their heavenly Father, knowing their need, would provide for them as He did for the fowls of the air and lilies of the field. The language is plain and unqualified, the figures bold, strong, and striking.

While the whole spirit of Christ's teaching seems to be against petitions that betray a want of confidence in the promises God has given to His children, and a want of faith in the assurance that He will provide all things needful, the liberty He has given to His own children is so great that if, in your heart, with full sincerity and faith, you can offer a prayer to God for all temporal good, for health, wealth, and honor, with the assurance that you *can*, and the determination that you *will*, use all for the glory of God, and in subservience to His grand design, there can be no objection to such a prayer. The question to be first settled by each individual Christian is, whether he can meet the responsibility involved in the possession of the good he prays for.

The teaching of Christ seems to be, that we are not to be concerned for our lives,—for that which may make them comfortable; we are not to dread evils which may befall us; but we are always to live in the simple faith that since He has placed before us "eternal life," He will certainly grant to us nourishment for the body, and will preserve the health and life, so long as they may be for His own glory and the good of the soul. What Christian could ask for a greater promise than this? Grant that we know not whence the bread and water for to-morrow's sustenance is to come, can our care and thought produce it? The Christian's faith is that his heavenly Father will provide it if it is needful; that He will guide into the use of just those means that will bring it. But, even though the morrow should come, and there should be no bread, it does not prove that God is unfaithful, for the absence of sustenance, and the pain resulting therefrom, and even the death of the body, may be the means by which God grants the greater good to the soul. Did not Christ, by His teaching, intend to form in us just that trust which is manifested by the birds of the air and the lilies of the field? They, unable to talk or think, trust His kind providence. Why cannot we trust Him, with an intelligent faith? This is not fatalism, but it is the faith of a soul so fully absorbed in God and in His work that it "takes no thought" of those things which the Father hath promised to grant.

The words, "Take no thought for the morrow," are full of meaning. Why should we be troubled about the things of the morrow, when the great God, the Benefactor and

Sovereign, has given His promise that He will not leave or forsake us? The duties of the present day are pressing upon us, and their faithful performance makes such demands on our time and energy, that we can spare none for anxious care about what may be to-morrow. The present moment is ours,—the next belongs to God. We have no right to take hold of the future, except as it relates to our own souls and the interests of God's kingdom.

It is evident that any scheme of Christian doctrine must inevitably hinge on Scripture testimony,—on the words of the divine Founder of Christianity, or of those who, having been under His teachings in life, were after His ascension governed by His inspiration. If the teachings of Scripture point a particular course of action, or reveal a certain path of duty, we are bound to accept and follow it; if we do not, we are false to the convictions of truth flashed upon our minds by the Holy Spirit.

A careful study of all Christ has spoken, of all the experience of the apostles as it has been recorded, will not reveal any warrant for special prayers for temporal blessings, or any assurance that they will be answered.

It is probable that the prayer of Christ in the garden of Gethsemane, "Father, if Thou be willing, remove this cup from Me; nevertheless, not My will, but Thine be done," might be adduced as a prayer for deliverance from a threatened danger. We would ask this one question: Did Christ, knowing all that could occur, fully conscious of all things, assured that the salvation of men could be secured only by His drinking all of that cup, pray that He might be delivered from that which was the one condition by which men might be saved from wrath, and be made subjects of the mercy of God? May we not rather gather from the passage,—the truth that sin was such an evil that nothing but the blood of God could deliver us from it; that sin was such an enormity, and its deserts so dreadful, that nothing less than the life, sufferings, and death of God Himself could deliver man from the punishment which he had brought on himself? Where would have been our hope if that cup of agony of our blessed Redeemer had been a prayer for deliverance from those very sufferings which He came to earth to endure? Legions of angels, we know, would have gladly gone to His rescue; would have, by their supernatural power, saved Him from the evil designs of men; but He did not ask this. His prayer was, that He might, by the grace and strength of His Father, fully accomplish that one purpose for which He became incarnate, and by which He might save from the power of the evil one, all those who would believe in Him.

The biographies of eminent saints, as they are recorded by inspiration, are for our instruction and for our reproof. The life of St. Paul is full of instruction to all who will study it, and the lessons there taught must not be neglected. After the conversion of Paul, he separated himself from the world, renounced all that in which he had formerly gloried, and consecrated himself and all his powers to Christ and the glory of His kingdom; he lost sight of his physical comfort and ease, and was only anxious to serve his Master. Although, by the faithful performance of duties placed before him, he was brought into great dangers and was compelled to suffer, we do not find him praying to be delivered from persecution, or from those enemies of Christ who would put him to death. His own hearty desire, and that for which he would have the Church to pray, was that he might preach the gospel; that it might run and have free course. His love for his brethren was so great that he wished himself accursed if they might be saved. However difficult it might be to comprehend his real meaning, we are assured that the desire for the salvation of the Jews overpowered every selfish and personal wish. That he was conscious of the evil desires dwelling in his own heart, and his tendency to rest on earthly things, is evident from 1 Cor. ix. 27: "But I keep under my body, and bring it under subjection; lest that by any means, when I have preached to others, I myself should be a castaway." And while conscious of the power of the old heart, he yet trusts in the grace of God; for in the context he says: "I therefore so run, not as uncertainly; so fight I, not as one that beateth the air." In another Epistle he says: "I am persuaded, that neither death, nor life, nor angels, nor principalities, nor powers, nor things present, nor things to come, nor height, nor depth, nor any other creature, shall be able to separate us from the love of God which is in Christ Jesus our Lord." (Rom. viii. 38, 39.) His confidence in God is so great that nothing can disturb it.

This same faith was displayed when Agabus took Paul's girdle and bound his hands and feet, and, moved by the spirit of prophecy, said, "So shall the Jews at Jerusalem bind the man that owneth this girdle, and shall deliver him into the hands of the Gentiles," for Paul, when his brethren besought him not to go up, answered, "What mean ye, to weep, and break mine heart? for I am ready not to be bound only, but also to die at Jerusalem, for the name of the Lord Jesus." When he went to Jerusalem, and suffered all manner of persecution and imprisonment, and was sent to Rome bound as a prisoner, and was "made a spectacle unto the world, to angels and to men," we have no record of any prayer for deliverance from the threatening dangers. In 1 Cor. iv. 9–14, 2 Cor. vi. 4–11, 2 Cor.

xi. 23 to the end, we have a record of his sufferings, yet we read no petition for temporal mercies. The experience of St. Peter is of a similar character, yet we do not hear of any such prayer from his lips. Now, the question comes up to the mind, Did Paul and Peter, as a free gift, have any more privileges to suffer for Christ than we now have? Or have we greater privileges than they, so that we may ask for temporal good, or deliverance from what we term temporal evil? Is it not true that Paul, who gave himself wholly to Christ, courted not the things of this world, did not desire the privilege of praying for them, and would not have used them if granted? Or is it that we have only partly come out of the world; have divided the heart between Christ and the world, and thus have need to petition for those perishable things that carry with them inherent evils and bring leanness to our souls? St. Paul accepted God's words, "My grace be sufficient for thee," as the truth, and, sustained by this faith, could bear all that the malice of his enemies could inflict. For him to die would have been gain, but to live was to spend a life of toil and suffering, that Christ might have glory and His Church be extended. Have not we, who are born of God, the same blessed privilege of suffering for His cause? Are we not striving to find the easiest and most comfortable passage to the heavenly Canaan,—yielding to the seductions of earthly pleasure, even at the expense of neglected duties and privileges? Are we willing that God should lead us in His own good way, through joys and sorrows, pleasures and pains, delights and disappointments, to the infinite happiness at His right hand? If not, your prayers are only the imaginations of the old heart. Jerusalem is not above your chief joy, but your great desire is to reach the New Jerusalem without trial and suffering. You would work out the way, and are not willing that God should "work within you to will and to do of His good pleasure." You may be saved, it is true, but it will be as by fire; but your education in the school of discipline on earth is not such that you will, on your entrance, be prepared to appreciate the glories of Heaven as you might. Will you be contented with a place of safety just within the bounds of the heavenly inheritance, when you might have gained the power of running, without weariness, on the endless road stretching out before you, and of making rapid progress through the eternal glories that are to be your possession? These are solemn thoughts,—they may soon be to you solemn realities. Are they not worthy of your careful reflection?

In the Lord's Prayer we have the most comprehensive one ever uttered,—a prayer to be reverently used by all men, of all ages, in all places, and in all times. Careful reflection on its deep import should prevent that careless and irreverent repetition which is too frequent with many. The preface, "Our Father which art in Heaven," should deeply impress the mind with a sense of the infinite perfections, truth, holiness, and justice of the great God, who cannot look upon sin or insincerity with any favor, so that the heart may cast off every cherished evil desire, and the conscience any secret sin, that would make these petitions nothing "but idle words upon a thoughtless tongue."

The main idea of the whole prayer is that of a deep longing for the glory and kingdom of God, expressing in the first three petitions God's relation to us, and in the others our complete dependence on Him, closing with the full faith that God, who is the highest good in Himself, will bring to pass the highest good, even His own kingdom. Let us examine the Prayer with a practical intent and purpose.

"Hallowed be Thy name." Is there in your heart an all-pervading desire that this Name should be revered and honored throughout the earth? Until you have really and truly hallowed it in your own heart, you cannot truly ask that it may be honored by others.

"Thy kingdom come, Thy will be done in earth as it is in Heaven." What are you doing to prove that this petition is from a sincere heart? How much of your time, labor, and wealth are you contributing to bring this glorious time to pass? Are you aiding it by the covetousness, ambition, and pride that would seek great things for yourself, and make you indifferent to or careless of all those interests of Christ's Church—the preaching of the Gospel, the enlightening of the ignorant, the education of the young, the providing for and protecting the widow and orphan, the alleviation of the distress of humanity—that are the divinely appointed means to the desired end? Have you a care for the universal good, or only for that which is local and selfish? There is no faith or sincerity, unless you are striving to perform the involved duties, and the petition becomes a mere phantom, except that it leaves your heart harder and more callous than before. Do not these petitions teach us that all the peace and comfort of our own spiritual life are to be found in entire self-surrender to God, and in seeking first that which will be for His glory?

"Give us this day our daily bread." As, in the first revelation of truth, we are taught, "That in the beginning God created the heaven and the earth," so at the introduction of the Gospel we are taught dependence on God for the supply of all that is needful for soul and body. This petition is not for mercies in detail, but is broad and comprehensive, embracing all material and spiritual gifts that may sustain the life of soul and body, and thus prepare us for our part in God's great plans. It is for simple food for this day only. We pray not for to-morrow's bread, for on the morrow we may need no bread. And do we not also pray that the material gifts of God's providence may by His blessing be transformed into spiritual food, and thus be made means of grace to us?

"And forgive us our debts as we forgive our debtors." This inherently-balanced petition regulates itself. The words "as we forgive" place upon us a responsibility from which we may not draw back, and one which we too often neglect. How can one who deliberately holds and cherishes unfriendly feelings, or an unforgiving spirit towards any fellow-mortal, take these words on his lips? As there is in the New Testament no other exhortation to ask directly for pardon of sin, except the words of the Publican, "God be merciful to me a sinner," Divine Wisdom gives us in this petition a direct warning against that unforgiving spirit that would oppose the Gospel spirit of love; and it is not in its essence so much a petition for pardon for our own sins, as a command to forgive the sins of others. As none but those who believe can realize what sin really is, only they can make a true and hearty confession, which in itself is pardon.

"Lead us not into temptation." In view of the declaration of James, that God does not tempt any man, and of other words of the same apostle, exhorting his brethren to count it "all joy" to fall into divers temptation, and his calling those blessed who endure temptation, this petition seems beset with difficulties. We would thus construe it: Leave us not to the power or allurements of our wicked hearts, or to the power of our spiritual enemies, by which we may fall into sin or be drawn away from the path of duty. We also pray God that, if the trying of our faith be needful, He would with the "temptation" (trial) grant us a way of escape.

"Deliver us from evil,"—not from natural troubles, physical sufferings, or providential afflictions; for these are the secondary means by which Christ educates and disciplines all His children, that they may be co-workers with Him in advancing the glory of His kingdom,—but from those real evils which are eternal in their results and ruinous to our souls. Death should never be an evil to the Christian, for it must be passed before he can enter on the fruition of all his hopes.

"For Thine is the kingdom, and the power, and the glory, forever. Amen." This doxology is the closing strain of glory to God, teaching that the foundation, the progress, and the final object of the whole prayer are God and His kingdom.

Certain practical deductions may be drawn from the whole subject. Every immortal being should realize the great responsibility resting on him from two important considerations: First, from the fact of his immortality, and, second, that an infinitely holy and eternal being has condescended to place a responsibility before him. We are not conscious of what a power we may be in the hands of an Infinite Sovereign, especially when we have fully opened our hearts and admitted Him, that He may work within us, to will and to do of His good pleasure. A thought, a word, or an act, may be the means of changing your destiny for time and eternity, or may alter the conditions of a family, community, or a nation. A rational being is bound, in view of this responsibility, to appreciate and improve fully every privilege that may come before him,—not for any selfish ends, dictated by ambition or selfishness,—but that, if he be in the path of duty, true peace, order, and prosperity may result legitimately to himself and his neighbor. Being, as we are, a part of a grand plan, the government and decrees of God, as they are connected with our various duties and relations in life, must be taken into consideration, and our whole course of action be brought into accordance with the perfect holiness which he has placed before us as the aim of life. The happiness which results from the holiness is its natural product; but if mere happiness be placed before the soul, as an object to be obtained, it will continually elude the grasp.

In the Eternal mind, our responsibilities are just in proportion to the light we enjoy and the talents intrusted to us; therefore, no one should imagine that he can be lost in the throng, and thus escape the fulfilment of these responsibilities. Neither should an imaginary sense of inferiority or weakness stand in the way of the performance of known duty. Let the thought take possession of the mind, that if you were the only fallen immortal creature, in a state of probation, in a school of discipline for a more perfect inheritance, your guilt is so great, and the love of Christ so infinite, that nothing less than His whole life of suffering and death of agony could make an atonement for you. His love for you is as great as the love He bears for the whole redeemed Church. Impressed with this truth, our prayers could scarcely be for anything but those spiritual blessings on the Church, and on the souls of Christ's redeemed ones, that would best promote the glory of God; for the whole economy of redemption involves the idea that, while we are praying for all those whom Christ has redeemed by His own blood, they are, at the same time, asking for the same blessing for us. Love is the one binding chain. While we may not ask for temporal blessings for ourselves, we have full liberty to ask for good, both temporal and spiritual, for the brethren, and have the assurance that all things needful will be granted. St. Paul reminds us, "Let no man seek his own, but every man the wealth of others;" hence, all selfishness is shut out from the soul of the saint, and he has neither heart nor time to be anxious about the supply of his own perishing wants, for God is faithful to grant what he needs. In God's benevolent designs, and in the plan of creation, every atom is called into being, not for its own special benefit, but to support, cherish, and sustain all the other atoms. It is so in the plan of redemption. If one member suffers all suffer with it. The Church of Christ is one perfect system,—a miniature of the universe.

The doctrine that the end sanctifies the means is a heresy most disastrous in its effects on the mind that receives it, when the motives to those means do not point to a perfect and holy end. In the moral world there is but the one perfect end, and that is the attainment of the holiness which is an attribute of God. The motives or the means can only be sanctified when in harmony with that universal principle, and this truth at once places the whole duty of man in harmony and symmetry with the holy will of God. Many in theory acknowledge the truth of this statement when it refers to religious matters, yet in that which relates to temporal matters often practically proceed on the contrary opinion. If any man in his actions maintains a mental reservation, or works secretly, or deliberately uses means that are contrary to the glory of God and the welfare of men, he is guilty of a breach of the great law of love, and is doing that which does not spring from faith. The inconsistency lies in the fact that he would sanctify the end for the means; he rejects an eternal for an evanescent good; he aims to make the most of time, and loses hold of eternal interests; he rejects eternal wisdom, and trusts to his own; he acts by sight, not by faith.

The Christian should not pray in detail for temporal blessings, because there is no promise that such petitions will be answered. There is no rule given by which it is possible for finite beings to determine how much they may need of perishing things, neither can they know how much of what is termed temporal good would be best for their souls. The anticipated trouble which the natural heart cries out to be delivered from may be, and in many cases is, the means by which God confers upon the soul His choicest blessings, while the prayed-for good, if granted, might prove an eternal curse to the soul. There is a path clearly marked out waiting to be filled up by each rational creature. It begins in time, but goes on through eternity. The circumstances of each are different from those of any other: no two paths can be alike. Scattered along each path marked out by Heavenly Wisdom, everything needful for the holiness and happiness of him who is to walk in it will be found at the proper time. These blessings are designed for, and adapted to, the particular individual, and for no other one. Each person, in the exercise of his free agency, can secure the path intended for him, and thus bring his life into full harmony with the plan of God; or he may fail to find it, and thus introduce confusion and disorder fatal to his happiness. The greater the good to be found, the greater will be the evil, if you fail to secure it.

If there was placed before you by revelation from God a true history of your life, with all its joys and sorrows, its pains and pleasures, from the cradle to the coffin, and you believed it true, would you make any attempt to change it? Would you, in view of it, seeing the connection between the circumstances and the final result, pray to be spared from natural temporal evil, or would you ask for a larger supply for the wants of time? And yet, if you are a child of God, your way is marked out, and it is just the path which will surely result in the salvation of your soul from sin and death. If you really believe that all God's dealings with you are holy, just, and good, why not trust Him for all things? Why not bring your actions and life into accord with your creed? Suppose that in order to experience the good which comes from temporal evils you were required to pray for them just as earnestly as you pray for spiritual blessings, would you do it? If you would not, where are your faith and love? Be thankful, then, that God, in the economy of creation and redemption, does not require you to pray for natural evils, even though they may be necessary for the perfection of your Christian character. You do, indeed, pray indirectly for them, in asking for spiritual good, which may sometimes be obtained only by them. Why should you, then, pray in detail and in particular for imaginary temporal good which, if granted, would be injurious to the health of your soul? It is a vain imagination of the natural heart to suppose that mere external circumstances can produce that happiness which is full satisfaction to an immortal nature. Yet, when a Christian's prayers are for earthly things, he confesses that from them he hopes to have his pleasure. He says that the love of God and all its fulness does not yield him what he wants; he acts as though there were sources of pleasures beyond God and His service.

The habit of praying for temporal good will certainly lower the tone of the Christian character. The Christian will be more influenced by his natural heart than by the Holy Spirit. His thoughts will be more concerned with the good asked for, as an end, than a means to aid him in his spiritual progress. Should his prayers be heard, as they may be, and answered in wrath, he may receive a rod of chastisement, or a curse, instead of that which he thought would be a source of happiness. We say it is answered, but it is answered in this sense,—that God has left the soul to its own vain imaginations, and to the delusion that God has heard his request, while the thing wished for has brought with it a train of inherent evils, and been transformed into a curse. God may leave one of His dear saints to pray for something which the natural heart desires, and may grant the desired object only to show to that saint the pride of his own heart, which, had it remained, would have caused spiritual death.

Another reason why a Christian's prayers should not be for temporal good may thus be stated: We know not the general character of our future earthly lives; but as all those events that we may often regard as trivial do have an important bearing on them and do often possess an importance we do not always fully estimate, it is wiser to leave them entirely to the disposal of Him who, to effect our salvation, through holiness and likeness to His own Son, delivered Him up to save us from our sins,—the only price by which our redemption could be purchased. That love, so pure and holy, should be met on our part by a love that is disinterested and unselfish. If it be in our power, we should exercise that affection which is free from all selfish motives. We should trust that love, even though some particular manifestations of it may in this present time and to our finite senses appear to be evidences of its withdrawal. Though clouds and darkness may surround our way, we may always have the confidence that a Father's love is guiding our course, and that the object of that love is our deliverance from sin, and, as a result, our entrance into perfect holiness and happiness. Why not, then, like an unconscious infant in the arms of a loving mother, trust all the events of our earthly life to the care of Him who hath in the past given us not only evidences of affection, but of His infinite wisdom that would choose only that which would be for our ultimate good? If this childlike trust—which is the precious heritage of every child of God—was in constant exercise, our prayers would be for deliverance from sin, for increase in grace, and for high attainments in holiness, and not for those things which, if obtained, would only increase our pride and draw us away from the source of true happiness.

A DARK PROBLEM.

AMONG the dark problems that have fascinated the minds of men for ages, none have been the subjects of more earnest thought and deep research than the reconciling of God's sovereignty and man's moral free agency, and the endeavors to reach the origin of evil. Knowing that "secret things belong to the Lord, but those revealed unto us and our children forever," I would not attempt to solve the mysteries, but only endeavor to gather up from revelation and experience some truths and facts bearing upon them. It is true that God did take from the Gentiles a people for His name. (Acts xv. 14–18.) He has also declared that He makes "His people willing in the day of His power." Christ clearly states the truth "All that the Father giveth Me shall come to Me," coupling it with the cognate truth, "And him that cometh to Me I will in no wise cast out." (John vi. 37.) In these and many other similar passages the doctrines of election and free sovereign grace for every sin-sick soul are plainly announced. There is no obstacle in the way of any soul's coming to Christ, whatever may be its merits or demerits. Speaking reverently, God, knowing that a rebellious race would not return to love and loyalty, had a right to select a people for Himself without infringing upon the moral free agency with which He had endowed them. A Church, perfect and entire, was therefore ordained before the foundation of the world, before the first law was proclaimed, or the first law-breaker had come into being. The special mission of this divinely-ordained Church was to be as a city set on a hill, whose light could not be hid; to proclaim to a rebel world that God was reconciled to man; to show forth the praises of its Lord; to call out from the world every sin-sick soul that would accept life, and to prepare it by a process of trials and purification for a high state of glory and happiness. The peace and rest manifested to every soul by the glad tidings of great joy were open to all who would come.

In this is evident the trinity of doctrines,—predestination, forcordination, and election. As the Holy Ghost proceeds from the Father and the Son, so does election flow forth from the first two doctrines. It is the only system from which can logically proceed man's moral free agency, by which he chooses eternal life or death.

To claim that God has decreed a soul to death, or that He uses any external constraint upon any dependent and defective, though rational and responsible, creature of His hand, is to destroy the very idea of a God, just as much as to say that He is striving for victory against a power equal or superior to Himself, or that He is subject to uncertainties and contingencies. The dependent being must have a liberty parallel with the responsibility placed upon him by the Creator, who, in justice, is incapable of causing a moral evil to fall upon the work of His own hand.

An Infinite, is the great First Cause, eternal in being, omniscient, omnipotent, omnipresent, perfect in thought, wisdom, and design. If there was an original "nothing" it would be so now; nothing can come out of nothing. An Infinite begins and ends in perfection, overruling what is called evil for good, even sin, and making the very wrath of man to praise Him. All life, thought, power, phenomena, emanate from Him, except sin, which is a coming short of, or a breach of law, an after-event.

Would Adam have been susceptible of eternal life if he had not fallen? The Jews committed the greatest sin the world has ever witnessed, but from it resulted that which is to be the salvation of the world.

Predestination required the Son of man to be perfected through suffering, that He should become the Son of God, a great High Priest and King. As Son of man he filled the office of a prophet. Yet He was a High Priest without a Temple, a King without a Kingdom. In heaven He became a High Priest. When He comes again he will be a King with a Kingdom, and perfectly fulfil all the offices of Prophet, Priest, and King.

Predestination is fact fixed. Foreordination is order, time, and limitation. Predestination is a straight and one-sided principle, always tending to perfection. When you place your hand in the fire it burns, but you do not say you were necessitated to do it. You knew that by the laws of fire and your own flesh pain and injury would be the result. If in a thunder-storm you refuse to enter the open door, you suffer the consequence. In ordinary life it is evident that in some way or other we are the authors of our own natural evils. Salvation is from God, condemnation from ourselves. (John iii. 18; xii. 47, 48.)

An Infinite is a law in Himself and to Himself, and cannot come into collision with what He has pronounced holy, just, and good. He must keep justice whole, not only for the good of the universe, but for the subject of punishment, which is not an arbitrary infliction, but a manifestation of infinite love. There is but one real original evil in the world,—sin, the parent of all evil. All natural evils, of which we are the cause, are for our final good, if we only believe and accept them as such. If your house is blown down it is by the elements on their proper mission for the universal good, and you suffer for others. In our government we give up certain natural rights for the good of all.

While the gospel proclamation is in force there can be no arbitrary judgments. The evils we now experience are from the breach of law or from the force of natural laws. If God manifests His dying Son to you as the source of life, and you, exercising free agency, reject Him, the divine perfections and omnipotence cannot prevent you from remaining in death.

To deny the misconstrued and much-abused doctrine of predestination as contained in the Bible, is tacitly to deny the existence of a great First Cause of all things, as well as the law of compensation which is involved in the whole system of creation and redemption, the consequences of which cannot be evaded. It is this which makes a rational being a responsible one, after the presentation of a simple law, with no promise of reward attached for observance, but a warning if broken. By the law was the knowledge of sin which worketh wrath. This law was to discover what was in man, and to reveal to man not only his lost, wretched condition, but that which he should be. While it could give him no aid, it demanded death or a substitute.

Why, then, did man, in full possession of the Word, having all that heart could wish, voluntarily depart from God? Because it was predestinated that if man loved death rather than life, an Omnipotent could not, consistently with perfect law, prevent him from choosing it. Adam was not obliged to eat the forbidden fruit, yet he did eat of it. Here at once are manifested predestination and free agency. Man had taken the first step in the exercise of moral free agency.

From the Fall to the Flood, God left man without any law, gospel, or restraint, with free liberty to improve or ruin himself. In the latter course he was successful, but his choice was not, as in the gospel, life or death. As a second step in the process of restoration, God, in pity for man, took him from the waste, howling wilderness and placed him in a school of law to train and discipline him for a higher sphere of glory. He sent holy men and prophets, who were rejected and persecuted. The more He did for men the worse and more wicked they became, until He said, "What have I not done to My vineyard which I could have done?" and the race was released from probation as incapable of returning to loyalty. Then God's love said, "Perhaps they will reverence My Son." The forerunner, John, came to prepare the way for the Messiah, but he was cut off. The Messiah came, but was crucified, and thus was prepared the way for the descent of the Holy Ghost,—God with us, remaining to the present period. In this third stage of the process the gospel of free and sovereign grace is manifested without money or price: only believe and receive. Yet, notwithstanding the fulness and freeness of the gospel plan, its blessings have been appropriated by a small fraction of the human race, and there is no hope from revelation that they will be the portion of the majority. The fourth stage will be when the last sin-sick or redeemed soul is brought home, when the proclamation of glad tidings ceases, when the Holy Ghost and the Church shall have left the world, and judgment, as naturally as by a law of gravitation, not by an arbitrary decree, falls upon the earth. What more terrible judgment can befall man than to be left to the imaginations of his deceitful heart, to be led by Satan, captive at his will?

The first Adam and the fallen race with liberty,—Israel

with the law—and now grace for the Jew and Gentile, for grace is simply the gospel; come and receive life whatever may have been your sins. All have failed, except for the redeemed Church of God. The Infinite Father may say: "When I gave my Son, I gave Myself; all I had to give. At an infinite cost have I presented life, but ye have chosen death. I would have incorporated you in my own life, love, and holiness, but ye would not." This is predestination without any infringement on man's moral free agency. What human power can make a man believe that which he does not believe? None. God only, by converting grace, can do it.

One fruitful cause of disagreement between those holding what may seem to be radically different views on these important questions, is the false conception of passages of Scripture. As an example, take 1 John ii. 2: "And He is the propitiation for our sins; and not for ours only, but also for (*the sins of*) the whole world." While not presuming to speak of the right or wisdom of the translators to interpolate the three words in italics,—the sins of,—we ask each one to read the declaration as it came from the pen of the apostle, and judge for himself what a change is made in the sense. Calvinists and Arminians have both rested in the error that *purchase* and *redemption* were one and the same thing. The Calvinist is right in the belief that redemption is limited to the household of faith. The Arminian is right in the belief that a purchase was made for every lost soul. Thus they differ, because each holds to a partial, one-sided idea of truth which the other denies.

The text in 2 Pet. ii. 1: "Even denying the Lord that bought them," clearly shows purchase, and taken in connection with Ps. ii. 8, John i. 3, Heb. i. 3, and Col. i. 16, makes it evident that Christ, the Creator of the universe, strengthened His right by purchasing with His blood. Take an example that could be drawn from the now extinct laws of a part of these United States. A slave-holder, owning one hundred slaves, having an absolute right to them by purchase, declares that all who will receive their freedom are relieved from bondage by accepting his offer. Half of them believe and accept, and are at once made free. The others, by declining to embrace the offer, are still his property and remain slaves. Light is thrown on the subject by Rom. iii. 22, where the righteousness of God is "*unto* all and *upon all* them that *believe.*" Here are predestination, foreordination, and election in perfect harmony with the exercise of moral free agency on the part of man.

It must be freely admitted that there are connected with Christianity many truths which the mind of man cannot fathom with its present capacities. They may be above reason, but they are not in conflict with it. As there are in the material world many influences and forces of the sources of which we are ignorant, and the results of which we have learned by experience, so there are in the spiritual world truths, influences, and forces, the presence and powers of which we must acknowledge and act upon in the same way that we do in the material. However men may theoretically deny the doctrine of predestination and assert the presence and power of free will, yet in the every-day affairs of life they practically admit the doctrine. The farmer plants his seed, confident in the belief that it will germinate and bring forth a crop, but he is just as certain that all things requisite to that anticipated result must precede it; the law which governs natural production—that of predestination—is so definite, so sure in its operations, that no man looks for a crop of wheat unless he sows wheat, neither does he expect wheat if he sows oats. There is no diversity of operations in the natural and spiritual worlds. Inexorable law pervades both. The confusion and disorders which prevail among men are simply the moral evils which spring from a breach of, or a coming short of, those laws, which are themselves only the manifestations of God's predestination.

In the mind of an Infinite all is fixed. These designs take form by two simple instruments in creation and redemption. Law in the material and grace in the moral, in proper time and order, manifest and fully develop the design. A broken law was the first development of sin,—an after-event in the history of man,—the first exercise of his free agency. Law is the simple instrument to draw the love of sin out of the heart of humanity. By it God subdues the world to His will. It breaks up the fallow ground of the heart, drives out self and the love of sin, so that the seed of divine grace can enter. As air rushes into a vessel when the water is poured out, so does grace come into the heart when sin goes out. When Satan's doorkeeper, the will, is discharged, the Holy Ghost enters.

Before a watchmaker begins to work with his materials he has in his mind a perfect idea of a watch, else he would not attempt to construct one. He is finite, but God infinite. This is predestination. Election proceeds from it, and foreordination. "Make your calling and election sure," is a general expression with reference to a final result. Compare this with, "Work out your salvation with fear and trembling, for it is God that worketh in you, both to will and to do of His good pleasure,"—both addressed to saints under instruction in the school of God. If salvation is not found in this school it cannot be worked out. As these texts are sometimes expounded from the pulpit they leave an impression upon the indifferent or awakened soul that it can, by the exercise of some inherent power, or by a voluntary act of the will, fit itself to be more acceptable to Christ,—an attempt as sure to end in failure as for a sick man to refuse the service of a physician until he cures himself. A soul conscious of its lost condition, convinced of guilt, and fearful of the consequences, yet hesitates and asks, "How can I know that I am one of the elect?"

Now surely such a question, which does not concern any soul honestly seeking light, must spring from mistaken conceptions of the doctrine. It awakens a doubt of its honesty, or at least betrays the fact that such a one has no real conception, in the gospel sense, of his peril while out of Christ. It is like a drowning man endeavoring to reach the farthest of two ripples in the offing. Aiming to be one of the elect as an object insures failure. It is a nonentity. One who starts for the goal naked, hoping to acquire the robe of Christ's righteousness will surely miss it, but one who starts with sin forgiven is clothed in the righteousness of God. One who asks, "How am I to know that I am one of the elect?" betrays the fact that he has not realized his lost, helpless condition, without the sense of which he cannot receive the grace of God. The exhortation of Peter, "to make your calling and election sure," is not a command in a legal spirit, but a kindly exhortation to avoid that which might be an obstacle in the way of receiving that grace which is granted, not for, but by, God's appointed and revealed means. The process is, come, believe, and receive life. The Holy Spirit enters into and possesses the soul, assumes all the responsibility: you yield to His leading, you obey, and are led into the presence of God, where there is fulness of joy and your election made sure. Law existed before grace; therefore, predestination is unchangeable, an inexorable law that no finite, rational creature can evade. Whatever theoretical difficulties may cluster about the doctrine, it is clear that the way of attainment of a state of peace and rest is plainly marked out in the Scripture, and that any human soul yielding to the divine influences exerted upon it will be led into the path of eternal life.

APHORISMS AND REFLECTIONS.

*The Gospel of Grace is not the Messianic or Judicial Gospel preached by Christ,—it is not the dispensation of the law in which works are a means to gain a good or avoid an evil. The works of a Christian are only the natural issue from, and fruits of, Grace.

Christ did not preach the Gospel of the Kingdom of Heaven to the Gentiles, neither did He permit His disciples to do so. The Messianic Gospel was preached by the Son of man to Jews only, and has exclusive reference to Christ's kingdom on earth. The Gospel of Grace was designed by the Eternal Mind before the foundation of the world, for a special purpose, separate from and independent of all other systems.

The Gospel of Grace, which is heavenly and spiritual, came by and through the Son of God. Crucified as the Son of man, He arose from the grave as victor, assumed His Divine character,—the Son of God,—and was visible only to believers.

The Gospel preached by Christ was one of works: "Inasmuch as ye have done it unto these (Jews) My brethren, ye have done it unto Me." "Go sell all thou hast and give to the poor, and come and follow Me." "Offer for thy cleansing, according as Moses commanded." The Gospel of Grace is life received by faith, and the works following are only the consequences or results.

It is not the faith that brings the life,—the blood of

Christ is the life given; faith is the channel through which the oil of Divine Grace flows. We are not to look at the *act* of our faith, but to the object of it, Christ; not to believe in our faith, but in that upon which it is fixed. We are not saved from sin *for* believing, but *by* believing. Nothing can be added to the work of Christ, for He did all. When the soul has received life it is ready to enter the school of God and be instructed how to live and walk in the new creation. When it believes it comes into everlasting life. It is not to be, or to come, but a present possession. You are not told, as in the law, "Do and live," but are instructed how to live. What is instruction to saints is not Gospel for the unbelievers, for to such the Gospel message is, Look, believe, receive life by faith. All of the Epistles are directed to those who have been redeemed by Christ, and to them only. They only are capable of receiving and understanding them.

The Blessing of Grace is not given as a reward for what we have done, or can do, in bringing the soul to a knowledge of Christ, or for efforts to increase the numbers of the visible Church, or for sufferings, afflictions, and martyrdom for Christ's sake. These are only the fruits of obedience. If any enter the Kingdom, it *must* be through much tribulation. Neither is it for prompt and careful attendance on public, social, and private worship, or for the exercise of benevolence and charity. These may strengthen the soul and edify the Church of Christ, and are the good works springing from the renewed heart.

It is no fruit of the pure Gospel when a Christian to whom has been given a large degree of temporal wealth and prosperity, measured by a worldly standard, regards himself as a special favorite of Heaven, and cherishes the idea that he has not been so unfaithful as his brethren.

He that would live godly in Christ Jesus must pass through affliction. What a rule to apply to Christendom, where the prevalence of legalism prompts the constant looking for earthly prosperity as a reward for so-called religious service!

Neither is it a result of the pure Gospel when a saint, who has reached a certain point in his Christian experience, settles into a peculiar feeling of self-complacency that all is right, that his salvation is fully secured,—a most dangerous ground to rest upon, for it gives evidence that he is standing upon the law. There is no resting-place in an enemy's country, for until the redemption of the body, we carry within us wicked and deceitful hearts, against which, aided by principalities and powers and spiritual wickedness, we must be in perpetual conflict.

The Gospel is not salvation from punishment, but from the bondage of sin and the law. It does not incite you to aim for eternal existence, but for eternal life. Eternal life is the incorporation of your own life into the love, holiness, and life of God.

The Gospel does not merely bring the soul into a condition of peace with God, but it brings the peace of God to dwell within the soul. The saint is not simply to believe the blessed fact that Christ was crucified, but he must be crucified, buried, and risen with Christ if he would attain the full stature of a man in Christ Jesus. He is not to aim for the crown by evading the cross. He is not to deliberately hold sin on the conscience unrepented of, or to believe that sin does not dwell in him, but he is not to dwell in sin that it should reign over him. It is not by a voluntary act of the will that he can make himself perfect, but it is by obedience and subserviency to the Divine Will that the grace of God makes him perfect.

The Gospel does not incite you to seek for happiness, a carnal desire, but for holiness, a heavenly spiritual desire. It does not encourage you to seek for peace outside of yourself, but to seek it only where it can be found, in your own heart. It does not influence you to live aright that you may thus avoid the evils of wrong-doing, but that by uprightness your life may be in harmony with the perfect life of Christ. It does not teach you to dread the evils of sin, but to dread sin as the parent of all evils. A legalist does good works to gain a reward and shun an evil. True religion begins with the forgiveness of sin, false religion labors to secure it.

The Gospel does not teach that God's salvation is a purchase to be made, wages to be earned, a work to be done, or a summit to be climbed, but simply a *gift* to be received. It teaches that if you are in grace it is of necessity, if in unbelief, by your voluntary choice. It does not teach that the visible Church on earth is a place of safety, but that the Church is an assembly of souls redeemed by Christ, who form and sanctify the Church. It does not teach that the saint should find his home in the world where Christ was crucified, but that those who possess the life of Christ should find their home where He is. It does not incline you to come to Christ by your own will, but by a realizing sense of your need and helpless condition. It does not teach that God can come and dwell in the heart before that heart is emptied of itself: self-renunciation must precede purification. It does not require you to be a believer before you are a listener, or to be a worker before you are a worshipper. It gives no encouragement for any soul to say there is no salvation for it. It gives no authority in the Epistles for a saint to neglect his own personal piety that he may be instrumental in directing souls to Christ. It does not incline you to reform and elevate crude humanity, in which there is nothing for God to admire, but to accept for yourself, and induce others to receive, an entirely new creation in Christ Jesus. It does not teach that doing is God's salvation, but that ceasing to do and accepting what Christ has done, is assured salvation for the soul. It teaches that the saints who now sit *in* heavenly places *in* Christ Jesus will in glory *sit with* Him.

The Gospel does not present Christ as fulfilling the law for us by His life. The sins of the believer are imputed to Christ, who is holy. Righteousness is imputed to us, who are sinful. He is made *all* our sin as truly as He had none of His own. We are made all His righteousness as truly as we had none of our own. It is *we*, wholly and completely, that are His sin; and it is He, wholly and completely, that is our righteousness.

It does not teach you to look into your own heart for holiness, for there nothing but sin can be found; but you are to look to Christ for pardon.

It teaches the saint to be ever dissatisfied with himself, but he is not doomed forever to be unsatisfied.

It declares that the saint is not a servant, but a freeman, a child, an heir. It places faith before repentance, death before life, receiving God's blessing before seeking it. To seek for life proves that you have no life, for life is requisite to acquire life.

The Gospel does not judge or condemn you for your sins,—that is the province of the law,—but because you reject the only medicine that can cure the disease, the end of which is death. It gives you nothing for what you have, but it will supply that which you realize you lack and need.

The Gospel does not insist upon external forms as essential to salvation. While recognizing sacraments as a means or channel of good, participation in them is not an absolute condition to the reception of the blessings they manifest. Abraham, the Father of the Faithful, was not baptized. The thief on the cross, an example of human depravity, was never baptized, never partook of the Lord's Supper, but, by Grace, was transformed into a saint without the aid of ordinances. The baptism of the Holy Ghost *is essential* to salvation.

It does not incline you to make the Lord's Supper a feast of bitter herbs, but encourages you to make it one of peace, joy, and gratitude. It requires no season of legal preparation, but it does form in each humble sincere saint a condition of mind and heart that makes him always ready for a happy and profitable participation.

The repentance of John was simply a change of mind. That of the Messianic Gospel, preached by Christ, was a turning from the wrong to the right,—that shown by the prodigal son. The repentance of a godly sorrow for sin, which is not to be repented of, is a deep sense of sin against God. This is the gift of God after you have become a believer, and something that can be exercised only when you have realized that you are a sinner. The repentance while under conviction is sorrow for the evils of sin, rather than a deep hatred of sin as the parent of all evil.

The Gospel does not require you first to *do* that you may believe, but to *believe* so that you may be taught how and what to *do*.

In the Gospel there are life-works,—God working within the heart of the saint. These, however, are very different in source and development from the law-works performed for wages or in an attempt to make one's self more holy. Law-works may be wrought without grace or love in the heart.

The Grace saint starts for the goal clothed in Christ's righteousness. The legalist starts naked for the other end of the course, hoping to gain the garment of righteousness, which he can never find or procure.

The Jews were not the Church, for every Jew, holy and unholy, enjoyed all the rights and privileges of the Theocracy by reason of natural birth. In the Gospel the Church is the Body of Christ, without spot or blemish. God dealt with the Jews as men in and of the world, but in the Gospel He deals with saints as jewels taken out of and separate from the world.

In the Gospel the believer, by keeping his eye of faith on Christ his life, is, *by*—not *for*—looking, transformed into the same image, from glory to glory, by the Spirit of the Lord, and thus unconsciously becomes conformed in moral perfection to the image of Christ.

In the Gospel those who compose the Church, *let* their light so shine that others are beneficially influenced. By their *patient continuance* in well-doing they put to silence the ignorance of foolish men, and, showing forth the praises of their Lord, become His faithful witnesses on earth. They are such by living in Christ.

In the Gospel there is a " name to live," but not a name to act or do. The believer, seeing his sins in the wounds of the body of Christ on the cross, is more absorbed in the " finished work" done *for* him than in that carried on *within* him by the Holy Ghost.

Law came by Moses; Grace and Truth by Jesus Christ.

The Law was not designed to make a man more holy, but the end of the Gospel is to redeem man from sin, and make him holy as God is holy.

The Law was not given to save the world, but to curse

it. The Gospel is to call out from the world all who desire to leave it. (Rev. xviii. 4.)

The Law hath dominion over a man as long as he lives. The Gospel takes him as dead to the Law, and through Jesus Christ frees him from its dominion.

Under Law there is no moral liberty. In Grace is moral liberty.

The Law demands perfect obedience, but gives no power by which that obedience may be attained. The Gospel holds out perfect liberty, love, joy, and peace in the Holy Ghost.

If the Jew worked on the Sabbath, the penalty was death. If the Christian does not perform spiritual work on the Lord's Day, the fruit or result is spiritual death.

Law never can subdue the human heart. A view of God's love by faith melts it into contrition.

The Law was proclaimed from a mountain's top amid thunderings and lightnings. The Gospel came without observation.

If the Jew went into the Holy of Holies while the High Priest was there, the penalty was death. Under the Gospel if one stays out of Christ it is spiritual and eternal death.

In the Law man was enjoined to love God, but the aim of the Gospel is to manifest God's love to man.

The Law says: Make you a new heart and a new spirit. The Gospel declares: A new heart I will give you, and a right spirit I will put within you.

Law curses every one who contrives not in all things written in the book of the Law to do them. Grace blesses the man whose iniquities are forgiven and whose sins are covered.

Law tells what man is to do for God; Grace what God has done for man.

Law: "Pay what thou owest." Grace: "I freely forgive thee all."

Law: Do this and thou shalt live. Grace: Believe and life will be given.

The Jew is looking for a Messiah and an earthly Kingdom of Righteousness. The Gospel gives a Saviour and fixes us in heavenly places, our lives being hid in God.

The law pronounces condemnation and death; Grace justification and life.

The Law addresses man's *old* nature; the Gospel man's *new* nature.

Under the Law man seeks an object to worship, but the Gospel seeks worshippers.

Under the Law the worship made the worshipper; under Grace the worshipper makes the worship.

The Law can neither create nor remove sin, neither can it form an aversion to it. The Gospel removes sin, creates a hatred to it, and brings peace to the soul.

In the old creation man belonged to death; in the new death belongs to man.

By Eve came life, by Eve came death. By the new creation death gives us all we need.

Law is condemnation; Grace is reconciliation.

Law reveals your danger, but points out no refuge; the Gospel holds out the sure refuge.

Under Law the Ten Commandments are a rule of life; to a Gospel saint they are a rule of death, for to him Christ only is a Rule of Life.

The Law is a work to do; the Gospel a word to believe.

The Law would induce you to avoid punishment; the Gospel delivers you from the *guilt* of sin *by* (but not *for*) believing.

Law inclines you to act from slavish fear; the Gospel from spontaneous grace and love.

Under Law one works *for* life; under Grace *from* innate life.

Under the Law the wages of sin is death; Grace makes the gift of God eternal life.

The Law claims everything and gives nothing; Grace gives all and claims nothing.

The Law worketh wrath, but Grace works blessing.

Under the Jewish Law life was to be attained; in the Gospel life is acquired and enjoyed.

God does not require Jews to go out in love that others might participate in their blessings, but Gospel saints cannot refrain from inviting sinners to come to Christ.

The Jews, as an elect nation under tutorage, are dealt with by discipline; under Grace saints, being in the school of God, are taught how to live and walk while there.

With Moses all is from man to God; with Jesus Christ it is all from God to man. Law is first, Grace second.

Christ, as Son of man in the flesh, addressed Himself to Jews and Gentiles; as the Son of God He reveals Himself to saints through the Holy Ghost.

Daniel, the Jewish prophet, was told to seal up the book to the time of the end; John, the Christian prophet, was told not to seal the book, for the time is at hand.

In Matt. iii. 3 we read that the Kingdom of Heaven is at hand, but in Luke xvii. 20, and xxii. 16-18, that the Kingdom of God cometh not by observation.

The first Sabbath was in commemoration of creation, was nullified by sin; the second Sabbath, that of the Law, on the seventh day, has not been abrogated; but the Gospel Sabbath, or Lord's Day, is the first day of the week.

The expectations of the Jew who keeps the Law, and

thus lives by it, are all of an earthly, perishing nature; the hopes of the Gospel saint are fixed on that incorruptible inheritance reserved in Heaven.

The foundation principles of the doctrines of Grace are found in Romans, from the third to ninth chapters. The doctrine of Justification is plainly recorded in the third and fourth chapters, the privileges of the believer in the fifth, his character and duties in the sixth, his conflicts in the seventh, and his glorious triumph in the eighth.

Some Christians flatter themselves that they have attained the condition described in the eighth chapter, while their true position is below the seventh. So deceitful are human hearts, and so powerful are the temptations of Satan, that many believers fall into a self-complacency which leads them to suppose they are special favorites of Heaven, and some are so far deluded as to imagine that they have passed beyond the power of temptation or the possibility of sin. They are, indeed, members of the one body, Christ, and receive a dividend of Grace *according to their faith,* but no more. As far as the inclination of the heart goes, to be perfect in spirit like Christ, the new man is perfect; but holding within himself the two antagonistic natures of flesh and spirit, he is subjected to a warfare continuing until the redemption of the body. Yet, he cannot hold unrepented sin on his conscience; if he does, it only proves that he was never born of God.

The Son of man is heir of all things; to Him all power and judgment are given; in Him are hid all the treasures of wisdom and knowledge.

Life, in its true sense, is not, and cannot be, purchased by man. Life is given to the believer as a free gift. God sees nothing in man to admire, but, looking upon him, sees what he lacks and what he needs in Himself.

No good or holy action can precede life, which is implanted when the Holy Ghost makes the body its temple.

No salvation *by* works; no salvation *without* works.

First the gift, then the result; first the tree, then the fruit; first the saint, then the service; first the life, then the action; first salvation, then the evidence.

Believing and receiving Christ require no preliminary works. With the first sight is "the accepted time." Christ has done all for you. Receive His testimony and live.

If you are *preparing* to enter heaven, you will never be ready. The Holy Spirit calls you into life, that you may be prepared and ready to enter into eternal life,—called into earthly life that you may enter into heavenly places in Christ Jesus, and be susceptible of enjoying eternal glories. The closing of earthly life is no time to prepare for another world, which, though certain, is unknown.

You say you cannot *feel* as Christians say they do, or as you think they ought; but feeling is not faith. Christ's work has been done, independent of your feelings. Faith comes first, feeling follows as a natural result. You pray, but do not believe you will receive that which you ask for because you do not feel. This is a carnal, legal spirit.

Faith is a fruit of believing and obeying God's Word without cavilling, questioning, or waiting to prove that it is true. There can be no preparation, dictation, calculating of consequences, or any aiming for a future object.

A humble, resolute saint is not so much aiming for perfection and holiness, as he is fleeing from and resisting the power and pollution of sin, and keeping his garments unspotted from the world. By striving to be unblamable and without rebuke, he would be ready at the coming of the Lord. While keeping his heart with diligence and continually rooting out his imperfections, he is constantly heading towards perfection, while not placing it before him as an object.

We must be listeners before we can be believers,—worshippers before we can be workers.

The saint's service is not that of an unwilling slave, but that of a sincere lover. God is not an exactor, but a loving free giver.

To believe in Christ's body—the Church—as our life and light is one thing, but to patronize the Church for personal comfort or the well-being of our families in time is quite another motive.

The Gospel of Grace touches many, but triumphs over few. Many are called but few are chosen to holy service and high reward.

One born of God may have sin dwelling in him, but he does not dwell in sin. There is a great difference between a soul *struggling* against sin which it hates, and one *wallowing* in sin which it loves.

There are in God's Kingdom Abrahams and Lots, Marys and Marthas; those whose hearts and affections are fully engrossed in Christ's present and future glory,—pilgrims and strangers, having no continuing city,—and those who are struggling between law and grace, or conscience and grace, heaven and earth, not having comfort, joy, and peace in the Holy Ghost, but having too much light to find satisfaction in things of earth.

Soon after Pentecost, when Christendom was of one mind and spirit, Christianity spread rapidly, and the number of souls converted was perhaps greater in proportion to the population than at any time since. As soon as it became popular and successful in a worldly sense, the Church was made the theatre for the exercise of selfish ambition, pride, and power. Errors of doctrine and practice crept in, and that unholy alliance between the Church and the world was formed, which has continued ever since. The Holy Spirit was grieved and departed. Since that time we do not believe there has been such an outpouring of the Spirit like that at Pentecost. There have been outpourings of the Spirit in measure, for the Spirit will bring home every soul redeemed by the blood of Christ. Judging from the lives of the great mass of those who have joined the visible Church, they might be called surface or galvanized Christians. Christendom has not continued in the goodness of her Lord, and must meet her doom (Rev. iii. 16 and xviii. 24), because she has left her first love.

A soul truly born of God will be kept by the power of God through faith unto salvation, and for such there can be no falling from grace. "He which hath begun a good work in you, will perform it unto the day of Jesus Christ." But one, impressed by the apparent application of the words, quotes 2 Chron. xv. 2: "The Lord is with you while you be with Him; and if ye seek Him, He will be found of you; but if you forsake Him, He will forsake you." This is consistent and true, for God is always accessible to, and may be approached by, the humble, sincere soul. But it is a perversion of truth to apply this statement to the Grace dispensation, for the passage in its connection was addressed to Jews, man in the world and the flesh, under law, and in a condition where he was being disciplined and prepared for a higher sphere. The Gospel saint is out of the world, dead to sin, the flesh, and the law. As well quote Ezek. xviii. 24–26. While it is good to be a subject of God's moral government, it is better to be a possessor of eternal life, and a subject of God's unchangeable grace. God makes the body of the saint the temple of the Holy Ghost, who wills and works within to do the whole work, and to give continual life to the soul. The subject works as if all depended on working, and believes as if all depended on faith in the blood of Christ. Yet he realizes that he can do nothing of himself, for Christ has done all. We are to discharge Satan's doorkeeper, the will; then the Holy Spirit applies Christ's finished salvation, the fruits of which are good works and a holy life.

Having entered the school of God, the Holy Spirit being our guide and teacher, we are exhorted to walk worthy of our vocation as heirs of God and joint-heirs with Christ. The saints do not perform good works to be made more holy, but because they are holy, separate from the world, and set apart by the Spirit for high service and holy duty. They do not work for life, but because they have received the life of Christ. The gracious encouragement to a saint to progress in the divine life is found in the fifth chapter of Hebrews, from eleventh verse to the close of the sixth chapter. This portion of Scripture is a parenthesis through which, by the Word and Spirit, we may be carried to unknown heights. We may attempt to mark out God's plan of salvation, may be able to argue logically on the doctrines of Divine sovereignty, or of prophecy, or of the resurrection and union with Christ by the Spirit, yet all may be simply an intellectual exercise that does not feed or strengthen the soul, and is destitute of humility and self-abasement, and not governed by perfect love to God and man. To be content with a name to live, without the indwelling of the life of Christ, is a sad dereliction of duty and obedience.

THE SABBATH.

An intelligent and scripturally-based appreciation of the Day of Holy Rest, involving, as it does, important practical results to both Church and State, is a subject worthy of careful research and deep thought on the part of those who are interested in the prosperity of either. To those who are component parts of the Church and State the "Sabbath question" will have a twofold importance, for it has an intimate relation with all that God has revealed to the Church in the Word, as well as a direct bearing on the temporal happiness of the citizens of the State.

Any conception of the Sabbath, that would thrust upon the freeman in Christ Jesus, the unyielding rigidity of the Jewish law, is as far removed from the spirituality of the Law of God written on the heart by the Holy Ghost, as is that rationalistic indifference or opposition which would make the day "an occasion to the flesh" and transform it into a season of sensual or merely intellectual satisfaction.

After a true appreciation of the Blood of Atonement, nothing in Revelation is more important to the Christian, than a proper understanding of all that is represented by the resurrection, the new creation, the descent of the Holy Ghost, and the Lord's Day.

These lovely features of the Gospel have been so shrouded by Judaistical legalism and human theology, that their pure light has been intercepted, and the Church itself, by holding a rod over the masses in announcing commands expressed by "you must" or "you shall," instead of presenting a bleeding Saviour on the cross as the manifestation of the love of God, has been a stumbling-block to the free course of the Gospel.

From the earliest ages of Christianity there has been ever present a strong disposition in the Church to rule arbitrarily over the faith and practice, not only of those who had yielded willing allegiance, but of those who were beyond its pale. This feeling has taken shape in the various creeds and confessions to which assent was demanded, and in those more modern organizations of human wisdom that have so frequently shown the same intolerance which Protestants bitterly condemn in Romanism. The Church, by methods resulting from these agencies, and by its course in presumptuously turning aside to do God's work instead of learning to depend on His counsel and do His will, has arrogated to itself the office of the Holy Ghost and assumed an authority never granted to man. The result, as far as the individual is concerned, has been an infringement on the personal liberty of the Christian, which has in turn reacted disastrously on the best interest of the whole.

Springing naturally from the hidden seeds of Judaism, this legal spirit has strengthened with the centuries, and is to-day more blighting in its results to the Church than positive opposition.

Among the dearest privileges which God has granted to His children—a divinely-given right which none can take from them—is that of being taught in all truth and guided in all duty by the Holy Ghost. This *Christian liberty*, with which all are endowed, and which Paul labors to make clear and plain as their inalienable possession (Gal. v. 1, and Col. ii. 16), is that perfect leading and guiding of the Christian by grace—that simple following of the law of

God written on the heart—which makes it impossible for any one to charge him with sin in religious principle, or by the flesh. It is beyond the judgment of another, it is an individual possession, "for why is my liberty judged of another man's conscience?" (1 Cor. x. 29.) " It is a very small thing that I should be judged of you, or of man's judgment: yea, I judge not mine own self." (1 Cor. iv. 3.) But while Paul so clearly sets forth the individual responsibility of the saint, and his perfect freedom from the restraints of external law, both in the spirit and the body, he at the same time gives wise counsel and plain warnings against the improper use of the liberty which he announces; and let it be marked that he does not write to Christians as though he would exercise any authority over them, but as one who would be a promoter and helper of their joys. He assumes as a fundamental principle " that every man be fully persuaded in his own mind," that there should not be a trace of doubt as to the propriety and wisdom of any particular course. He declares there should be no judging of a brother in any selfish spirit. He warns the Corinthians (1 Cor. viii. 8–10) not to indulge in that which, although in itself harmless and innocent, might yet be a stumbling-block in the way of a weak brother; and not, under any circumstances, " to use their liberty for an occasion to the flesh." Of similiar import are the directions of Peter, who, while declaring the freedom of the saints, cautions them against " using their liberty for a cloak of maliciousness," and tells them to use their high privilege " as the servants of God."

We have, therefore, in the inspired writings of the Apostles, two general principles clearly enunciated,—viz., That there is for all the children of God, a true Christian liberty, founded on redemption through Christ, spiritual in its nature, tending to full deliverance from error and sin, and uniting to God and His Word by bands of love; and that by the yielding of the whole nature, body, mind, and soul, to the enlightening and guiding influence of the Holy Ghost, accompanied by an earnest desire to know the will of God as it is revealed in His Word and Providence, with a constant exercise of fervent love towards God and man, the Christian is prevented from using his liberty in any other way than that which the Father intended in the bestowal of the gift.

Assured of these truths, we wish to demonstrate by Scripture that Christ is the end of the law for righteousness to every one that believeth; that His incarnation, life on earth, death, resurrection, and ascension form the sure foundation of the Christian's hope; that love in the heart, flowing spontaneously from divine grace, is the fulfilling of the law; and that, as a consequent, a soul redeemed by the blood of Christ is free from the constraint and commands of any external law, and is subject only to the law of God, written on his heart by the indwelling of the Holy Ghost.

Governed by this ever-present divine influence, the outward life of a believer must necessarily be the manifestation of the indwelling principle, and his conduct be always in accord with the Divine Will; any dependence upon human strength or wisdom, involving, as it does, departure from the source of all truth, must result in confusion and failure.

From the time of the ascension of Christ, those who were His disciples seemed to have been strongly tempted to walk in the old beaten paths of Judaism. A brief review of the history of the Church will make evident the constant presence of legalism. While it is probable that the legal spirit of the Jewish nation influenced in some degree the primitive Christians of the first two centuries, yet it appeared most prominently in the third and fourth centuries, when Constantine took both the Christian and Pagan religions under his fostering care, and made the Church the channel through which he dispensed his patronage, and the theatre on which he displayed his ambition. *Then* it was that men, under the name of the Church, but in the spirit of the old legalism, introduced those human plans and measures, the apparent success of which was measured by the quenching of the Holy Spirit's influence.

The Church, which claimed to be the possessor of the truth, and, therefore, its most powerful ally, having departed from the principles declared by Christ, was unable to manifest them in its practice, and thus became an obstruction to the progress of the Gospel. Losing sight of the fundamental principle of Love as an element of transcendent power, it accepted and used in its stead a legal arbitrary spirit, which naturally produced the two classes of formalists and sceptics. The one believed that salvation was the result of strict adherence to law, and the scrupulous observance of ceremonies; the other, convinced that obedience was impossible, and that no virtue could be lodged in a ritual, and failing to catch the truth on which both were primarily based, rejected the whole as an effete superstition.

These classes are represented to-day in every community; they stand side by side with those who have accepted Christ as their deliverer from the Law, and yielded themselves to the guidance of the Holy Spirit. Nominally part of the same visible Church, their ideas of truth, springing from different sources, are essentially different in character, and must therefore so affect their conduct and lives, that union and harmony, even if desirable, would seem impossible under such conditions.

It is important, in the discussion of any point of religious truth, that the difference between the old dispensation of law and the new dispensation of grace should be clearly marked, although the contrast between their spirit and method has been made evident by Paul. Christians of the present age have sadly mingled both, so that it is no easy task to separate them, and yet the Gospel of Free and Sovereign Grace is as simple as Infinite Love could make it. It is manifested to all,—all can see it without labor or effort. It is salvation "*by*," not "*for;*" it is looking, believing, and receiving eternal life, freely presented in the Gospel. The soul may choose eternal life,—or refuse and remain in eternal death. The soul that desires to be a child of God is such, for desire means sincerity. He who believes that God so loved him as to give His Son to atone for his sins, is born of God. The Holy Ghost takes up His abode in his heart and affections, and makes his body a temple for His indwelling. According to the promise, the Holy Ghost writes the law of God upon his heart; God, working within him, to will and do of His good pleasure, so that he delights in the law of God, after the inner man, and thus he is freed from the law of sin and death. This is not the work of the subject,—it is all of God, because Christ is the end of the law for righteousness to every one that believeth, and love is the fulfilling of the law, "that the righteousness of the law might be fulfilled in us, who walk not after the flesh [our own will], but after the spirit." (Rom. viii. 4.) It is not the righteousness *by* the law which is fulfilled, but the righteousness *of* the law, which, being holy, just, and good, can be fulfilled only by a Gospel saint. No external moral law can have any binding force on such a one, for he is a free man in Christ Jesus, who, "walking by faith and not by sight," keeps his eye of faith on Christ, his life and light, and beholding, as in a glass, the glory of the Lord, is changed into the same image from glory to glory, even by the Spirit of the Lord, and, although unconscious of it himself, is being conformed to the image of his Lord and Master. It is impossible for man to make men accept as truth that which they do not believe; it is God's prerogative to effect this work, not in the way of restraint, but by the presentation of His Son on the cross, by which the soul, being drawn, subdued, and melted, is induced to yield a loving and voluntary consent. As one of the redeemed, the soul has died with Christ,—has been buried with Him, and, by resurrection, made a subject of the new creation in Christ Jesus. Having thus died unto sin, the flesh, and the law, the saint has entered into the service of a new Master, and is free from all that enchained him before. Having been forever purified and sanctified, he has ceased from his own works, and all his active efforts are *from* life, and are not *for* life. The battle for life has been fought and won in Christ, and now the saint *lets* his light so shine that he becomes a living preacher; absorbed in God's love, he forgets himself, and thinks not of the light which is streaming from him; dependent upon God, he is independent of the world, and lives the life of a pilgrim in the country where his Lord was crucified. His course is accurately marked out by Paul, in Heb. vi. 1–4, and in Philippians iii. 9–15.

The first record we have in the Word of a period of rest is in Genesis, after the history of Creation, in these words: "And He rested on the seventh day from all the work which He had made: and God blessed the seventh day and sanctified it, *because* that in it He had rested from all His work."

This is the substance of the record,—of its origin and purpose. The Sabbath, as a period of time, was "blessed" and "sanctified" because during it God "rested." There is no intimation that it had any connection with man; we can discover no rule or appointment for its observance by man; it is not made evident by the Scriptures that the patriarchs paid the slightest regard to the day. The silence of Scripture may justify the conclusion that the first Sabbath was connected with a purpose for God's glory, without any reference to mankind.

The first Sabbath was commemorative of the creation of the material world, at a time when man was in the Garden. Very soon the curse came upon the world, and the significance of the day—if any had been attached to it—was lost under the new conditions of humanity.

While we may not add to or take from the Word, yet, when we have the statement in Hebrews iv. 15, "For where no law is there is no transgression," and Hebrews v. 13, "Sin is not imputed where there is no law," followed immediately by the statement of the fact (verse 14) that, "nevertheless, death reigned from Adam to Moses," we may with reason infer that this Lord's Day of Rest had another and much higher object than observance by man. Its spiritual significance, in relation to God's purpose of grace to men, is referred to by Paul in the fourth chapter of Hebrews, tenth verse: "For he that is entered into his rest, he also hath ceased from his own works, as God did from His." The Sabbatarians—and by this general term we mean those who believe that the Jewish Sabbath, either in spirit or letter, is still binding on the Christian—narrow the meaning of this "rest" to that supposed to be referred to in the millennium in the future; but taken in connection with the second verse, "For unto us was the Gospel preached, as well as unto them," and verse third, "For we which have believed do enter into rest," we prefer to regard this Sabbath of Rest as a type of that Eternal Sabbath of Rest experienced by the saint when he is made the subject of the new creation in Christ Jesus, and enters upon a rest from the power of sin and Satan and from the bondage of the law. He has surely ceased from his own works, has left the world, and has been *made* meet for the inheritance of the saints in light. He is united with his great High Priest in Heaven, and "sits in Heavenly places in Christ Jesus," and, although groaning within himself, is looking for the redemption of the body, when he will be glorified. It is the rest of the soul from the dominion of sin, which is *in* him, but not *on* him; sin indeed *dwells* in him, but he does not *dwell* in sin.

All saints will agree that the first text that introduces the spirit of Grace (Matt. xi. 28–30), "Come unto me, all ye that labor," etc., refers not only to the Jewish dispensation, but also to that of Grace. The latter is the conversion of a soul by the Blood of Christ; when the soul comes Christ will give it rest; when it takes the yoke, or is fully initiated by the Spirit, it will *find* rest without seeking for it.

The first intimation that we have in the Bible of a "Sabbath" in connection with men—the first use, indeed, of the word Sabbath—is found in Exodus xvi. 23. When the children of Israel murmured against Moses and Aaron, charging them with having brought the whole assembly into the wilderness to kill them with hunger, the Lord gave Moses directions for gathering the manna which was to be rained from Heaven. A double portion was to be gathered and prepared on the sixth day, "and it came to pass that on the sixth day they gathered twice as much bread: *and all the rulers of the congregation came and told Moses*," who repeated the words of the Lord: "To-morrow is the rest of the holy Sabbath unto the Lord." Then Moses gave the people special directions for the proper observance of the Sabbath, which was evidently a new institution among them.

While the Mosaic Sabbath was in commemoration of the deliverance of God's elect nation from physical bondage, it had also a distinct reference to and was a type of that Kingdom of Heaven which was to be established on earth. This, while it was the fulfilment of all that was promised, is the foreshadowing of that Grace or Heavenly Kingdom which is prayed for in the petition, "Thy Kingdom come, Thy will be done on earth," as it is in the spiritual kingdom of Heaven, where Christ will be not only the King of the Jews, but King of Nations. The curse will have been removed from the earth and death destroyed. The Jewish Sabbath will be restored,—the seventh day, not the first day,— "and it shall come to pass that from one Sabbath to another shall all flesh come to worship before me, saith the Lord." (Isaiah lxvi. 23.) The fourteenth chapter of Zechariah is a statement of the same truth confirmed in Isaiah lxvi. 19–20, and emphasized by Christ, as recorded in Acts i. 8. This judicial Gospel will be preached throughout the world by the returned elect remnant of the Jews *after* the Church has been taken to Heaven. The Jewish Sabbath has never been changed, abrogated, or abolished by any explicit Divine command. It is the seventh day, and not *one* day of the seven. Its object is stated in Revelation, and the mode of its observance plainly set forth and enforced by severe penalties. If the Sabbatarian admits that Christ, by

His obedience, fulfilled nine parts of the law for him, and yet holds to the binding force of the one,—the Fourth Commandment,—he tacitly assumes that Christ is *not* the end of the law for righteousness to every one that believeth; that He did not make a finished salvation, and, therefore, he must himself fill up the remainder. He will also admit that no one can acquire rest or manifest true love for his enemies by keeping the Ten Commandments. While the law is thus powerless, we admit and are assured that no redeemed soul can receive life under the Grace dispensation, without being governed by the Spirit and imbued with the essence of the law, which in itself is holy, just, and good. The body of the saint being the temple of the Holy Ghost, God's law is in the heart, and love is the fulfilling of that law.

It may be noticed that all the passages of Scripture bearing on the point (such as Rom. viii. 4; viii. 2; Gal. v. 18; ii. 19; iii. 2, 12, and 21; Rom. iii. 21, 22; xiv. 23; Gal. iii. 24; 2 Cor. v. 21; Rom. iii. 28–31; Gal. iv. 9; v. 1; ii. 15, 16; Col. ii. 14, 16, 17, and 20; Rom. viii. 15) do not refer to the righteousness *by* the law, but to the righteousness *of* the law, which the Holy Ghost works in human hearts.

It would seem to be evident from these texts, that the one object the Apostle Paul had in writing was to convince and assure the believers in Christ that they were *absolutely free* from any and all restraints and demands of the Jewish law, and entitled to the full liberty of the children of God.

The "Lord's Day" did not come from any Divine command or appointment. It was not ordained by Christ,— its observance was not enjoined by the Apostles. It was not a simple change of time for the performance of prescribed duties from the seventh to the first day of the week, neither is it the continuance of the Mosaic Sabbath under different circumstances and conditions. Its origin, progress, and culmination are different from, and higher, holier, and purer in every respect than, those of either *God's day of holy rest* or the *Sabbath given to the Jews* in the wilderness. We accept the "Lord's Day" as the gift of the Holy Ghost, a product of the Third Person of the Trinity working upon the hearts of believers in Christ, a result of the Gospel of glad tidings, an evidence of the death of the law, a proof of the new creation in Christ, and the consequent liberty of those who are united to Him. That the Holy Ghost, moving upon the hearts and minds of believers in the apostolic age, did lead them into the acceptance and observance of a day of rest, different in spirit and signification from all that had preceded it; and that the change was not arbitrary, but founded on events and examples that would appeal most strongly to the principle of love, on which the Gospel is based, will be apparent from a careful examination of the four Gospels and the Book of Acts.

The example of Christ, or rather His lying in the grave until after the Jewish Sabbath had passed, was the death of the old law, as far as its demands related to the new spiritual creation. His resurrection from the grave—the fact on which is based the Christian's assurance of immortality—on the first day of the week immediately marked it as a memorable day for all His disciples. Christ's visit to the Disciples on that day, the custom of the primitive Christians of meeting together on that day, of one accord, by the guidance of the Holy Spirit, the preaching of Paul and Peter, the collection of alms, the Revelation of Jesus Christ given to John on the "Lord's Day," are all indications of the presence of a Divine influence on the hearts of believers. Since the morning of the Resurrection until the present time the Holy Ghost has preserved this Day of Rest through and for His children, and yet we cannot find in the New Testament any absolute or even implied command in relation to it. There is here, as in everything connected with the Gospel of Glad Tidings, an absence of that legal spirit expressed by "must" and "shall." The "Lord's Day," springing from love, is to the saint the Day of days, when, free from the labor which is necessary for the supply of temporal needs, he can refresh the soul with spiritual food, and at the threshold of the week start out with invigorated ardor in his Lord's service. Its duties and pleasures are anticipated with delight, and its services strengthen and edify the soul. To one that observes it as a form, or in obedience to an inexorable law, it is a fear that bringeth torment,—a bodily labor that profiteth nothing,—a service that brings leanness to the soul. Such an one can have no clear and true conception of the spirituality of the law which God writes upon the heart,—of that Divine influence which is the "unity of the Spirit," to be kept in the bonds of peace, so often referred to as an ever-present power in the hearts of the early believers, as in Acts i. 14, ii. 1-46, iv. 24, v. 12, viii. 6, xv. 25, and Philippians ii. 2. Will that spirit of "accord," which was the characteristic mark of the undivided body of Christ in the early ages, serve as a thermometer of Christendom of the present century? If the Church will still hold to law and grace, neither being complete law or full Gospel, it will reach that point to which Laodicea, the last of the visible organizations of Asia, came, "neither hot nor cold," and be spued out of the mouth. That old spirit of Judaism,—naturally the resort of the unrenewed man, and too often of the enlightened soul,—which Paul labored so hard in the Epistles to the Romans and Galatians to induce the believing Jews to throw off, is still prevalent in the Church, in the face of the completed Scripture and the experience of eighteen centuries. Had the Church yielded to the guidance of the Holy Spirit, the resulting light and knowledge would have freed it from the grievous bondage.

Many of the provisions of the Jewish law may seem trivial and useless to those who do not care to look into their hidden significance. All who read of the paschal lamb do not immediately connect it with the Christ of whom it was the type and symbol. But while this particular feature, and others equally striking, are at once recognized as component parts of one grand plan of love and mercy, there are in the Jewish economy many minor details of much moment that are passed by without thought.

The frequent reference made in Scripture to the *eighth day* strengthens the conviction that it has an important practical bearing on the time which the Holy Ghost seemed to have marked as the Day of Rest.

Believing that all the ceremonial observances of the Jewish law, as well as most of the historical events recorded of God's ancient people, are connected with and receive their great significance from the earthly human life of Christ,— the ordinance of circumcision being divinely fixed on the eighth day after birth, the "wave offering" on "the morrow after the seventh Sabbath," the "Feast of Tabernacles" continuing eight days, but culminating in solemnity and interest on the eighth day in the Hosanna Rabbah,— all have a spiritual meaning which ought not to be disregarded. The consummation of the vow of a Nazarite on the eighth day; the feast of seven days and the "solemn assembly" at the dedication of the Temple on the eighth day; the purging of the altar during seven days and the consecration of the priests on the eighth day; the sanctifying of the House of the Lord in the reign of Hezekiah on the "eighth day of the month,"—these, with other instances that might be cited where the *eighth* day was particularly designated by Divine command for the performance of duty, may justly be claimed to have a connection with that eighth day which the people of God have sanctified by their holy worship. If the burnt offerings and sacrifices, the tabernacle and all things therein, the priests and their garments, together with all the statutes and judgments of the Jews, in their life and worship, were spiritually connected with a promised and clearer revelation of God to men, the special importance which seems to have been attached to the *eighth day* gives a strong, although not a direct or authoritative, reason for its observance as a marked day under the Gospel.

Although the Sabbath of the Jews, given to them by Jehovah, was prominent in the law, and so closely associated with the Temple service that its observance was made a test of faithfulness and an infringement severely punished; although it was an ordinance of which the Jews were peculiarly jealous as a national gift,—a mark that distinguished them from all other nations,—its claims, although so powerful to them, cannot be connected with the Lord's Day of the Gospel in any other than a general way.

Accepting the Sabbath—the seventh day—as one of the ordinances of the law given by God to the Jews in commemoration of their deliverance from Egyptian bondage, and as a type of that Kingdom of Heaven to be manifested on the earth, it may be regarded as the representative of a large class. It must stand or be swept away with other provisions of the law. The reasons for its maintenance are no stronger, and can have no greater force, than those which might be urged for the continued observance of the Passover, with its slain lamb and sprinkled blood. Indeed, the Passover, regarded as commemorative and typical, has claims to a binding force that equal, if they do not outweigh, any arguments for the Sabbath. Both were parts of Divine Revelation to the Jews, and to this day are religiously observed by pious Israelites.

• By common consent, founded with good reason on the declarations of the Apostles, Christians have always believed, and do still believe, that the Jewish Sabbath was destroyed and abrogated for them by the resurrection of the Lord and His after-appearance on another and a different day. They have connected it with a new creation, have made it the beginning of a new life, thus involving an entire change in everything relating to the external. The Lord's Day, introduced by the Holy Ghost, is, in its truest and deepest sense, the realization of all that had preceded it. It is the spirit and life of the form, the substance of what had been foreshadowed. Having grasped the substance, who will care for the shadow? having taken hold of the kernel, who will look after the husks?

It is erroneous to suppose that the construction of the law on which we insist will weaken the power of the Gospel. Instead of making void the law, we would the more firmly establish it on a surer, firmer basis than that of command,—would base it on the "righteousness of God,"—the very essence of the law,—which is conferred upon every redeemed soul. By this divine gift each soul fulfils the law, not by walking after the flesh, but after the Spirit.

The law was for the Jew, and is for every natural man. Its restrictions and requirements had reference only to the outer man,—they did not extend to the motives of the heart. In the Gospel saint the fruits that appear are the products of divine love working within him, the development of a principle constant and uniform in its expansion. It may be urged by some good men that this sweeping away of the law, which seems to be the object of Paul in his Epistle to the Churches, has reference only to the "ceremonial" law,—to that part of divine revelation intended primarily for the Jews,—and can have no application to the "moral" law, which, as they claim, is eternally binding on all. The burden of proof must rest on those who make the objection. With the broad, general declarations of the Apostle before us, we simply ask that they make evident from the "Word" that an external law has now any binding force on a soul that has accepted Christ by faith and been made a partaker of His righteousness. In God's hands the law and Gospel are one,—the life and essence of the former are perfectly manifested in the latter by the one principle of love, through and by those whom Christ has redeemed by His blood. The soul must die before it can live unto Christ,—must die to the law before it can be married to Christ, and, by virtue of union to Him, become a participator of His righteousness. Its freedom must come only from death. Christ—who in His being was beyond and above the law, became obedient to it, perfectly fulfilled it, gave His life for those whom the Father had given Him—hath forever delivered them from bondage who trust in Him. If the soul is under the Jewish law its life must be one of fear, which bringeth torment, and its end death. The attempt to gain happiness is futile,—the earnest struggles only carry it farther from the haven; for the law never contemplated satisfaction for man in union with God. The best the law can produce and offer to God is the righteousness of man.

If the Christian, who, by faith in and union with Christ,

is made the recipient of full liberty and glorious privilege, claims that he is still alive to the law, and therefore bound by it, does he not thereby deny that he is a partaker of that new and divine life which is hid in Christ? Failing utterly to appreciate the value of his dearly-bought liberty, and carelessly ignorant of the spirituality of the divine law of love written by God on his heart, he turns to that external rule of conduct which God had given as a guide to men before He made the full revelation of Himself in His Son. Living in the bright light of noonday, he is still looking for the rush-lights of early morning.

The soul that is under grace, that has received the power of Christ's righteousness, that has been made one with Him, is at perfect peace with God and stands in Christ without condemnation.

The birth of such a soul is a great mystery, an advent of a new creation, a death to all that had preceded it, a part of that plan by which God took out from the Gentiles a people for His name.

The institutions and usages of the Gospel resulting from the Grace Dispensation were in accord with its idea. Prominent among these was that period of time scripturally termed the "Lord's Day." This was new in its origin, commemorating a new event, and was observed in a new manner. It needed no appointment, command, or consecration. It was simply the product of the Holy Ghost moving upon the hearts of believers. We venture to say that any *command* to observe the "Lord's Day" would not only *not* be in harmony with the Gospel Spirit, but would present the basis for an argument for the binding force of the law as a whole. The observance of the Jewish Sabbath and the "Lord's Day," springing from opposite motives, are attended with different results. Those who remembered the Sabbath obeyed a Divine command, and received a blessing in fulfilment of a promise. The day was holy, and the soul became a partaker of all the good which was involved in the day. Now, the soul that is united to Christ makes the day holy by the observance and enjoyment of it. As under the old economy the altar sanctified the gift, so in the new dispensation the gift itself, being inspired by the Holy Ghost, is holy and sanctifies the altar. The contrast might be advanced one step and the claim made that, while under the law, connection with the Jewish Church made holy the soul, under the Gospel the Church is made holy by the faith of the soul in Christ, its Head. In the Jewish Church there was no room for the exercise of personal faith. The law was absolute, the ceremonial observance was strictly enjoined, the rewards for obedience were promised. Incorporation with the Church was essential to salvation. The Church was the only ark of safety,—the only channel through which God conveyed spiritual blessing to men. Light dwelt only within its borders,—beyond its pale was deep darkness.

Under the Gospel all is new. Religion, holy life, salvation, the conditions of immortality, are no longer the results of a connection with a Church, its sacrifices and priesthood. They spring from and are governed by the faith of the individual soul. Faith is the basis of an individual transaction between Christ and the soul. The Church—the body of Christ, the company of those who have accepted Him—is only the result of the faith of those who compose it.

The Sabbatarian claims that the Jewish Sabbath was merged into the "Lord's Day,"—that the two uniting have, like the different scenes of a dissolving view, formed that which they term the Christian Sabbath. This we conceive to be a mere human inference, without foundation in the Word, and in what we have written have endeavored to show that the two days were altogether different in origin and character, that one was an essential part of law, while the other was the product of grace, and that on every soul out of Christ the old Sabbath still held its binding requisitions. We believe that the Jewish Sabbath—the seventh day—is now, and will be until the end of time, binding on all out of Christ, and that the Lord's Day—the first day—has been, and to the end of time will be, the day of rest for Gospel saints,—that it has not been and will not be changed.

It may be charged that we are erratic in theory, censorious in disposition, and uncharitable in judgment. We earnestly disclaim such charges in motive, and declare that we are not opposed to persons or associations in any selfish sense, even though we disapprove of any certain course of action which may make withdrawal from such seem an imperative duty, but would, as far as in us lies, endeavor, by presentation of the truth as it has been apprehended by us, to combat and weaken the erroneous principles which Satan has injected even into the Church. We desire to suggest the causes from which we believe the events of the age spring, and the laws by which they are modified and governed. We lay no claim to the position of a brother's keeper in any selfish spirit, but do sincerely wish that each for himself would search the Scripture, and be fully satisfied in his own mind in regard to the truths on which we have touched; but especially do we hope that each Christian may intelligently decide for himself whether he is a subject of law—the law, undoubtedly of Divine origin, which governed the Jews—or a partaker of "*that liberty* wherewith Christ makes His people free,"—a participant in the blessed privilege which the Father hath granted to all who are united by faith to His Son. While clear conceptions of truth on this fundamental principle do have a most important bearing on *all* the relative duties of Christian life, their significance seems to be vastly increased when connected with a real and proper observance of a period of rest, be it a "Sabbath" or a "Lord's Day." Differing widely in origin, constitution, and life, it would be wise for the adherents of each to examine carefully the foundations on which the observance of either is based, and the principles by which such observance is governed. We have the greatest respect for the sanctified motives of either class of Christians regarding the whole question of a Sabbath. Both have the same object in view,—the keeping holy unto the Lord one day in seven, as authorized by the Holy Spirit. Both are equally zealous to have it strictly maintained, not only on the lower utilitarian ground of good to the physical organization of man and beast, but that it is a means of grace to the soul, and will be for the advancing of Christ's Eternal Kingdom of Glory. The difference between them must be found in the motives by which they are governed. In one it is command, in the other it is love. But those who would be guided by command—by some external law explicitly laid down for their guidance—cannot find in the New Testament any *positive law* enjoining observance of a Sabbath, be it seventh or first day. They find the Sabbath, with its typical significance and its dread penalties, in the Old Testament, but no such institution is discovered in the New Testament after Christ had ascended. If the days were identical in all except the mere period of time, why should the Sabbath be in the Old Testament but not in the New? or why should the Lord's Day shine out from the New and not appear in the Old? Running through the Decalogue, the ruling idea of prohibition, expressed by the words "Thou shalt not," presupposes a tendency, on the part of those to whom it was addressed, to act in a manner contrary to its teaching,—a disposition to run counter to it. It surely will not be claimed, especially in reference to the Lord's Day, that the children of God, redeemed by the blood of Christ and enlightened by the Holy Ghost, are so influenced by evil that they, having no earnest desire to observe the "*Lord's Day,*" will do so only when an absolute law is presented to them. Sorry day, if this be so! God's chosen children are sanctified to an obedience springing from the love deeply implanted in their hearts, which is not only in essence, but in practical results, far beyond and above that which comes from an external law.

The radical and the biblical distinction seems to be that *Sabbath* represents *Creation* and *Law*, while the "*Lord's Day*" stands not only as the symbol, but the realization of *Resurrection* and *Grace*. When the idea of the Sabbath rest—the Lord's Day—is brought into connection with the ordinary routine of daily life, which involves an application to specific action, reference must be made to *that perfect liberty which every Christian enjoys under the guidance of the Holy Ghost.* If he is under the law the Spirit has no room for exercise of His power. Liberty is only a myth,—a phantom of imagination. But if he is under grace this *liberty* is followed by a corollary of equal importance springing from and governed by the demonstrated truth,—viz., that *under the Gospel no man possesses the right to judge his brother.*

And by this corollary we simply mean to say that if any brother, led by the Spirit, chooses to do that which is not contrary to the revealed Word, even though it be opposed to the practice we have followed for half a century, we have no right to judge him. To his own Master he standeth or falleth.

We are conscious that there may be those who will regard any views that seem to come in conflict with the idea of the Sabbath held so tenaciously by the majority of the Church as the product of an infidelity which should be deprecated by all Christians. We are fully aware that the ground on which we are treading is at present beset with peculiar difficulties, and that the words written are liable to misconstruction. We are not ignorant of the fact that some most worthy Christians, whose well-regulated lives bear testimony to the presence of a divine power in their souls, will class *us* with those who desire to cast down the barriers which restrain the outbreaking of immorality. We are prepared for the charge that the tendency of the idea which we endeavor to present is the destruction of the Day of Rest, the sweeping away of old landmarks, the abolition of long-cherished and dearly-valued privileges. We are sorry to differ from many who, recognizing the necessity of Divine guidance, and earnestly seeking it, are yet led to directly opposite conclusions as to the actual teachings of Scripture on points that have a practical bearing on the Christian life and character. It is our earnest desire, as far as it may be in our power, to set forth what we conceive to be a scriptural truth in two aspects: that Christ, by His divine-human life, death, and resurrection, has, first,—negatively,—delivered His children from the bondage of the law, and, second,—positively,—perfected salvation for all who accept Him by faith. We are striving for that freedom given to the children of God, so clearly proclaimed by Paul in his Epistles to the Romans and the Galatians. We are advocating the spirituality of the law of God written on the heart of the redeemed man, which, while delivering the soul from bondage, is an active principle, leading the subject far beyond and above all that could be achieved by obedience to any external law. We would, in short, substitute *Love* for *Law*,—urge the acceptance of a general principle of universal application in the place of a rule given to men as a preparation for the full revelation of Divine Love and Wisdom in Jesus Christ. We would, if it be possible, lead Christians from an attachment to a law designed for a *nation* to a surrender to a living principle that will bind the *individual* soul in close union with the loving Father. This is high ground; these are principles that may, by enthusiastic perversion, be made germs of evil in individual cases. They are, however, carefully guarded in Scripture by cautions against a wrong use of the heavenly gift. If any would imagine that he is living in a "higher life" than his brethren, and is therefore removed from the sphere of temptation, that he is not dependent on the truths of God's Word, that the indwelling of the Spirit renders prayer useless, that the exercise of faith and the enjoyment of spiritual ecstasy relieve him from the performance of all the duties of ordinary morality, he has forgotten the cardinal truth that he is a transgressor, —a transgressor reconciled to God by mediation. He hath need to ponder carefully Paul's exhortation, "Wherefore, let him that thinketh he standeth take heed lest he fall."

Knowing that some of the ideas in this essay—suggested but not fully developed—may be regarded as foreign to the Sabbath question, if not altogether irrelevant to the point under discussion, but being well assured, we nevertheless claim that the Christian view of the perfect life to be attained, and the liberty enjoyed by those who have a proper and scriptural appreciation of the spirituality of the law of God as written on the hearts of His children by the Holy Ghost, springs from and is governed by the individual conception of the plan of redemption as set forth in the Gospels and Epistles.

Two ideas only can find place,—viz., *Law* or *Grace*. On one or the other the daily life must be based. Men are forced to accept the Pentateuch or the Gospels; they must either *work out their own* salvation or accept that which *Christ* has worked out *for them*. If the first be accepted the *Old* Testament must be the rule. If the latter, the *New* Testament must be received as living truth. While one supplements and completes the other, the underlying principles of each are so different that a transfer is logically impossible. In the *Old* men vow unto God; in the *New* God makes promises to men. In one man *gives*, in the other he *accepts*. It would doubtless be more satisfactory to the natural heart if something might be offered as equivalent for salvation, but grace *is grace*,—that which is given freely, but which cannot be purchased.

Two important facts of revelation must be borne in mind,—viz., that God, in the manifestation of Himself and the display of His glory, selected a peculiar people—the children of Israel—as the medium of communication, to whom He gave special privileges, and upon whom He placed special obligations; and, second, that corresponding with this selection under the system of law, He has, under the Dispensation of Grace, visited the Gentiles, "to take out of them a people for His name," an elect people, redeemed by the blood of Christ, sanctified and enlightened by the Spirit, unto whom He manifests Himself individually, and who, by His grace, are sustained and enabled to hold out faithful to the end, when they will receive the Crown of Life. "Against such there is no law."

SUFFERING.

The past history of mankind, as well as the experience of each individual soul, attests the truth of Paul's statement that perfection is to be attained only through suffering. In the natural as well as in the spiritual world suffering seems to be requisite as an element of purification, a process essential to the development of strength and power. By death comes life is a principle in constant operation. In the coal we are burning to-day we are consuming the life and essence of the vegetable products which in past ages clothed the earth with beauty. The rich stores of knowledge of which all may be common partakers were not gathered without toil and suffering. The liberty we are enjoying is the good fruit springing from the seeds of heroic suffering and painful death. Our hope of salvation bases itself on the suffering of Him who died for us.

Notwithstanding the fact that suffering is all-prevalent, universal, and unavoidable, there has been implanted in each breast an instinctive dread by which we naturally shrink from physical pain. We feel thankful for the provision by which a slight twinge of pain warns us of and preserves us from a greater evil. But yet, in spite of this shrinking and of this gracious premonition, how many rush recklessly into moral evil, which not only causes the most intense physical suffering in the life that now is, but awakens in the soul a vivid consciousness of future retribution, —that remorse which must be a foretaste of the misery to follow!

In the Divine Government of the universe, as it has been revealed to us in Holy Writ and in the operations of law, suffering seems to be a secondary, at least, if not an essential means in the process by which fallen rational creatures can be restored to the Life, Love, and Holiness of God lost by sin. Man, having voluntarily departed from loyalty and plunged into misery and woe, cannot claim that God is the author of sin or the cause of the suffering that inevitably follows the breach of law. But the love of God, which never deserted man, has, by the wisdom of a self-adjusting system, brought order from confusion, good from evil, and praise from the wrath of misguided men. While unable to comprehend this vast design of justice, love, and mercy in all its height and depth, yet we know enough to enable us to rest in the calm confidence that the ultimate purpose of an Infinite Being will be one of perfect good, and that by a wise overruling and governing, in strict accordance with the laws made known to us in Scripture, all evil, as it now appears to us, will be a means in accomplishing His final ends.

But the present purpose is not to seek the cause of evil, or even to trace its development, but rather to look at its results, and discover in some degree the purpose and effect of suffering as it is so intimately connected with human existence. The history of the family and people of Jacob is full of instruction on this point. In the hands of cruel Egyptian task-masters, suffering all that could be inflicted by a despotic tyrant, they were brought to a condition when they were ready to accept help from any source. When God took their part He did not at once by the exercise of omnipotent power snatch them from the hands of Pharaoh, but He placed a choice before the king in the words, "Let My people go, that they may serve Me." In the presentation of truth and right, there was an opportunity for the exercise of moral free agency on the part of Pharaoh, submission to God, and the avoidance of impending disaster. By refusing the manifested truth, which like the sun hardens or melts, the king's heart was hardened. By a natural course of events God's designs were accomplished in either direction,—the proud will of Pharaoh was broken, and a Father's love was made evident to the Israelites. God's omnipotence was displayed, and yet as far as men were concerned it was made dependent upon the choice of a human being. Released from bondage, Israel passed through a long struggle in an enemy's country, undergoing a process of discipline and trial resulting in the death of an entire generation, ere the nation entered upon the promised land.

Although enjoying the Divine favor to a degree beyond any other nation of the earth, the history of Israel is marked by periods of discipline involving great and long-continued suffering,—a process which resulted, for a time at least, in purification from grievous sin into which the people had fallen, and a means by which they were more fully prepared for their predicted mission of blessing to the world. At this point may be marked the great difference between the Lord's dealing with Israel and other nations. Other nations have rebelled or by perverseness stood in the way of the progress of the Divine plan, and they have been swept from the earth, for judgments on nations must be executed in time. Israel, under greater light and under more favorable circumstances, had frequently been guilty of flagrant rebellion; but the infinite love of a Father made the evils which came upon the nation a severe chastisement working out a positive good.

Just as we may in their past history trace the process by which God's declared purposes of making them His earthly portion and heritage, and their settlement in the promised land were accomplished, so may we trace in prophecy, connected with the facts of their national life, God's ulterior purpose of making the Jews a blessing to the earth in the latter days,—a blessing in a high and spiritual sense, as it was clearly foretold in the Old Testament. But the fulfilment of the promise made to Abraham, in its broadest sense, is yet in reserve. Israel is now passing through a long-extended period of suffering, which, bitter and continued as it is, would seem to be but a prelude to that sharp, intense trial by fire through which they must pass, and from which but a remnant will emerge,—a remnant purged and purified, prepared not only to acknowledge the Lord as their God, but to appreciate and fully enjoy that Kingdom of God upon the earth which, but for their apostasy, might have been their portion when the Messiah appeared. This refining process by intense suffering is explicitly stated in the following passages, with their contexts and parallels,—viz.: Isaiah xxiv. 15; xxvi. 8 and 9; ix. 8 and 9; ix. 14 and 15; xxx. 11 and 24; xxxi. 2; xxxiii. 14; xxxiv. 8; xlix. 3; lvii. 16 to 18; Mal. iii. 2 and 3; Zech. xiii. 7–9. It will be evident from these that judgments and suffering must precede the attainment of the promised glory by the chosen people.

Every principle of Divine Government relating to men is of universal application. The operations and results of law are simply God's manifestations of Himself to men. They are inexorable, and cannot be evaded by human wisdom or power. Although the revelation of Himself in Jesus Christ and the proclamation of salvation by Grace were a new development of the love of God, a simpler and more effective method of bringing men into union with the Divine nature, yet the process in no wise involved the elimination of suffering as one of the chief elements of discipline and purification.

The inherent depravity of the human heart, the pride of the human will, and the love of that which is contrary to holiness, must be eradicated ere the Holy Spirit can implant the positive seeds of righteousness, or enter into and fully possess the soul with the feeling of absolute and unconditional submission to the will of God. Any idea of a Christian life separate and apart from suffering is contrary not only to the individual experience of the Apostles, but to the plain declarations of Christ, while it includes the seeds of peace and joy, and carries within itself the elements of highest and purest satisfaction, the rich fruits of which are brought to maturity only by a course of tribulation exercising every part of human nature, body, mind, and soul. Were it possible, would any Christian ask to be delivered from that which, however painful in itself, will make him meet for the full enjoyment of his Lord? or ask to pass through this life, which in fact is nothing but a preparation for eternity, without being subjected to the discipline that will purge his soul from the love of sin, so closely connected with the flesh, which, continuing to bear sway, would separate from the love of Christ?

As suffering is a natural consequence of sin, a result inevitably following a cause, an evil flowing from a voluntary departure from God, it cannot therefore come from any arbitrary will of God, but is in His loving hands a means by which we are brought back to the bosom of His love and favor. It is insanity to refuse it, ingratitude to reject such a manifestation of love. Let us rather rejoice that the Heavenly Father, far from willingly afflicting the children of men, has provided and clearly opened the way by which the very fall of man into sin and woe has been made the sanctified means of leading him into eternal life and glory.

We have no doubt that the most godly saints in heaven are those whose sufferings on earth increased in the same ratio as their faith, and whose graces were developed in the furnace of affliction. It is a mistaken impression that a life of faith is one of comfort in a carnal sense; that it is to be honored in the Church and applauded by the world; that its possessor is to be blessed in earthly riches, and that his children, following in the same path, are to be partakers of similar blessings. This temporal good, which may at times be the portion of God's children, is profitable when sanctioned by the Holy Ghost, but is at the same time a strong temptation to feelings of self-complacency and self-satisfaction which are not conducive to humility or edification of the soul. The very reception of these benefits lays upon the subject a burden of responsibility heavy to bear.

In addition to the never-ceasing conflict going on in the heart, many a godly saint has an ever-present cause of pain and sorrow in the contemplation of humanity suffering under the evil of sin,—of the Church apparently given up to worldliness and living so far below its high vocation,— a pain the more intense because it is pent up in his own breast and cannot be shared by those about him, who think they can see a bright future in store for the world before the appearing of the Lord, and the times of trouble that are to come upon the earth. Such an one, by his belief in what he reads so clearly in Scripture, sees the dark cloud impending not over the world, but over the visible organization, which is too often regarded as the Church of the Living God. He is in a great degree separated from those who profess to be the followers of the Master, but who care not for His blessed appearing, and regard those who hope and long for it as the victims of some strange hallucination. It is an unspeakable pain to him to have that "hope" which is so prominently held up to believers, treated as a thing of little worth,—a mystical or fanatical idea, having no relation to the Christian life or to the glory of his Lord and Master.

* There are certain principles of action applicable to suffering. To avoid suffering at the sacrifice of obedience and a conviction of duty is as absurd as to refuse to submit to an amputation of a limb that the life may be saved. Any effort to avoid suffering which is plainly in the way of duty, is indirectly to place your human will in opposition to God's revealed will. It is duty to avoid suffering when such a course will not come in conflict with any known duty. To court, or to heedlessly run into suffering, is an impulse of the flesh savoring of self-glorification and self-righteousness. To experience suffering for your neighbor's sake is noble; but it may be prompted by mere human sympathy and not by Grace. To court suffering to prove your love for Christ may be only a desire for merit. To welcome and patiently bear suffering by, and when in obedience, is from Grace in the heart,—a high and holy privilege by which the purity of faith may be tested and an opportunity given of rejoicing in the Lord.

While the infirmities of our physical nature cause us to involuntarily shrink from approaching suffering, yet Grace is promised by which the corrupt nature may be controlled and brought into subjection to the Divine will. The blessed consciousness and sure conviction that the sudden withdrawal of earthly good, the powerful temptations of the world, the fiery darts of the evil one, and all the other multiplied trials which are so often the portion of the

Christian in this world,—the secondary means by which the soul may be prepared for glory,—spring only from the seeds of Grace planted long before by the Holy Spirit, and developed in a greater or less degree by the Divine influence. Without this inwrought conviction and assurance, trials may harden rather than melt the heart. The faith which will sustain in suffering, and enable the soul to regard it as an evidence of love, is not the faith that can be taken up into exercise or laid down in quiet rest by an arbitrary choice of the will. To be effective it must be an ever-present abiding principle, an active controlling power in the life. That soul only is ready for the death which separates it from the body, when it has been previously prepared for a holy life by the power of the Holy Ghost.

There can be no condition of human life so painful that consolation cannot be drawn from the facts, that Christ by His sufferings and death has forever delivered His brethren from the bondage of sin, Satan, and the law,—that by those sufferings Christ hath gained for us all temporal and spiritual blessings that may be needful for us in this life, with a clear title to all that the Father hath in reserve for them that love Him,—that in the suffering, we are the companions of Him who hath trodden the same path and of whose glory we shall be partakers.

In looking closely and critically over his past life, we suppose there is no Christian who will not acknowledge to himself, if not to others, that many of the so-called troubles of his course have been in some degree the results of his own acts; or, if they have not been thus positively produced, have been the correctives of some course of action which, persistently followed, might have resulted in ruin. In the light of after-events he can see that pride, covetousness, ambition, or love of the world had darkened his faith, drawn off his affections from Christ, and brought him into a state of careless indifference fatal to piety, from which he was awakened only by some sharp, sudden affliction, causing the more intense pain because the soul had been living in a temporary separation from its source of life and peace, and had thus been cut off from the channel through which alone a true child of God could gain consolation. Then he realized, perhaps as never before, his own weakness when not living in close union with God, and could see how he had been led through thorny paths of suffering until he reached a steadfast dependence on Christ. He can trace the method of suffering which mercifully preserved him from that which would have wrecked his hopes and left him to despair. The result of such a retrospect ought to be a feeling of calm assurance that God's way of leading the soul is the best way, however dark it may appear at the time.

In the Divine order of man's life, the saint must pass through three stages before he enters upon the high glory which is to be his eternal portion. In each he is subject to the same law of suffering, and cannot escape from it until he is taken home. Born of the earth, he is earthy. Born of the Spirit and thus made a subject of Grace, he is purged, purified, and educated,—is being prepared for his eternal glory. Heavenly and earthly elements are conflicting within his soul. But the time comes when the process, as far as earth is concerned, is completed; when the love of sin is eradicated; when the affections are fixed on Christ, and the desires placed on His glory; when the will is brought into sweet conformity to the Divine will. Then the conflict is over, for Heaven has entered into the soul, and it is heavenly, perfected, waiting for an abundant entrance to the glory of the Lord. By his own loving and voluntary consent, the Holy Ghost has made his body a temple and dwelling-place, so that his whole nature has been transformed into the moral image of Christ,—not by any act of the will; not by any human effort; not by striving for any particular point or object in the future; not by vain and useless strugglings to attain to any imaginary state or condition. It is by the simple yielding of the whole nature to the influence and guidance of the Holy Ghost, by steadfast reliance on the Divine promises, and by absolute confidence in the eternal and infinite love of God so fully manifested in Jesus Christ. The earthly trials which often press thickly about his course, are not borne in any stoical spirit, but are regarded—as what in truth they are—as the instruments in a Father's hands of accomplishing a purpose of love. He finds a solace in the faith, that patient endurance of suffering is not only a purifying process resulting in increased fruitfulness in the earthly life, but that by constantly expanding his Christian experience it makes him more capable of appreciating Infinite love, prepares him for more rapid advance and higher service in the future life. Such a soul has reached a very high point in Christian experience when it can truly say with St. Paul, "I am crucified with Christ, nevertheless I live; yet not I, but Christ liveth in me." Then is such a one, although bereft of all that might seem to yield comfort in an earthly sense, and filled with all that is an intolerable burden to mere flesh and blood, manifesting in a spirit of self-renunciation, the fruits of Divine holiness implanted and cherished in the heart by God's grace and love.

While it is true that suffering does come upon the children of God in consequence of sin,—or, to speak more accurately, that Christians by departures from obedience and by actual violations of God's law do bring upon themselves the evils which are inseparably connected with sin, and are thus made subjects of suffering which as moral free agents they might have avoided,—yet it is a blessed truth that there often lies in the earthly pathway of some favored souls a burden of suffering, which is a peculiar glory and honor, for it is a portion of that bitter cup which the Master did not refuse to drink. It may be that these highly-favored souls are not conscious of the dignity which the Heavenly Father hath bestowed upon them, for it has been their highest happiness to yield lovingly to the Divine will as it was revealed to them by the Holy Spirit, and to accept gladly as the best way, the way in which God led them. But when, in the light of eternity, the things of earth and time shall assume their proper proportion, it will be made evident that these are they who have been baptized with Christ, and have been partakers with Him of that very cup from which His human nature shrank in the Garden; then, and perhaps not until then, will be apparent the blessedness of those whom God hath chosen to be participants in the suffering of His Son.

CRIMINALS AND PRISON REFORM.

AMONG the many objects claiming the attention of the Christian and philanthropist, none are assuming greater importance than efforts to repress crime and to reform the criminal. Aside from the love for men as immortal beings, which is the moving impulse in a Christian heart, motives of self-preservation should press the subject home on every citizen. Indifference and carelessness on the part of those whom Providence has favored with an abundance of worldly goods, will be followed by evils which prompt and decided action might have prevented or at least greatly mitigated. The vast and constantly-increasing army of criminals is not only making taxation more burdensome, but rendering life and property more insecure. Too often the very methods by which society punishes offences, become the means of preparing the offenders for other and more serious crimes. While there can be no doubt that society must inflict summary punishment on offenders, yet that right and power involve a responsibility which does not end when the transgressor is securely confined within stone walls and iron bars. If, when his term of confinement has expired, the convict comes out more hardened and desperate than when he went in, society has gained nothing but a brief immunity from violence. If, during his imprisonment, he has not been subjected to moral influences and industrial training which would awaken and cherish some principles of self-respect and right action, as well as habits of labor, placing it within his power to earn a subsistence, then his imprisonment has, indirectly if not positively, been a failure both to convict and society. There are no sadder or more hopeless persons in the world than many released convicts as they leave the prison-door. Shunned by those who have a knowledge of his crime, regarded with indifference by all others, penniless and therefore unable to reach a place where a fresh start may be made, the stigma of prison utterly shutting out hope of employment, the former convict feels that he must starve, or enter at once upon some new course of crime. Almost by necessity he begins again to prey upon society. These men are our brethren, having a claim upon our sympathy and substantial assistance. If for no higher reason than the promotion of our own peace and safety, assistance should be freely granted to them. While some of them are the children of worthy parents whose counsels have been disregarded, the majority have not had the advantages of education, good example, or moral influence, so that their lives have been the unrestrained development of a depraved human nature. But if we, by the mercy and restraining grace of God, have been preserved from the contamination of the same moral diseases, the fact places us under a solemn obligation to exercise Christian benevolence and sympathy towards those whose different circumstances have made it so much easier to fall into crime, and incites us to put forth active efforts to rescue them from degradation. It is a sphere of Christian effort which must necessarily be attended with comparatively small results and with much discouragement from repeated failures; but surely it is a labor of love for which there is Divine warrant and promise of sustaining grace.

It must be acknowledged that there are peculiar difficulties surrounding effort in this direction, from the fact that there are no institutions under the control of the State where convicts after serving a term, or a part of a term of imprisonment, may for a time be legally placed under a system of training, where they may, by moral influences, be prepared to re-enter the world, free from those tendencies and circumstances which so almost irresistibly drive them to the course of life which so many of them dread and, if possible, would escape from. Such an intermediate home would, perhaps, have to be established by individual action and subscription,—the State only providing by legislative enactment, for the legal detention for a time of those who had been convicted of crime, thus placing them under a modified restraint for their own moral benefit. It is rather anomalous that in a Republican government, all needful measures may be taken for the prevention of physical disease, but any legal course for the prevention of moral evil and crime against society, is opposed on the ground of a tendency to union of Church and State. There are also dangers that false and spurious humanitarian feelings may place the criminal in the position of a martyr—a victim of circumstances—to a great extent not responsible for the evil he causes or falls into. Reformers of this class are not true friends of either the community or the prisoner, for they incline to measures that would rob Justice of her due and take the sting from the penalty of the law. In most cases the prisoner is suffering justly for breach of law, and it would be wrong to endeavor to relieve him of the penalty which he has drawn upon himself, but at the same time the worst criminal is one that may be reformed by the application of moral means. The only system that will be of real advantage to society and the reformation of the criminal, must be pervaded by Gospel principles, with truth and love as weapons. The offender must be regarded as a rational, immortal being, capable of appreciating and receiving the love of Christ. The fact that he is susceptible of transformation from the position of a law-breaker into that of a law-abiding, peaceful citizen, must never be weakened in the breast of any who would be the friend of the prisoner. Kindness and love are the only effective means. Let the worst man only be assured that you are his sincere friend, laboring for his good without any ulterior or selfish motive, and you gain a firm hold upon his heart.

The Gospel and the principles of sound philosophy teach that, while you are following the right impulses of the heart in striving to promote the present and eternal happiness of all to whom your influence may extend, you are taking the only effectual course to secure your own present and ultimate happiness, and thus indirectly, and without any selfish design, attaining the true end of life. The resulting happiness is the consequence, not the object. No man has found, or ever will find, true happiness when it is made the object of his search. The state of heart which produces it results from faith in and reliance upon the Almighty. Man is not of himself, and cannot be for himself, but was placed upon earth for the glory of his Creator and the good of the universe. If a man's plans are made with reference only to material wealth and the pleasures derived therefrom, he will discover—too late, perhaps, to remedy the evil—that he has mistaken the intent of life, and has utterly failed to gain its realities. The true end of life can be found only in the path of wisdom. All designs for temporal good are proper and legitimate when they are made tributary to the proper primary design, and when they include a purpose of good to all men. Wealth, honor, and pleasure, the objects of devotion in the attainment of which of all laws, except those of policy, have been trampled on, will not only fail to yield the desired satisfaction to those who seek them, but become sources of evil to society by the very process by which they are gained. Wealth, honor, or position gained by a strict adherence to the laws of eternal wisdom will not injure the possessor or any who may be his neighbors. In a word, when a large part of any community is busily engaged in the prosecution of purely selfish purposes, regardless of the best interests of those who may be below them in intelligence and morality, careless of any means for the prevention of evil, that portion of the community is really preparing the crime which the individual will commit. Their failure to properly meet the responsibility resting upon them as component parts of the state, whose individual interests are identified with and affected by the welfare of all others, must suffer the consequences arising from the presence of a constantly increasing army of criminals. In this sense it is true "that no man liveth unto himself," for if he fails to meet the obligation resting upon him he must meet the evil. As the moral sense and moral activity of the community is only the aggregated moral sense and activity of its individual members, each individual in the community must bear his proportion of the responsibility; and that responsibility will be just in proportion to the education, talent, or wealth of which he may be the possessor.

Those who have made the growth and repression of crime and pauperism a study, have marked the fact that both evils have increased in times of unusual worldly prosperity. With increasing wealth come corresponding pride and indifference to those about us. The lines of separation between the richer and poorer classes become more strongly marked. Wealth assumes still greater importance to the minds of all. Many are tempted to attain it by some other methods than those of industry and economy, and unsustained by moral principle are led on to a course ending in forgery, embezzlement, or kindred crime. In a small community where good order and morality prevail, and where there is but a shade of difference in the social position of those who compose it, there will be found but little poverty, and but seldom any outbreaking crime, because there is in the breast of each a benevolent and sympathetic feeling for the best interest of the whole. If one suffers by loss or affliction, all suffer with him, for all are mutual helpers of each other's good. If one member of such a community suddenly acquires great wealth, and for that reason imagines he is a better man by reason of its possession, or entitled to more respect and deference than before, he places a false estimate on the value of material objects, and is taking the first step that will certainly cut off the sympathy and confidence which had existed between himself and those whom he now considers below him in social rank. As he rises in this false position, he either despises or becomes indifferent to those with whom his social interests were once so happily identified, and gradually, but surely, feelings of envy, discontent, and open antagonism displace the love and sympathy which formerly bound them closely together. Let these cases be multiplied, and such a community will present a miniature picture of the process which seems to be going on in all parts of our country,—a process which is gradually loosening the foundations of the whole fabric, generating antagonistic feelings between the richer and the poorer classes which must in the end be fatal to the best interests of all. The rich men becoming richer, the poor becoming poorer, the aggregation of capital, and often the oppressive measures which unscrupulous capitalists can enforce, making it more and more difficult for the laboring-man to gain an honest subsistence, and thus producing the almost inevitable conflict between capital and labor, are bringing about a condition of society that will be most prolific in pauperism and crime. If the strong, the educated, and wealthy part of the community will not learn by experience and observation, that one who resolves to injure another by that very act injures himself, and that if they do not in all things regard the moral as well as the temporal interests of the poor, the weak, and the ignorant, they are forging chains which will bind on them and on their children a most intolerable burden, and introduce a turbulent element of anarchy and confusion, the full development of which may sweep away their earthly wealth and be attended by acts of murder and rapine before which even the horrors of the French Revolution may seem insignificant. While unwise or evil acts of government may be the cause of crime in the older and more complex civilizations of Europe, the most prolific source of crime in this country is the selfishness of the individual, the unjust combination of capital, and the growing and all-prevalent indifference to the public good. The wisest statesmen of England are alarmed at the heavy burdens of crime and pauperism now pressing on that country. The soil and territory of England being limited, the crisis there may be reached within the present century. The vast unoccupied territory of America, affording an outlet for those in some parts of our land where the pressure has become intolerable, acts as a safety-valve, and may postpone for a time the culmination of the evils which are now so evident to the observing eye. But as surely as God has ordained and made known to men good and perfect laws, unalterable and inexorable in operation and penalty, just so surely will a breach of these laws, or a failure to come up to their requirements, work out their own disastrous results and produce confusion in the social economy. Any one who has read in the Old Testament the denunciations there written against the ancient nations, and has followed the course of history, has witnessed the fulfilment of the prophecies. The same laws still operate, and the same penalties are attached to them. •The oppression of the weak, the neglecting of duty to the poor and ignorant, are everywhere mentioned as causes of severe denunciation; as an example, read eighth chapter of Amos. Wisdom and prudence would suggest that the most effectual method to overcome a growing evil would be the destruction of its cause. Seal the fountain and the stream will soon cease to flow; kill the root and there will be no more fruit or seed. All will agree that the most effectual measures which can be adopted to check crime are those of a preventive character,—taking hold of the young. But the question now pressing for an answer is, How can the criminal of adult age be transformed into an honest, self-supporting member of society? In the answer to this important question, leaving out of view all the influences that might or should have been brought to bear upon the criminal in childhood and youth, accepting the facts that the various complex bearings of our civilization and the indifference of society to the interests of those who compose it, have both indirectly and positively fostered the development of open crime, we cannot forget that the army of criminals is being daily recruited by the men and women who are convicted in our courts and sentenced to periods of imprisonment which place them, for the time at least, in a position where good influences may be exerted,—influences the more potent because the subjects are removed from the temptations to crime which have hitherto been so powerful, and are surrounded by the circumstances which may be made favorable to the development of all that is good.

Evil and wicked as these criminals may be, ignorant of all but that by which they may accomplish the sinful purposes of their depraved hearts, they are by the very fact of conviction of and sentence for crime, placed under the care and guardianship of the community against which they have sinned. What, then, shall be done with them? Lock them up securely for two or three years, and by this locking up accomplish two good ends,—protect society from depredation and make the criminal feel the absolute justice which follows an outraged law. These results are good as far as they go, and their value must not be disregarded. Iron bars and high walls have protected the community from the outbreakings of violence,—the narrow cell, the scanty fare, the deprivation of liberty, and the constrained labor ought to convince the prisoner that the way of transgressors is hard. An incidental advantage from the punishment of an offender lies in the fact that imprisonment deters others from evil-doing. But, granting the threefold benefits arising from the punishment of an offender against good and wholesome laws, we still have the question staring us in the face, "What shall be done with the convict?" If during the period of his incarceration, the treatment and discipline to which he has been subjected have been such that the convict leaves the prison threshold more hardened than when he came in, with a mind more fully determined on evil, with a heart inflamed with hatred against the community which has inflicted a just punishment, with hands ready to commit new crimes, with a conscience seared as with a hot iron, we have utterly failed in accomplishing that which should be the essential purpose in the process of punishment,—the reformation of the criminal,—and have by the imprisonment added an element to the increase and development of crime.

Experience has conclusively proved, that merely external appliances have but little effect in the process of reformation, and that the duties of enforced servitude of prison life, however faithfully performed, do not inculcate habits of industry which will sway the conduct when the outward pressure is removed. It is therefore evident that we must look for something better, for some impulse from a higher source, for some principle which, implanted in the heart, will be a seed producing good fruit, an element of continuous power which will transform the heart, mind, and life. The root and spring of all genuine reformation, be its place of exercise the pleasant home or the criminal's cell, are the consciousness of sin and the apprehension of the love of God as manifested in Jesus Christ,—a consciousness of individual sin which convinces the subject that he is not, and under existing circumstances cannot be, a subject of Divine favor, and at the same time an apprehension of the infinite love of Jesus Christ, which assures the soul that humble, honest confession of sin insures pardon for past offences and gives promise of grace for the future. While it may be wisest and best to impress upon the mind of the criminal that the penalty of the law must follow its infraction, and to make clear to the community the fact that the committing of crime will be certainly and promptly followed by the threatened penalty, yet, if the criminal and the public are both to be benefited by the infliction of a penalty, the process and result of the punishment should be of such a character that the subject of penalty will be returned to the community, after its infliction, in a better condition, physically, mentally, and morally, than he had been when he entered the prison-door. It is easy to thus state the proposition, the truth of which none will deny; but the practical solution of the problem demands careful thought and persistent labor on the part of the community by which and whom, for its own protection, some of its members are placed within prison-bars.

It is evident that the process of discipline and labor which tends to reform the criminal is that which will reduce crime, and therefore be of the highest good to the community. The benefits arising from any system producing such results, will accrue to both convict and community. If accepted by both, the problem would be easily solved; if the parties on either side were satisfied that the arrangement would be of mutual benefit, the contract—if a term of imprisonment can be so called—would be quickly ratified. But unfortunately there is a great difference of sentiment at this point. The convict does not, and, perhaps, will not, admit that his actions are deserving of punishment, and, consequently, will not acknowledge the justice of the penalty or the right by which it is inflicted. The community, convinced by the results of injury they have suffered from the acts of the convict, that breach of law should be followed by penalty, cry out for justice, and, ordinarily, are satisfied when sentence is pronounced and judgment inflicted, regardless of the result of the penalty. Now, in fact, if any good is to follow the infliction of penalty,—any permanent results to be made evident in the avoidance of evil and the following of good on the part of the convict,—any acceptance of the fact that the penalty has been inflicted by society, and acknowledgment of the obligations thereby incurred on the part of the community,—such good fruits must come from the united action of the parties concerned; the convict and the community must be of one mind, must work together in harmony. In truth, there must be mutual confessions of wrong-doing,—on the part of the convict, that he has been guilty of breach of good laws; on the part of the community, that, by selfishness and by indifference to those who are ignorant and weak, it had presented temptations to the very crimes it is now punishing. There can be no true reform without these mutual concessions, expressed or implied. The first step in the process, as far as the convict and the community are concerned, is the removal of the antagonism which, unfortunately for both, is so prevalent.

The community must take the first step. It is the stronger party. The convict is comparatively powerless when he becomes its prisoner. It has all the power springing from education, wealth, culture, and experience, as well as the absolute control of legislative enactments. If, with all these advantages, the community cannot devise some system of punishment of crime which will combine the elements of retribution for breach of law, and the inculcation of some principle which will tend to deter from a breach in the future, we must reluctantly confess that our boasted civilization is not competent to remedy the evils which it brings in its train,—that it is, in spite of all that may be claimed for it, a failure when it comes into direct conflict with that which it so often tends to nourish, and which is so detrimental to its best interests.

Granting, as is claimed by those who have most carefully studied the matter of Prison Reform, that the pain of imprisonment proves to the convict that the loss of crime overbalances its gain, that such imprisonment deters others from the commission of offences, that it protects the community from the evils of crime by violently restraining those who would commit them, and that by imprisonment the desire on the part of the convict of committing crime is lessened by the breaking up of previously formed evil habits, aided by the influence which steady labor and submission to wise regulations tends to induce, there yet remains to be considered a principle of tremendous power, without the presence of which there can be no genuine reformation. This principle, divested of all that may be sectarian, may be thus stated, in its threefold aspect,—viz., a consciousness that man is a sinner,—in a position where he does not enjoy the favor of God,—a consciousness that God in the person of Jesus Christ has manifested a way of escape from the evil of sin, and a consciousness that by faith in the Lord Jesus Christ the individual soul may not only be delivered from the guilt and consequences of past sin, but may receive the grace by which it may be enabled to avoid sin in the future. Any genuine reform must be preceded by a consciousness of sin, a faith in a way of escape from its evil, and an acceptance of the Divine power which alone can transform the heart and be an ever-present impulse to good.

The transcendent power of the Grace of God to renew the vilest heart will scarcely be denied. Without this there can be no hope of permanent improvement among criminals; and that they should be placed under the influences, constant and unremittent, of the Gospel of Christ, seems to be the duty of those called to control their punishment.

Into this wise system of control so many elements enter, and so many principles of apparently conflicting purposes seem to act, that their reconcilement and harmonious development make penal reform one of the most difficult spheres of philanthropic effort. The question of prison labor, as an element of moral reform, as well as a matter affecting the interests of the community, is one demanding careful consideration by those who are placed in the position of managers of prisons. It may seem just that society should demand from the offender an equivalent for the loss or injury sustained by those who have suffered by the perpetration of crime, and, the criminal, having nothing with which he can satisfy this demand, society has an absolute right to so control his action that a repetition of the same or a similar crime may be prevented. And just here come in the questions, Should the offender, by reason of his offence, be made a burden on those whom he has injured? should the process of punishment be such that the cost involved must be borne by those who have committed no crime? While it may not yet be definitely determined whether it is best for the interest of all concerned that the labor of convicts should be made a *source of income* to the State, and thus indirectly interfere, it may be, with some form of labor outside prison-walls, it has usually been conceded that any power or skill which the convict possesses may be properly used in paying for the cost of his own maintenance during imprisonment. Simple equity would seem to prove that honest labor ought not to be taxed for the support of offenders. But, leaving out of view the many difficulties connected with prison labor as it may affect outside industry, there can be no doubt of the fact that steady, persistent labor is a most important element in any system of prison reform,—that without it any hope of reformation by imprisonment is absurd. Henry Cordier, Superintendent of the Allegheny County, Pa., Work-House, in his report for 1873, makes the following statement as the result of his own experience: "The inmates of our penal institutions should under all circumstances be treated with kindness and humanity, but there is no reason why their labor should not be controlled and utilized so as to prevent them from being a constant and heavy burden to the tax-payers. Prisoners, if able-bodied and healthy, should at once be taught a wholesome lesson of the value of industry by being obliged to pay by honest labor at least for their board and keeping. It is true the reformation of the offender should be the principal aim of imprisonment, but reformation, if permanent, must be based upon a well-directed system of labor,—labor profitable and remunerative. Make a man industrious, and you make him virtuous." He follows this opinion with the statement that *all self-sustaining prisons*, of which he names several, "are also model institutions for good discipline and reformatory success." Whether or not industry produces virtue, the testimony of Mr. Cordier is clear as to the value of labor as an element of prison reform. It may be stated in this connection that the original idea of the Allegheny County Work-House, was that it should be made a *reformatory* institution, and that its superintendent, appreciating the philanthropic intentions of those with whom he was associated, devoted to the new enterprise all the energies of his heart and brain, and by his sagacity and experience soon placed it among the self-sustaining prisons of the country. His success was so remarkable, that Rev. E. C. Wines, D.D., the Secretary of the International Prison Reform Congress, prepared a statement of the results as far as they could be gathered by his personal inspection, and published it for the information of prison superintendents and managers in Europe as well as in the United States.

The practical application of the principles of prison reformation to convicts, may perhaps, be left to those who have made penology a study and are in a position to carry out their ideas. But the responsibility of the community for the care and proper treatment of those who have transgressed its laws cannot be placed entirely upon those who inflict the penalty and have control of its conditions. By the infliction of penalty, by the very process of imprisonment, society assumes a responsibility involving certain duties. The fact that certain members of society have, for perhaps good reasons, been selected to take especial charge and care of all who may be convicted of crime, does not release the community from an interest in, and concern for, those whom its laws have imprisoned. Each one who cares for the general good, should use active effort to secure the election or appointment of intelligent and worthy men who will wisely use the power delegated to them,—managers who will not permit the prison to be turned from its legitimate reformatory intent, by being used for selfish or political ends, or its positions of trust to be used as rewards for party services. The institutions which have been most successful as reformatories, are those where the public has extended sympathy and practical aid in the way of personal visitation, and in generous benevolence, for purposes which do not come within the scope of the law.

Surely, it is not too much to ask of the public, an interest in and care for that which so deeply affects its own material welfare as the reformation, or at least the control, of its criminals. We would rather base a claim for the criminal and all that concerns him on the ground that, depraved as he may be, he is still a child of the Heavenly Father, placed by his crime in circumstances where the blessed influences of the Gospel of Jesus Christ may be thrown around him with peculiar force, and which, entering into his soul, may return him to society prepared to enter upon an honest, useful life.

THE END.

www.ingramcontent.com/pod-product-compliance
Lightning Source LLC
Chambersburg PA
CBHW031941230426
43672CB00010B/2004